1000
Vegan
& Vegetarian Meals

1000 Vegan
& Vegetarian Meals
EVERYDAY RECIPES TO MAKE
HEALTHY EATING EASY

CHARTWELL
BOOKS

Inspiring | Educating | Creating | Entertaining

Brimming with creative inspiration, how-to projects, and useful information to enrich your everyday life, Quarto Knows is a favorite destination for those pursuing their interests and passions. Visit our site and dig deeper with our books into your area of interest: Quarto Creates, Quarto Cooks, Quarto Homes, Quarto Lives, Quarto Drives, Quarto Explores, Quarto Gifts, or Quarto Kids.

© 2021 Quarto Publishing plc

This edition published in 2020 by Chartwell Books,
an imprint of The Quarto Group
142 West 36th Street, 4th Floor
New York, NY 10018 USA
T (212) 779-4972 F (212) 779-6058
www.QuartoKnows.com

Conceived, designed, and produced by The Bright Press, an imprint of The Quarto Group
The Old Brewery, 6 Blundell Street, London N7 9BH, United Kingdom
Tel 00 44 (0)20 7700 6700

Publisher: James Evans
Art Director: James Lawrence
Senior Designer: Katherine Radcliffe
Designer: Ginny Zeal
Editorial Director: Isheeta Mustafi
Managing Editor: Jacqui Sayers
Senior Editor: Caroline Elliker
Editorial Assistant: Chloe Porter
Photographers: Michael Dannenberg, Ian Garlick

Image credits:
Shutterstock: Julia Sudnitskaya 11; Svetlana Klementyeva 12; food.kiro 74
Stockfood: Jim Scherer 94

Recipe contributors: Susannah Blake; Deborah Gray; Michael Keogh

10 9 8 7 6 5 4 3 2 1

Chartwell titles are also available at discount for retail, wholesale, promotional, and bulk purchase. For details, contact the Special Sales Manager by email at specialsales@quarto.com or by mail at The Quarto Group, Attn: Special Sales Manager, 100 Cummings Center, Suite 265D, Beverly, MA 01915, USA.

ISBN: 978-0-7858-3900-2

Library of Congress Control Number: 2020942083

Printed in Singapore

contents

A Meat-Free Diet

Contemporary vegetarian and vegan cooking has been transformed by the widespread availability of a vast range of ingredients and the general move away from a purely meat-based diet by health- and environmentally- conscious consumers. Gone from the menu too are the largely Eurocentric vegetarian options, and in have come vegetable and grain dishesinfluenced by the South-east Asian flavors of lemongrass and ginger, and Middle Eastern favorites such as sumac and za'atar.

Into the mix has also come fusion food, which combines foods of different international cuisines and origins to make some of our most exciting meals. Overenthusiasm can sometimes override common sense, however, and such foods should be combined for good culinary reasons—or there is a danger the palate may feel conflicted. The emphasis, as in all vegetarian and vegan cooking, should be on flavor, contrasting textures, and the exploitation of good-quality ingredients. When cooking, taste and adapt the balance of saltiness to sweetness, along with the sour and spicy notes, as personal preference is the key to good results and to your enjoyment of what you have prepared.

The recipes in this book make the most of the explosion of flavor in supermarkets, and demonstrate the use of a range of readily available ingredients that are not necessarily incorporated into our everyday eating habits. However, ever mindful of the size of readers' cupboards and pockets, the list of ingredients has been limited to those that are most useful. The format of the book lends itself to this exploration, as the base recipes featured are supplemented by variations, which show that changing a few ingredients or the cooking method can subtly or quite dramatically change the flavor, mode, or ethnicity of your cooking. These variations are not exhaustive; the hope is that they will give you ideas and that you will develop your own take on the recipes, thereby extending your cooking repertoire even further.

Vegan recipes

Ⓥ indicates that a recipe is vegan or can be prepared using only plant-based ingredients following the substitution advice. Many recipes simply need an adaptation such as using nut, oat, coconut, or soy-based dairy alternatives, or replacing honey with agave syrup. Suggestions for vegan alternatives are indicated in the list of ingredients. Other recipes that are not marked as vegan can be adapted if vegan cheese or egg substitutes are used instead of their dairy equivalents.

Gluten-free recipes

ⒼⒻ indicates that a recipe contains no gluten or can be adapted to be gluten-free. Many recipes in this book are naturally gluten-free. For others, adaptations are indicated in the ingredients list, such as using gluten-free oats or tamari in place of soy sauce. It is assumed that gluten-free substitutes may be made to more of the dishes, opting for gluten-free pasta or bread, for example. In this context, soy sauce should have a special mention. Most soy sauces contain gluten as they are made from wheat as well as soy beans; however, some are gluten-free and labelled as such. Generally, the Japanese soy sauce tamari is less likely to contain wheat and more likely to be gluten-free but always check the label before use.

Likewise, remember to read ingredients lists on items such as stock and stock powders, mustards (especially Dijon) and other condiments, which might use wheat-based malt vinegar. Recipes using Dijon mustard are not labelled as gluten-free, but those using vegetable stock are. If an item may have been thickened, check that a maize- (corn-) based thickener and not a wheat-based one was used; this applies to items such as yogurt, dressings, and sauces. To be on the safe side, when buying items for recipes that will be served to anyone who avoids gluten ensure that all ingredients are labelled as gluten-free.

CHAPTER 1

Breakfast & Brunch

The recipes in this section will arm you with a range of wholesome dishes with which to start the day, as well as make-and-take-with-you ideas for those days when you are on the run. There are also a few snack ideas to keep hunger pangs at bay.

DAIRY-FREE SUBSTITUTES

A challenge for vegans or those avoiding dairy is that traditional breakfast options are often based on cow's milk—café latte, cereal, and pancakes all usually contain dairy milk. However, there are a number of options for substituting non-vegan dairy milks on the breakfast table.

The most commonly used non-dairy milk is soy milk, but oat milk, almond milk, and rice milk are also easily available. All may be used in cooking and in beverages. Non-dairy milks are usually sold in the refrigerated section of most grocery stores and in nonrefrigerated, boxed form on the shelves. Non-dairy milks are available in vanilla and chocolate flavors; always check the package to be sure the flavored milk is non-dairy. Always seek the advice of a health professional before using non-dairy milks for infants.

Almond milk

A lightly sweet milk good for cereals, beverages, and baking. Contains high levels of vitamin A and other vitamins and minerals and omega fatty acids, but is lower in protein than soy milk. Most are not soy-free because they use soy lecithin. Almond milk is free of cholesterol and saturated fat.

1 cup (140 g) raw almonds   1 tbsp. brown rice syrup
1¾ pints (1 liter) water   pinch salt

Blend the ingredients in a blender until creamy and smooth. Pour through a fine mesh bag or a cheesecloth into a bowl, squeezing the bag to force through all the liquid. Chill.

Makes 1¾ pints (1 liter)

Coconut milk

A sweet milk naturally found in the heart of the coconut. Rarely available fresh, most varieties are made by squeezing the liquid out of coconut flesh and then adding water. Coconut milk is high in saturated fat but low in calories and protein.

1½ cups (150 g) shredded   3 cups (700 ml) hot (not
   coconut   boiling) water

Combine the coconut and water in a bowl; cool to room temperature. Pour through a fine mesh bag or a cheesecloth into a bowl, squeezing the bag to force through all the liquid. Chill.

Makes 2½ cups (600 ml)

Oat milk

Of the non-dairy milks, oat milk performs best at higher temperatures. It will reduce and thicken slightly. It is cholesterol-free. Note that not all brands are gluten-free.

1 cup (90 g) oats (not quick-   1 tbsp. raw sugar
   cooking)   ½ tsp. vanilla extract
1 tsp. cornstarch   pinch salt
5 cups (1.2 liters) water   pinch ground nutmeg

Combine the ingredients in a pan. Bring to a boil over a medium-high heat, reduce the heat, cover, and simmer until the oats are well cooked, approximately 10 minutes. Cool, then put in a blender, and blend until smooth; let stand for 1 hour. Pour through a fine mesh bag or a cheesecloth into a bowl, squeezing the bag to force through all the liquid. Chill.

Makes 5 cups (1.2 liters)

Rice milk

Thinner and sweeter than soy milk and higher in carbohydrates than cow's milk. Rice milk is also cholesterol-free and saturated fat-free. Rice milk is good on cereals and in beverages. It does not perform well in cooking without the use of stabilizers. Available fortified with calcium and vitamins A and D.

1¾ pints (1 liter) water   ½ tsp. vanilla extract
½ cup (100 g) brown or
   white rice

Combine the ingredients in a pan. Bring to a boil over a medium-high heat, reduce the heat, cover, and simmer until the rice is very soft, about 25 minutes. Cool, then put in a blender and blend until smooth; let stand for 1 hour. Pour through a fine mesh bag or a cheesecloth into a bowl, squeezing the bag to force through all the liquid. Chill.

Makes 1¾ pints (1 liter)

Soy milk

Rich, higher in fat, fiber, and protein than most non-dairy milks and probably the best all-round dairy milk substitute. It cooks well due to its stability at high temperatures. However, its taste is less successful in some delicate sweet dishes. Soy milk is cholesterol-free and saturated fat-free, but it has a high concentration of omega-3 fatty acids.

Quick & Easy Breakfast Bars

Makes 12 bars

3 oz. (75 g) quick-cooking rolled oats
4 oz. (125 g) whole wheat flour
4 oz. (125 g) brown sugar
¼ tsp. baking soda
¼ tsp. salt

¼ tsp. ground cinnamon
pinch ground nutmeg
4 tbsp. sunflower seeds
4 tbsp. shredded coconut
4 tbsp. dried cranberries

1 tbsp. flax seeds
1 tbsp. sesame seeds
4 fl oz. (125 ml) canola oil
3 tbsp. cranberry juice

1 Heat oven to 325°F (160°C) and lightly oil an 8x8-in. (20x20 cm) baking pan. Combine all the dry ingredients, then stir in the oil and cranberry juice and mix well.

2 Press the mixture into the baking pan and bake for 30–35 minutes until browned. Let the loaf cool for 5 minutes, then cut into slices. Will keep for 1 week in an airtight container.

WITH APPLE & WALNUT
Prepare the basic recipe, using 2 oz. (50 g) dried chopped apple in place of the cranberries, 2 oz. (50 g) walnuts in place of the coconut, and apple juice in place of the cranberry juice.

WITH MANGO
Prepare the basic recipe, using 2 oz. (50 g) dried mango in place of the cranberries, 4 tbsp. pumpkin seeds in place of the sunflower seeds, and mango juice in place of the cranberry juice.

WITH CHOCOLATE
Prepare the basic recipe. Melt 4 oz. (125 g) dairy-free vegan chocolate and spread over the cooled bars.

WITHOUT GLUTEN
Prepare the basic recipe, using spelt flour in place of the whole wheat flour.

Get-up-and-Go Energy Balls

Makes approximately 16

5 oz. (150 g) pecans
14 oz. (400 g) pitted Medjool dates
(about 16 dates)

1 tbsp. coconut oil
2 tbsp. unsalted peanut butter
2 tbsp. cocoa powder

pinch of salt
1 tbsp. water
3 tbsp. desiccated coconut (optional)

1 Place the pecans in a food processor and pulse until crushed.

2 Add the dates and coconut oil and continue to pulse to mix. Add the peanut butter, cocoa powder and salt, then pulse again. If the mixture doesn't come together (this will depend on the moisture content of the dates), add a little water to combine.

3 Take 1 tbsp. of the mixture and roll it into a ball. Place on a sheet of baking paper set on a small tray or plate. Repeat until all the mixture has been used. Roll the balls in the desiccated coconut to coat, if liked.

4 Place the rolled balls into the fridge for around 1 hour, then remove from the paper and store in an airtight container in the fridge for up to 2 weeks.

WITH TROPICAL FRUIT
Omit the cocoa powder. Replace half the dates with 6 oz. (175 g) tropical dried fruit mix and 2 tbsp. desiccated coconut. The mixture will require 1–2 tbsp. water to enable it to combine.

WITH CACAO & CASHEW
Replace the cocoa powder with raw cacao powder and the pecans with toasted, unsalted cashew nuts. Add ½ tsp vanilla extract to the mixture. Roll the finished balls in cacao nibs instead of coconut.

WITH ALMOND & CRANBERRY
Make the balls as directed, using blanched almonds instead of pecans, and almond butter instead of peanut butter. Use 12 dates and add 3½ oz. (100g) dried cranberries and 1 oz. 25 g gluten-free porridge oats.

WITH TAHINI & MANGO
Make the balls as directed, using 12 dates and 3½ oz. (100 g) dried mango, and replacing the peanut butter with tahini. Add ½ tbsp. fresh grated ginger to the mixture and roll the finished balls in toasted sesame seeds instead of coconut.

Frozen Berry Oat Smoothie

GF
Use
gluten-free
oats and
granola

V
Use non-dairy
yogurt and milk,
and agave
syrup instead
of honey

Using frozen fruit makes for a well-chilled smoothie, great for waking up the taste buds. But don't reserve this two-in-one smoothie for the mornings—the combination of fruit and cereal gives a great energy boost at any time of the day. If taking to work, place in a flask or thermal cup, leaving at least ¾ in. (2 cm) free at the top to enable a good shake before drinking.

Serves 2

9 oz. (250 g) frozen mixed berries
8 fl oz. (250 ml) full-fat Greek yogurt or non-dairy substitute
3½ fl oz. (100 ml) semi-skimmed milk or non-dairy substitute

1 oz. (25 g) porridge oats
1–2 tbsp. agave syrup or honey, to taste

1 Place the berries, yogurt, milk and oats in a blender and pulse a few times to break up the berries, then purée until smooth.

2 Taste and sweeten with agave or honey, as required. Divide between two glasses.

OVERNIGHT OAT SMOOTHIE
Make the frozen berry smoothie as directed, then cover and keep in the fridge overnight. In the morning, give it a quick whip with a balloon whisk, adding a little extra milk if required, as it will thicken slightly on standing.

WITH BANANA, DATE, CHIA
Replace the frozen berries with 1 large banana, 2 pitted Medjool dates and 1 tbsp. chia seeds. The dates are very sweet, so omit the honey in this version.

WITH BLUEBERRIES & GRANOLA
Use frozen blueberries, blueberry yogurt and granola in place of the mixed berries, Greek yogurt, and oats. Use a high-speed blender to avoid lumps.

WITH ALMOND
Use almond milk in place of semi-skimmed milk and add 1 tbsp. almond butter to the blender with the other ingredients.

Green Morning Smoothie

(GF) (V)

Full of antioxidants and hydrating fruits, which are great for waking up the system. White tea is added to this smoothie as it is thought to speed up the metabolism. If time is short, use cold water instead.

Serves 2

6 fl oz. (175 ml) not-quite-boiling water
1 white tea bag
2 Granny Smith or other sharp apples, peeled and cored
3-in. (7.5 cm) piece cucumber, peeled

2 oz. (50 g) spinach
⅓ oz. (10 g) fresh mint leaves
1 tbsp. lime juice
1–2 tbsp. maple or agave syrup

1 Pour the hot water over the tea bag in a jug and set aside to cool. Meanwhile, chop the apple and cucumber into chunks and place in a blender with the spinach, mint, and lime juice.

2 Once cooled, remove the tea bag from the jug and add the tea to the blender. Pulse a few times to break up the ingredients, then purée until smooth.

3 Taste and sweeten with maple or agave syrup, as required. Thin the smoothie with a little cold water if too thick, then divide between two glasses.

WITH COCONUT
Replace the water and tea with 3½ fl oz. (100 ml) coconut water, and add 2½ fl oz. (75 ml) coconut yogurt to the blender with the other ingredients.

WITH FIG & FLAX SEED
Make the smoothie as directed, replacing 1 apple with 2 fresh figs, stalks removed. Stir 1 tbsp. pure flaxseed oil into the smoothie before serving.

WITH ORANGE & CHILI
Make the tea with 3½ fl oz. (100 ml) water. Add 2½ fl oz. (75 ml) orange juice and ½–1 tsp seeded, chopped jalapeño or other mild chili (to taste) to the blender with the other ingredients.

WITH ALOE VERA
Make the tea with 3½ fl oz. (100 ml) water. There is no need to peel or core the apple and cucumber, just roughly chop. Using a juicer, press the juice from the apple, cucumber, spinach, and mint. Stir into the tea with the lime juice and add 2 tbsp. aloe vera and a pinch of salt. Sweeten with the maple or agave syrup, to taste.

Berry Smoothie Bowl

(V)
Use non-dairy
yogurt and milk,
and agave
syrup instead
of honey

This recipe is very easy and quick to prepare. Using frozen berries makes it deliciously cool and refreshing, but also invigorating.

Serves 2

4 tbsp. frozen mixed berries, plus extra to serve (optional)
1 large banana, sliced
4 fl oz. (120 ml) whole milk, or non-dairy substitute

2 scoops plain or vanilla protein powder (of choice)
seeds, nuts and berries (of choice)

1 Place the frozen berries and banana in a blender and blend on low until just small bits remain. Add a little milk and the protein powder and blend on low again, scraping down the sides of the blender as needed. Add the rest of the milk and blend until the mixture has a soft consistency.

2 Divide between two serving bowls and top with seeds or nuts and perhaps some extra berries.

WITH ALMOND MILK
Prepare the basic recipe, substituting almond milk for the whole milk.

WITH STRAWBERRY, ALMOND & OATMEAL
Prepare the basic recipe. Substitute 5 oz. (150 g) frozen strawberries for the mixed berries, and almond milk for the whole milk. Also add 1 oz. (25 g) rolled oats to the blender with the milk and protein powder, and blend until smooth.

WITH MANGO & CARDAMOM
Blend 6 fl oz. (175 ml) milk with 2 scoops protein powder and 8 oz. (225 g) yogurt, add 1 tbsp. honey, a pinch of dried cardamom, and 5 oz. (150 g) frozen mango, and blend until smooth.

WITH PINEAPPLE
Blend 6 fl oz. (175 ml) milk with 2 scoops protein powder and 8 oz. (225 g) yogurt. Add 2 tbsp. honey and 5 oz. (150 g) frozen pineapple. Blend until smooth.

Baked Oat & Nut Granola

Ⓥ

This granola is baked in the oven until it is golden and crispy. Add a little milk and a few berries for a delicious healthy breakfast.

Serves 6

13½ oz. (385 g) rolled oats
3½ oz. (100 g) chopped mixed nuts
3½ oz. (100 g) wheat germ
2 oz. (50 g) flaked or desiccated coconut
2 oz. (50 g) sunflower seeds

1 oz. (25 g) sesame seeds
75 g (3 oz.) brown sugar
5½ fl oz. (160 ml) water
5½ fl oz. (160 ml) sunflower or rapeseed oil
1 tsp vanilla extract
½ tsp salt
berries, to serve

1 Preheat the oven to 375°F (190°C).

2 In a large roasting tin, combine the oats, mixed nuts, wheat germ, flaked coconut, sunflower seeds, sesame seeds, and brown sugar.

3 In a medium jug, whisk together the water, oil, vanilla, and salt, then add to the dry ingredients and stir until well combined.

4 Bake in the oven for 20–30 minutes, stirring occasionally, until crisp and golden. If it starts to brown too much, turn the heat down for the last 10 minutes. Remove from the oven and leave to cool completely. Store in an airtight container for up to a week. Serve sprinkled with fresh berries.

WITH GOJI BERRIES & SULTANAS
Prepare the basic recipe. Add 2½ oz. (60 g) goji berries and 2½ oz. (60 g) sultanas to the roasting tin 10 minutes before the end of the cooking time.

WITH CRANBERRIES & MACADAMIA NUTS
Prepare the basic recipe. Add 2 oz. (50 g) chopped macadamia nuts to the mixture before baking, and 2½ oz. (60 g) dried cranberries to the mixture 10 minutes before the end of the cooking time.

WITH COCONUT OIL & PECANS
Prepare the basic recipe. Substitute 2 tbsp. coconut oil for 2 tbsp. sunflower oil, and add 2 oz. (50 g) chopped pecans.

CRANBERRY & CINNAMON GRANOLA BARS
Warm together 3½ oz. (100 g) dairy-free spread, 3½ oz. (100 g) agave syrup, and 5 oz. (140 g) brown sugar. Add 6 oz. (175 g.) rolled oats, 3½ oz. (100 g) sunflower seeds, 2 oz. (50 g) sesame seeds, 2½ oz. (60 g) chopped walnuts, 1 tsp ground cinnamon, and 5 oz. (140 g) dried cranberries. Press into a greased and lined 7 x 11 in. (18 x 28 cm) tin and bake at 325°F (170°C) for 30 minutes. Cut into 12 bars.

Breakfast Parfait

Serves 4

1¼ pt. (750 ml) soy yogurt
2 fl oz. (50 ml) maple syrup
10 oz. (300 g) cooked wheat berries

8 oz. (225 g) fresh strawberries, sliced
4 oz. (125 g) fresh blueberries
4 tsp. flax seeds

1 Mix the yogurt and the maple syrup together. Arrange the ingredients in layers in 4 large glasses. First, put one-third of the yogurt in the base of the glass, followed by wheat berries, then top with the fruit. Sprinkle 1 tsp. of the flax seeds over the top of each.

WITH GRAPE & BRAZIL NUT
Prepare the basic recipe, using 6 oz. (175 g) each of halved seedless red and green grapes in place of the berries and 3 oz. (75 g) chopped Brazil nuts in place of the flax seeds.

WITH GRANOLA
Prepare the basic recipe, using granola in place of the wheat berries.

WITH APRICOT COMPOTE
Prepare the basic recipe, using apricot compote in place of the berries. To make the compote, halve and pit 12 oz. (375 g) apricots. In a pan, dissolve 2 oz. (50 g) sugar in 6 fl oz. (175 ml) water, add the apricots and cook over a gentle heat for 12–15 minutes. Remove and let cool before making the parfait.

Coconut & Mango Chia Pots

Serves 4

4 fl oz. (125 ml) coconut milk
2 tbsp. chia seeds
1 tbsp. maple or agave syrup

5 oz. (150 g) mango chunks
1 tbsp. cacao nibs

1 Combine the coconut milk, chia seeds, and half of the maple or agave syrup in a bowl. Whisk for 1 to 2 minutes until well combined and the chia is beginning to swell. Cover and chill for at least 1 hour, stirring once or twice.

2 Combine the mango chunks and remaining maple or agave syrup in a food processor or blender and blend until smooth.

3 Spoon the chilled chia mixture into four small glasses or jars. Top with the mango purée, sprinkle the cacao nibs over the top, and serve immediately.

WITH EARL GREY
Steep an earl grey tea bag in 2 fl oz. (50 ml) boiling water for 1 minute, then remove the bag and leave the tea to cool. Combine the tea with 3 fl oz. (75 ml) coconut milk, the chia seeds, and half of the maple or agave, and proceed as for the base recipe.

WITH APPLE & RAISIN
Make the chia base as directed. Top with apple and raisin compote (see page 17) in place of the mango purée. Omit the cacao nibs.

WITH STRAWBERRY & ORANGE
Make the chia base as directed. Place 5 oz. (150 g) strawberries in a bowl and roughly mash with a fork. Sprinkle over 1 tsp maple syrup and the grated zest of ½ small orange. Use in place of the mango purée with the cacao nibs.

OVERNIGHT CHIA POTS
Make the chia base and fruit toppings the night before. Cover and chill separately overnight before layering in the jar. If making the pots to take out with you, do not worry if the layers mix.

Bircher Muesli with Figs

V
Use non-dairy
yogurt and milk,
and agave
syrup instead
of honey

Herr Bircher-Benner, a Swiss physician, served muesli to his patients before most meals for its health-giving properties and because soaked oats are easier to digest. It will take just a few minutes to prepare this variation of the original in the evening... then wake up to a tangy, well-balanced meal that will keep you satisfied until lunchtime.

Serves 2

2 oz. (50 g) porridge oats
2 dried figs, finely
    chopped
6 fl oz. (175 ml) apple
    juice
2 dessert apples
pinch of salt
2–3 tbsp. semi-skimmed
    milk or non-dairy
    substitute

1 oz. (25 g) almonds,
    roughly chopped
2 tbsp. plain full-fat
    yogurt or non-dairy
    substitute
honey or agave syrup
    (optional), to taste

1   The evening before required, place the oats and dried figs in a bowl with the apple juice. Cover and leave to soak in a cool place overnight.

2   In the morning, coarsely grate the apples into the bowl and add a pinch of salt and sufficient milk to bring the mixture to a loose, porridge-like consistency.

3   Sprinkle with the nuts and add a spoonful of yogurt, plus a drizzle of honey or maple syrup, if desired. Serve immediately.

WITH ALMOND
Replace the milk with almond milk and stir 1 tbsp. almond butter into the oat mixture before resting.

WITH SEMI-FROZEN BERRIES
Make the muesli as directed substituting 2 tbsp. dried cranberries for the figs. Omit the nuts and use 3 oz. (75 g) mixed berries. Place the berries on a plate and allow to defrost for 15 minutes. Scatter these over the prepared muesli before topping with the yogurt and honey or syrup.

INSTANT BIRCHER MUESLI WITH FIGS
Put all the ingredients, except the yogurt and honey or syrup, in a bowl and mix to combine. Allow to sit for 2 minutes, then mix again before serving, topped with the yogurt and honey or syrup.

ON-THE-GO BIRCHER YOGURT POTS
Make the bircher muesli as directed, omitting the spoonful of yogurt. Place one quarter of the muesli in each of two sealable pots or jars, top each with 3 tbsp. yogurt. Repeat to form four layers. Fill the jar to the top with a layer of halved black seedless grapes, to keep everything stable while transporting.

Apple & Raisin Compote

Use non-dairy yogurt

Cooked apple is much easier to digest than its raw counterpart. Freeze this compote in individual portions and reheat in the microwave for a quick, satisfying breakfast. It is also great on pancakes or with porridge for a more substantial start to the day, or as a quick pudding served hot with vanilla ice cream.

Serves 4

2 lb 3oz. (1 kg) Gala or other firm apples, peeled, cored and sliced
2 tbsp. water
2 oz. (50 g) raisins
1 tsp vanilla extract

2 tbsp. brown sugar, or to taste

To serve
Greek or non-dairy yogurt
mint leaves

1 Place the apple slices in a heavy-based saucepan with the water, raisins, vanilla and sugar. Cook over a medium heat, stirring frequently until the apples are hot, then reduce the heat, cover and simmer until they are tender but still hold their shape, around 10–15 minutes.

2 Taste and add more sugar, if required, but do not over-sweeten; the tartness of the apple and the sweetness of the raisins makes for a great contrast. Cook, stirring, until any added sugar has melted, then remove from the heat. Alternatively, for a smooth compote, cook for a few more minutes until the apples become pulpy, then beat with a wooden spoon to finish.

3 Serve the compote warm or cold with the yogurt and garnished with mint leaves. The compote will keep chilled and covered for several days in the fridge.

WITH CINNAMON
Make the base recipe as directed, replacing the raisins with dried cranberries, and the vanilla with 1 tsp. cinnamon.

WITH RHUBARB, ORANGE & GINGER
Use the same cooking method but replace the ingredients with 11 lb 11 oz. (750 g) chopped rhubarb, the grated zest and juice of 1 small orange, 2 tbsp. water, 3 oz. (75 g) soft brown sugar, and ½ tsp fresh grated ginger. Reduce the cooking time to 10 minutes, or until the rhubarb is just tender.

WITH PEACH & VANILLA
Use the same cooking method but replace the apples with 4 skinned, stoned and sliced peaches. Omit the raisins.

WITH PEAR & CRYSTALLIZED GINGER
Use the same cooking method but replace the apples with 4 medium ripe but firm pears, peeled, cored and sliced. Replace the raisins with 3 cubes of crystallized ginger.

Cranberry, Raisin & Hazelnut Breakfast Bread

This loaf is moist and nutty, with succulent raisins and a hint of orange.

Makes 1 loaf

9 oz. (250 g) all-purpose flour
1½ tsp. baking powder
1 tsp. baking soda
½ tsp. salt

3 oz. (75 g) chopped toasted hazelnuts
3 oz. (75 g) dried cranberries
3 oz. (75 g) raisins
2 fl oz. (60 ml) canola or sunflower oil

1 egg, room temperature
6 fl oz. (180 ml) orange juice
6 oz. (175 g) sugar
butter for greasing

1 Preheat oven to 350°F (180°C) and grease a 1 lb. (450 g) loaf pan with a little butter. Dust the pan lightly with flour. In a large bowl, sift together the flour, baking powder, baking soda, and salt. Add the hazelnuts, cranberries, and raisins, and stir until the nuts and fruit are well coated with flour.

2 In a small bowl, whisk the oil and egg together, and in another bowl, mix the orange juice and sugar together. Make a well in the center of the flour, add both the egg mixture and the orange juice mixture, and stir quickly and lightly until the batter is just blended. Pour the mixture into the pan and bake for about 50–55 minutes, until golden brown and a toothpick inserted into the center comes out clean.

WITH CHERRY, RAISIN & MACADAMIA NUT
Prepare the basic recipe, replacing the cranberries and hazelnuts with dried cherries and chopped macadamia nuts.

WITH RASPBERRY, RAISIN & WALNUT
Prepare the basic recipe, replacing the cranberries and hazelnuts with fresh raspberries and chopped walnuts.

WITH MANGO, RAISIN & PECAN
Prepare the basic recipe, replacing the cranberries and hazelnuts with chopped fresh mango and chopped pecans.

WITH BLUEBERRY, GOLDEN RAISIN & WHITE CHOCOLATE
Prepare the basic recipe, replacing the cranberries, raisins, and hazelnuts with fresh blueberries, golden raisins, and white chocolate chips.

Chocolate Chip Banana Muffins

Everybody loves the smell of freshly baked muffins in the morning... and these are more nutritious than most. The bananas are high in potassium, an essential micronutrient for regulating blood pressure, and there is plenty of fiber in there, too.

Makes 12

4 oz. (125 g) all-purpose flour
1 tsp baking powder
1 tsp bicarbonate of soda
3½ oz. (100 g) whole wheat flour
½ oz (15 g) wheat bran
2½ oz. (60 g) soft brown sugar

3 oz. (75 g) chocolate chips
2 eggs
4 tbsp. semi-skimmed milk or orange juice
1 tsp vanilla extract
3 ripe bananas, mashed
4½ oz. (125 g) unsalted butter, melted

1. Preheat the oven to 375°F (190°C). Line 12 holes of a muffin tin with muffin cases.

2. In a large bowl, sift together the all-purpose flour, baking powder and bicarbonate of soda. Stir in the whole wheat flour, wheat bran, sugar and chocolate chips. In a separate bowl, lightly beat the eggs, then stir in the milk or orange juice, vanilla extract, mashed bananas, and melted butter. Pour the wet ingredients into the dry ingredients and stir until just combined. Do not overmix; the mixture should still be a bit lumpy, as this will keep the muffins light and fluffy.

3. Spoon the mixture into the muffin cases, filling them to ½ in. (1 cm) below the rim.

4. Bake for 20 minutes, until golden brown and a cocktail stick inserted into the center of the muffins comes out clean. Cool for 5 minutes in the tin before removing to a wire rack. Eat warm or leave to cool.

WITH ORANGE
Make the muffins as directed, using orange juice instead of milk, and adding the grated zest of 1 orange.

WITH CHOCOLATE & PECAN
Make the muffins as directed, using 2 oz. (50 g) chocolate chips and adding 2 oz. (50 g) chopped pecans.

WITH COCONUT
Make the muffins as directed, using 2 oz. (50 g) chopped flaked coconut or desiccated coconut in place of the chocolate chips, and melted coconut oil in place of the butter.

WITH BLUEBERRY
Make the muffins as directed, using 3½ oz. (100 g) fresh blueberries or frozen blueberries (without defrosting) in place of the chocolate chips.

Orange Marmalade Bran Muffins (v)

These high-fiber muffins are deceptively light and flavorsome. The batter keeps for at least two weeks in an airtight container in the refrigerator, so make a double recipe and bake a fresh batch each morning.

Makes about 10 large or 16 small muffins

2 oz. (50 g) wheat bran
4 fl oz. (125 ml) boiling water
4 fl oz. (125 ml) canola oil
6 oz. (175 g) brown sugar
egg replacer or egg substitute for 1 egg (see page 223)

8 fl oz. (250 ml) soy milk
5 oz. (150 g) whole wheat flour
1¼ tsp. baking soda
½ tsp. salt
10 oz. (300 g) orange marmalade

1 Preheat the oven to 400°F (200°C). Line a muffin pan with paper muffin cups.

2 In a bowl, mix together all the ingredients. Spoon into the muffin cups, filling to about the three-quarters level. Bake the muffins for 20–25 minutes until well risen and springy to the touch. Cool for 5 minutes, then transfer the muffins to a wire rack to finish cooling.

WITH RAISIN & MAPLE SYRUP
Prepare the basic recipe, using 5 oz. (150 g) raisins in place of the marmalade. Reduce the brown sugar to 4 oz. (125 g) and add 3 fl oz. (85 ml) maple syrup.

WITH FIG & GINGER
Prepare the basic recipe, using 4 oz. (125 g) chopped plump dried figs (presoaked if directed to do so on the package) and 4 tbsp. chopped crystallized ginger in place of the marmalade.

WITH CARROT
Prepare the basic recipe, using 4 oz. (125 g) grated carrot and 1 tsp. apple pie spice in place of the marmalade.

WITH PEANUT BUTTER
Prepare the basic recipe, using 9 oz. (250 g) peanut butter in place of the marmalade.

French Toast Maple Syrup Muffins

Soft in the middle and crunchy on the top, these make the perfect breakfast.

Makes 12

9 oz. (255 g) all-purpose flour
5 oz. (140 g) brown sugar
2 tsp baking powder
½ tsp salt
1 egg, lightly beaten
8 fl oz. (240 ml) whole milk
3½ oz. (100 g) butter, melted
1 tsp maple flavoring

for the french toast topping
3 tbsp. whole milk
1 egg, lightly beaten
6 slices bread, crusts removed, cut into
    ½ in. (1.5 cm) cubes

for the sugar topping
2 fl oz. (60 ml) maple syrup
2 tbsp. granulated sugar
½ tsp ground cinnamon

1 Preheat the oven to 375°F (190°C), and either grease the holes of a 12-cup muffin tin, or put 12 muffin cases into the holes.

2 In a large bowl, stir together the flour, brown sugar, baking powder, and salt. Make a well in the center and pour in the egg, milk, melted butter, and maple flavoring. Stir with a wooden spoon from the center, slowly incorporating the flour from the sides. Spoon the batter evenly into the prepared tin.

3 Combine all the French toast topping ingredients together in a bowl, then spoon evenly over the top of the muffins. Press each one down slightly, and bake in the oven for 20 minutes, until golden brown. Remove from the oven and generously brush the tops immediately with maple syrup.

4 Combine the sugar and cinnamon together in a bowl. Sprinkle over the glazed muffins, cool for 5 minutes, then remove from the tin. Serve warm.

WITHOUT DAIRY
Prepare the basic recipe. Substitute 1 oz. (25 g) rolled oats for 1¼ oz. (30 g) flour, dairy-free margarine for butter, and coconut milk for milk in the mixture. Also, add 1 mashed banana to the mixture and proceed as before. Omit the topping.

WITH CHOCOLATE CHIP & PECAN
Prepare the basic recipe. Add 6 oz. (175 g) chocolate chips and 2¼ oz. (60 g) chopped pecans to the muffin mixture, and omit the topping.

WITH BLUEBERRY & WHITE CHOCOLATE
Prepare the basic recipe. Add 3½ oz. (100 g) blueberries and 6 oz. (175 g) white chocolate chips to the muffin mixture, substitute vanilla extract for maple syrup flavoring, and omit the topping.

WITH CHERRY & ALMOND
Prepare the basic recipe. Add 6 oz. (175 g) dried cherries, 2¼ oz. (60 g) chopped almonds to the mixture, and substitute almond flavoring for maple flavoring.

Fluffy Pancakes

(V)

What a treat to start the day with these light and fluffy pancakes. Be sure to use all-purpose white flour, because whole wheat flour will make the pancakes heavy.

Makes 8–10 pancakes

8 oz. (225 g) all-purpose
   flour
2 tsp. baking powder
½ tsp. baking soda
pinch salt
2 tbsp. sugar

8 fl oz. (250 ml) soy milk
½ tsp. vanilla extract
sunflower oil, for frying
warmed maple syrup, to
   serve

1 In a large bowl combine flour, soy flour, baking powder, baking soda, salt, and sugar. Add the soy milk and vanilla, and stir until you have quite a thick batter.

2 Lightly oil a nonstick skillet or griddle with sunflower oil and place over a medium heat. Gently pour a ladleful of batter into the pan. Wait until bubbles appear all over the surface of the pancake, then flip it over and cook on the other side until golden brown. Continue with the remaining batter while keeping the cooked pancakes warm under a clean cloth.

3 Stack the pancakes on small plates, and serve with warmed maple syrup.

WITH SPICY CURRANTS
Prepare the basic recipe, adding 3 oz. (75 g) currants, 1 tsp. ground cinnamon, ½ tsp. ground ginger, and ¼ tsp. ground allspice to the batter.

WITH RASPBERRY & VANILLA
Prepare the basic recipe, stirring 3 oz. (75 g) crushed raspberries into the batter. Also use the seeds scraped from 1 vanilla bean in place of the vanilla extract. Serve garnished with whole raspberries and soy yogurt.

WITH "BACON"
Prepare the basic recipe. Serve with 8 slices of vegan bacon alternative, pan-fried in a little sunflower oil, and patted dry with a paper towel.

WITH BLUEBERRIES
Prepare the basic recipe, adding 3 oz. (75 g) fresh blueberries to the batter. Serve with blueberry syrup and garnish with extra blueberries.

Oaty Apple Pancakes

(V)

These healthy, low-fat pancakes are a tasty way to start the day and are very quick to make. They are delicious with cranberry syrup or try them with warmed applesauce.

Makes 10–12 pancakes

2 oz. (50 g) all-purpose
    flour
3 oz. (75 g) quick-cooking
    oats
2 tsp. baking powder
1 tbsp. brown sugar
1 tbsp. vegetable oil
8 fl oz. (250 ml) oat milk

or apple juice
1 medium-tart apple,
    shredded
1 tsp. ground cinnamon
1–2 tbsp. sunflower oil,
    for frying
warmed maple syrup,
    to serve

1 Mix flour, oats, baking powder, sugar, vegetable oil, oat milk, shredded apple, and cinnamon together in a large mixing bowl. Lightly oil a nonstick skillet or griddle with sunflower oil and place over medium heat.

2 Carefully pour half a ladleful of the pancake batter into the pan. Fry until lightly browned on one side, then flip and cook the second side. Keep warm. Repeat with remaining batter. Serve with warmed maple syrup.

WITH APRICOTS
Prepare the basic recipe, using 4 oz. (125 g) chopped, plump, dried apricots in place of the shredded apple and 1 tsp. orange zest in place of the cinnamon. Orange juice may also be used in place of the apple juice.

WITH SWEET SPICES
Prepare the basic recipe, using 1 tbsp. maple syrup in place of the sugar. Also use ½ tsp. ground cinnamon, ¼ tsp. ground nutmeg, and ⅛ tsp. ground cardamom in place of the cinnamon.

WITH BLUEBERRY & BANANA
Prepare the basic recipe, using 1 tbsp. maple syrup in place of the sugar and 1 small mashed banana with 3 oz. (75 g) blueberries in place of the apple.

WITH EXTRA FIBER
Prepare the basic recipe, using whole wheat or buckwheat flour in place of the all-purpose flour. Serve with applesauce and raisins.

Stuffed Veggie Loaf

(V)

Filling and wholesome, I defy anyone not to absolutely love this lunchtime treat!

Makes 1 loaf

1 tsp. sugar dissolved in 8 fl oz. (250 ml) warm water
2 tsp. active dry yeast
13½ oz. (385 g) white bread flour
1 tsp. salt
2 tbsp. sugar

2 fl oz. (50 ml) + 2 tbsp. olive oil
1 large onion, finely chopped
4 cloves garlic, finely chopped
¼ tsp. chili powder
1 tsp. ground cilantro
½ tsp. garam masala

2 green chilis, deseeded and finely chopped
1 large potato, peeled, diced, and parboiled
1 large carrot, peeled, diced, and parboiled
4 tbsp. canned red kidney beans, crushed
1 oz. (25 g) cooked and drained spinach

1 Line a large cookie sheet with parchment paper. Sprinkle the yeast into the sugar–water mix, and set aside for 10–15 minutes, until frothy.

2 In a large bowl, combine the flour, salt, and remaining sugar. Make a well in the center, pour in the yeast liquid, add 2 fl oz. (50 ml) olive oil, and mix until a dough begins to form. Knead for about 10 minutes to make a silky dough. Transfer the dough to a large lightly oiled bowl and turn to coat it all over. Cover and put in a warm place for an hour or so, until doubled in size.

3 While the dough is proofing, make the filling. In a large skillet, heat the oil and sauté the onion for 5 minutes, until softened. Add the garlic, chili powder, cilantro, and garam masala, and cook for 2 minutes. Add the remaining ingredients and cook for a further 5 minutes. Set aside to cool completely.

4 Preheat the oven to 400°F (200°C). Turn the dough out onto a lightly floured work surface and punch down. Press flat and roll out to a large rectangle. Place the filling down the center, and fold up the sides. Lift onto the cookie sheet, brush with beaten egg, and bake for about 35 minutes, until golden brown. Cool on a wire rack, or serve hot.

WITH ROASTED VEGETABLES
Prepare the basic recipe, replacing the filling with 1 lb. (450 g) roasted Mediterranean vegetables.

WITH MIXED BEANS
Prepare the basic recipe, replacing the kidney beans with the same quantity of canned mixed beans.

WITH MOROCCAN SPICES
Prepare the basic recipe, replacing the chili powder, ground cilantro, and garam masala with 2 tsp. Moroccan spice flavoring. Mix 2 tsp. each of ground nutmeg, cumin, and ground cilantro. Add 1 tsp. each of allspice and ground ginger, and ½ tsp. each of cayenne pepper and cinnamon. Store excess in a jar with a lid for up to 1 week.

WITH VEGAN SAUSAGES & BEANS
Prepare the basic recipe, replacing the filling with 4 chopped cold vegan sausages mixed with half a can of baked beans.

Overnight Blueberry French Toast

Blueberries in crispy French toast, that burst on your tongue, and a sweet blueberry sauce combine to make a delicious breakfast.

Serves 8

oil or butter, for greasing
12 slices day-old bread, cut into 1 in. (2.5 cm) cubes
1 lb. (450 g) chilled cream cheese, cut into 1 in. (2.5 cm) cubes

3½ oz. (100 g) fresh blueberries
12 eggs, beaten
16 fl oz. (475 ml) whole milk
2 tsp vanilla extract
3 fl oz. (75 ml) maple syrup

for the sauce (optional)
8 oz. (225 g) granulated sugar
2 tbsp. cornflour
8 fl oz. (250 ml) water
3½ oz. (100 g) fresh blueberries
½ oz. (15 g) butter
7 oz. (200 g) crème fraîche, to serve

1 Lightly grease a 9 x 13 in. (23 x 33 cm) baking dish. Arrange half the bread cubes in the dish and top with the cream cheese cubes. Sprinkle all the blueberries over the cream cheese, and top with the remaining bread cubes.

2 In a large bowl, combine the eggs, milk, vanilla extract, and maple syrup. Pour over the bread cubes, cover and refrigerate overnight.

3 Take the baking dish out of the fridge 30 minutes before baking. Preheat the oven to 350°F (180°C). Cover the baking dish with a lid or foil, and bake in the oven for 30 minutes. Uncover and continue baking for 25–30 minutes, or until the center is firm and the surface is lightly browned.

4 For the sauce, place a medium pan over a medium heat, and combine the sugar, cornflour and water. Bring to a boil and cook, stirring continuously, for 4–5 minutes. Add the blueberries, reduce the heat and simmer for 10 minutes, until the blueberries burst. Stir in the butter and pour over the baked French toast. Serve immediately with a dollop of crème fraîche.

WITH CINNAMON & STRAWBERRIES
Prepare the basic recipe. Use cinnamon swirl bread in place of the day-old bread, and omit the blueberries, substituting strawberries. Serve with warm maple syrup instead of blueberry sauce.

WITH RASPBERRIES
Prepare the basic recipe. Use brioche or challah bread in place of the day-old bread, and omit the blueberries, substituting raspberries. Serve with maple syrup and a knob of butter.

WITH BANANA & BUTTERSCOTCH SAUCE
Prepare the basic recipe, substituting 1 sliced banana and a few chocolate chips for the blueberries. Serve with a butterscotch sauce. In a pan, heat together 3½ oz. (100 g) butter, 2 oz. (50 g) golden syrup, 9 oz. (250 g) brown sugar, 10 fl oz. (300 ml) single cream, and 2 tbsp. lemon juice. Keep on a rolling boil for 5 minutes, stirring occasionally.

WITH ALMONDS
Prepare the basic recipe, substituting almond extract for vanilla and sprinkling the French toast with 2 tbsp. flaked almonds before baking.

Scrambled Tofu

Serves 4

14 oz. (400 g) firm tofu
1 tbsp. vegetable oil
1 small onion, chopped

1 clove garlic, minced
1 tsp. powdered turmeric
1–2 tbsp. soy sauce

black pepper

1 Drain the tofu and crumble it with your hands into a bowl. Heat the oil in a skillet over a medium heat and gently fry the onion and garlic until softened, 4–5 minutes. Add the turmeric, then stir in the tofu. Reduce the heat slightly and season with soy sauce and black pepper to taste. Serve hot.

WITH VEGETABLES
Prepare the basic recipe, adding ½ zucchini, ½ red bell pepper, and ½ green bell pepper with the onion, and ½ tsp. dried Italian herbs in place of the turmeric.

WITH CHILI BEANS
Prepare the basic recipe, adding 1 chopped green chili with the onion and 1 peeled and chopped tomato with the turmeric. Serve with refried beans.

WITH MUSHROOMS
Prepare the basic recipe, adding 3 oz. (75 g) sliced mushrooms and ½ tsp. thyme to the softened onion, and frying until mushrooms have cooked.

IN PITA BREAD
Prepare the basic recipe. Divide it between 4 split pita bread pockets along with sliced tomato and alfalfa sprouts.

Mushrooms & Crispy Sage on Toast

Serves 2

8 sage leaves
½ oz. (15 g) butter or 2 tbsp. olive oil, plus extra olive oil for frying

6 oz. (175 g) portabello or other mixed mushrooms, sliced
1 garlic clove, crushed
2 tbsp. chopped fresh parsley

4 slices sourdough or good-quality whole wheat bread
salt and freshly ground black pepper

1 Wipe a frying pan with a little butter or olive oil and fry the sage leaves over a medium heat until crisp then remove from the pan and set aside.

2 Melt the butter or heat the olive oil in the same pan and add the mushrooms. Cook for 2 minutes, stirring, then add the garlic. Continue to cook for another 2–3 minutes, until the mushrooms are tender. Stir in the parsley and season with salt and pepper, to taste.

3 Meanwhile, toast the bread and pile the cooked mushrooms on top. Scatter over the crispy sage leaves to serve.

WITH EGG
Make the base recipe, as directed. Poach or fry an egg and slip on top of the mushrooms piled on the toast. Omit the sage leaves.

WITH ONIONS
Once the butter has melted, add 1 sliced red onion and cook over a medium heat for about 5 minutes, turning often until soft and just beginning to turn golden. Add the mushrooms and continue as directed.

WITH PASTA
Prepare the mushrooms (or the mushrooms with onions, left), as directed. Stir in 4 tbsp. crème fraîche and toss over 4½–5¼ oz. (125–150 g) cooked pasta.

CHEESE & MUSHROOM WRAP
Place 2 thin slices of Cheddar cheese in the center of each of 2 wraps. Spoon the mushrooms on top of the cheese, then crush the sage and sprinkle over the top. Tuck both sides in and roll. Cut in half down the middle.

Onion & Arugula Frittata

(GF)

Arugula is a peppery lettuce leaf containing vitamins and fiber. It has numerous health benefits, including raising good cholesterol, so is an excellent choice to start the day.

Serves 4

1 tbsp. olive oil
2 sweet onions, halved and thinly sliced
¼ tsp crushed chilies
1 x 2½ oz. (60 g) packet arugula
4 eggs

3 egg whites
3 fl oz. (75 ml) whole milk
2 oz. (50 g) grated or crumbled goat cheese
salt and freshly ground black pepper

1 Preheat the oven to 350°F (180°C).

2 Heat the oil in a large frying pan and fry the onions for about 30 minutes, until they are golden brown and caramelized. Add a little salt and freshly ground black pepper and the crushed chilies, and stir to combine. Add the arugula and cook for 2–3 minutes, until the leaves are wilted.

3 In a medium bowl, whisk the eggs, egg whites and milk together. Raise the heat to medium–high. Pour the eggs into the pan and cook for 2–3 minutes to set the base. Sprinkle the goat's cheese on top of the egg mixture. Transfer the pan to the oven and bake for 15–20 minutes, until the frittata is cooked through and set. Remove from the oven and serve immediately.

WITH CHEDDAR & TOMATO
Prepare the basic recipe, substituting Cheddar cheese for goat's cheese and adding 2 chopped tomatoes to the mixture before baking.

WITH BROCCOLI & PARMESAN
Prepare the basic recipe, substituting 6 oz. (175 g) chopped broccoli for the arugula, and adding 2 tbsp. grated Parmesan to the mixture before baking.

WITH "CHORIZO"
Prepare the basic recipe, adding 3 oz. (75 g) chopped vegetarian chorizo-style sausages to the pan after the onions have cooked for 25 minutes. Proceed as before.

WITH "BACON" & RICOTTA
Prepare the basic recipe, adding 4 chopped vegetarian bacon-style rashers to the pan after the onions have cooked for 15 minutes. Whisk 2 oz. (50 g) ricotta with the eggs and milk, and proceed as before.

Corn Fritters with Avocado & Tomato Salsa

(V)

Fresh herbs and an avocado and tomato salsa really complement the sweetness of the corn in these delicious fritters.

Serves 4

1 ripe medium banana
8 oz. (225 g) canned corn, drained
1 egg
4 scallions, finely sliced
½ tsp ground cumin

4 tbsp. chopped cilantro leaves
pinch of cayenne pepper
3¼ oz. (85 g) self-rising flour
salt and freshly ground black pepper
olive oil, for shallow frying

for the salsa
1 ripe avocado, stoned, flesh removed and
    cut into cubes
2 plum tomatoes, chopped
2 tbsp. chopped cilantro leaves
1 tbsp. olive oil
½ tsp salt

1 Preheat the oven to 300°F (150°C).

2 In a large bowl, mash the banana, then add the corn, egg, scallions, cumin, cilantro leaves, and cayenne pepper. Season with salt and freshly ground black pepper to taste, and stir until well combined. Stir in the flour to form a loose batter.

3 In a large frying pan, heat the olive oil and, when it is hot but not smoking, spoon in 2 tbsp. batter at a time to form the fritters. Cook the fritters in batches, for 2 minutes each side, or until golden and cooked through. Keep warm in a low oven while you finish cooking them all.

4 In a clean bowl, mix together the avocado cubes, tomatoes, cilantro leaves, olive oil, and salt until well combined. Serve the fritters with the salsa on the side.

WITH PEAS
Prepare the basic recipe. Omit half the canned corn and substitute fresh or frozen peas.

WITH GARLIC & CHILI
Prepare the basic recipe, adding 1 crushed clove of garlic and 1 chopped red chili to the mixture.

WITH PINEAPPLE SALSA
Prepare the basic recipe. Omit the avocado salsa. Mix 8 oz. (225 g) chopped fresh pineapple with ½ red pepper, chopped, 2 tbsp. chopped cilantro, ½ jalapeño, chopped, 1 tbsp. chopped onion, and 1 tsp lime juice.

WITH PEACH SALSA
Prepare the basic recipe. Omit the avocado salsa. Mix 8 oz. (225 g) chopped fresh peaches with ½ red pepper, chopped, 2 tbsp. chopped cilantro, ½ jalapeño, chopped, 1 tbsp. chopped onion, and 1 tsp lime juice.

Muffin Tin Frittatas

(GF)

Great straight from the oven, or equally delicious eaten cold for a packed lunch or picnic. The frittatas freeze well and can be reheated in a few seconds in the microwave.

Makes 6

1 tbsp. olive oil, plus extra for greasing
1 large carrot, grated
1 garlic clove, crushed
2 scallions, chopped

2 oz. (50 g) baby spinach, finely chopped
1¼ oz. (30 g) frozen peas
4 eggs
pinch of salt and black pepper

1½ oz. (40 g) Cheddar or Parmesan-style cheese, finely grated
fresh tomatoes, to serve

1 Preheat the oven to 350°F (180°C). Grease 6 holes of a muffin tin with oil, then line each hole with muffin cases, or alternatively use a disc of baking paper cut to size.

2 Heat the oil in a frying pan over a medium heat. Add the carrot and cook for 2 minutes, then add the garlic, scallions, and spinach and cook for an additional 2 minutes, stirring to prevent sticking. Stir in the peas and remove from the heat. Leave to cool slightly.

3 In a bowl, beat the eggs with the salt and pepper and stir in the cooked vegetables. Spoon the mixture evenly between the prepared muffin cases and sprinkle over the cheese. Bake for 18–20 minutes, until the frittatas are set and golden. Do not overcook—they should retain a very slight wobble in the center. Allow to cool slightly before removing to a wire rack. Serve hot or cold with fresh tomatoes.

WITH CARAMELIZED ONIONS
Replace the vegetables in the base recipe with 2 finely sliced medium onions. Heat 1 tbsp. butter (omit the olive oil) in a frying pan and cook the onions over a low heat for 10 minutes, stirring frequently until softened. Add 1 crushed garlic clove and ½ tsp dried thyme, then sprinkle over ½ tsp brown sugar. Continue to cook, stirring, until the onions are soft, golden and caramelized. Omit the cheese.

WITH POTATO & SAGE
Replace the vegetables in the base recipe with 6 oz. (175 g) unpeeled new potatoes. Cook the potatoes in slightly salted water for 10 minutes. Add 1¼ oz. (30 g) peas and continue to cook until the potatoes are tender. Cool until they are easy to handle, then finely dice. Meanwhile, wipe a small frying pan with a little oil and fry 6 large sage leaves until crispy.

WITH SPINACH & SUN-DRIED TOMATOES
Replace the vegetables in the base recipe with 3½ oz. (100 g) fresh baby spinach. Wipe a small frying pan with a little oil and sauté the spinach until wilted, then leave to cool slightly. Stir in 1 oz. (25 g) sun-dried tomatoes, drained of their oil and roughly chopped.

WITH MUSHROOMS & CHIVE
Replace the vegetables in the base recipe with 3½ oz. (100 g) roughly chopped chestnut mushrooms, fried in the oil until just wilted, then add 1 crushed garlic clove and 2 chopped scallions and cook until tender. Add 1 tbsp. chopped fresh chives.

Fried Eggs on Ciabatta with Parsley & Chili

These fried eggs have an Italian twist and are spiced up with the heat of a red chili.

Serves 4

4 plum tomatoes, thickly sliced	4 eggs	4 tbsp. chopped parsley
4 thick slices ciabatta	3 cloves garlic, thinly sliced	1 tsp balsamic vinegar
6 tbsp. olive oil	1 small red chili, thinly sliced	salt and freshly ground black pepper

1 Preheat the oven to 300°F (150°C). Heat a large non-stick frying pan over a medium heat. Lightly brush the tomato slices and the bread with a little olive oil. Cook the tomato slices first, for at least 5 minutes. When hot and tender, keep warm on a plate in the oven, lightly covered with foil.

2 Add a little more oil to the pan and toast the bread on both sides. Transfer to the oven to keep warm. Add a little more oil to the pan, and when hot, crack in the eggs. After a minute, add the garlic and chili, and cook for a further 2–3 minutes, spooning the hot oil over the eggs until they are cooked to your preference.

3 Remove the toast and tomatoes from the oven and place the toast on four serving plates, then spoon the tomatoes on top.

4 Throw the parsley into the pan with the eggs and splash in the balsamic vinegar. Season generously with salt and freshly ground black pepper, and slide the eggs onto each piece of toast. Drizzle over the pan juices and serve immediately.

WITH PEPPERS & CILANTRO
Prepare the basic recipe. Add 1 sliced roasted red pepper from a jar to the tomatoes in the pan. Replace the parsley with chopped fresh cilantro, and proceed as before.

WITH SWISS CHEESE
Prepare the basic recipe, sprinkling the slices of ciabatta with a little shredded Swiss cheese before keeping warm in the oven. Proceed as before.

WITH PESTO
Prepare the basic recipe. Omit the parsley and balsamic vinegar, and drizzle the tomatoes with a little pesto. Proceed as before.

WITH SOURDOUGH & SPINACH
Prepare the basic recipe, substituting sourdough for ciabatta. Add a few baby spinach leaves to the pan with the tomatoes, and proceed as before.

Cheese & Mushroom Omelette

(GF)

This recipe serves just one person, as this is the best way to make a perfect omelette: one at a time.

Serves 1

1 tbsp. olive oil
3½ oz. (100 g)
    mushrooms, sliced
2 oz. (50 g) grated
    Cheddar cheese
2 tbsp. chopped parsley

½ plum tomato, chopped
2 eggs, lightly beaten
salt and freshly ground
    black pepper

1   In a large non-stick frying pan, heat ½ tbsp. olive oil. Add the mushrooms and fry over a high heat, stirring occasionally, for about 5 minutes, until golden. Transfer to a bowl and combine with the cheese, chopped tomato and parsley.

2   Place the pan back on a medium–high heat and add the remaining olive oil. When it is hot, add the beaten eggs. Cook for a minute or so, swirling with a spatula now and again until set to your liking. Season to taste with salt and freshly ground black pepper.

3   Spoon the mushrooms and cheese onto one half of the omelette and, using the spatula, flip the other half of the omelette over to cover the mushrooms. Cook for a few seconds more, slide onto a plate and serve immediately.

WITH CHEESE & POTATO
Prepare the base recipe. Add 3 oz. (75 g) diced cooked potato to the pan before the mushrooms. Fry for 5 minutes over a high heat until browned. Lower the heat, add the mushrooms, and proceed as before.

WITH ZUCCHINI, ONION & FETA
Prepare the base recipe. Omit the mushrooms and substitute 4 tbsp. diced zucchini and 1 chopped scallion. Omit the Cheddar cheese and substitute with crumbled feta.

WITH ASPARAGUS & SWISS CHEESE
Prepare the basic recipe. Add 4 tbsp. chopped asparagus to the pan with the mushrooms, and substitute Swiss cheese for the Cheddar.

WITH "BACON" & GREEN BELL PEPPER
Prepare the basic recipe. Omit the mushrooms and add 2 chopped vegetarian bacon-style rashers and 4 tbsp. chopped green bell peppers to the pan. When the "bacon" is cooked and crispy, and the peppers softened, proceed as before.

Farinata with Date Caramel Sauce

These chickpea pancakes are called "farinata" in Italy and there is a spicy version called "besan chilla" in India. The batter needs to rest to enable the flour to absorb the water, so is best made the night before it is needed, which makes them perfect for breakfast.

Serves 4

9 oz. (250 g) gram (chickpea) flour
generous pinch of salt
15 fl oz. (450 ml) cold water
olive oil, for frying

for the date caramel sauce
10 oz. (300 g) Medjool or other soft dates

3 tbsp. almond or cashew butter
2 tbsp. coconut oil, melted
1 tsp vanilla extract
pinch of salt
4 fl oz. (120 ml) almond milk, plus a little extra if required

1 In a large bowl, whisk together the flour, salt and water until smooth. Cover and leave in a cool place for at least 1 hour, or overnight.

2 Put all the ingredients for the sauce in a food processor. Pulse to combine, then process until you have a smooth, thick but spreadable paste, so you may need to add a little more milk.

3 When you are ready to cook the pancakes, place a heavy-bottomed frying pan over a medium heat and use an oiled piece of kitchen paper to grease the surface. Once hot, pour a ladleful of batter into the pan and swirl it around to make a pancake about ¼ in. (5 mm) thick. Once the base is golden, flip it over and cook the other side. Transfer to a wire rack to keep warm while you cook the remaining batter, wiping the pan with a little more oil for each pancake. Serve warm with the sauce.

WITH VEGAN CHEESE & CHIVES
Make the chickpea pancakes (or the besan chilla above) and serve with 8 oz. (225 g) shredded vegan cheese sprinkled with fresh chives.

WITH WARM MARMALADE SAUCE
Put 4 oz. (125 g) marmalade and 4 tbsp. orange juice in a small saucepan and heat gently until the marmalade melts. Serve over the pancakes.

WITH AVOCADO SALSA
Chop the flesh of 2 avocados into chunks and put in a bowl, then toss in the juice of ½ lemon. Add 2 diced tomatoes, 1 sliced red chili, ½ red onion and a handful of chopped cilantro. Season with salt and pepper and serve with the pancakes.

CHAPTER 2

Super Salads

Salads are incredibly versatile and come in a seemingly endless array of colors, shapes, and sizes. Whether you're looking for a side dish, a filling main meal, a healthy snack, a wholesome lunch, a luxurious and indulgent treat smothered with creamy dressing, or a luscious fruity dessert, there's always a salad that's just perfect for you.

Most often thought of as a cold dish, salads can also be served warm—featuring fresh greens topped with hot or warm broiled poultry or fish, or perhaps tossed in a warm dressing just before serving. They can be light and leafy, consisting primarily of one of the many salad greens now available at most large supermarkets, or hearty and wholesome, based on cooked rice, pasta, or beans. Salads can be a meal-in-one—including eggs, tofu, or another protein—or they can be an appetizer course, whetting the appetite for the meal to come.

SALADS FOR ALL OCCASIONS

Salads are perfect for almost any occasion. Sweet, fruity salads such as Minted Watermelon & Feta Salad (page 52) are wonderful for breakfast, brunch, or as a dessert, while a lighter salad such as Spiralized Salad with Cashew Nuts & Thai Dressing (page 63) can be a delicious choice for an appetizer. There are simple salads that appeal to children, such as Arugula & Peach Salad (page 53), and more sophisticated salads, like Warm Puy Lentil Salad with Charred Squash & Beets (page 68). There are the classic salads of different cuisines, whether it's Montagnard Goat Cheese Salad from France (page 47), Spring Rain Salad from Asia (page 53), Middle Eastern Fattoush (page 60), or Green Salad & Ranch-Style Dressing from the U.S. (page 42). And there are all those main-dish salads featuring a good balance of nutrients, vegetables, carbohydrates (such as pasta, potatoes, or bread), and protein (such as lentils, chickpeas, tofu, eggs, or cheese).

INGREDIENTS

There's no limit to the type or quantity of ingredients you can put in a salad. You're likely to use lettuce or some type of salad greens, but even these aren't essential. Here are some ideas you might like to try:

Salad greens: There are countless types of salad greens, all with their own distinct taste, texture, and appearance, and all providing a great base for other salad ingredients. Some, such as iceberg or Romaine, are far more common than others, but look more closely at the produce section of your supermarket or shop at a farmer's market to find some of the more unusual varieties.

Iceberg, green- or red-leaf lettuce, and baby spinach leaves will give you a mildly flavored salad, while nutty arugula leaves, peppery watercress, Belgian endive, escarole, and radicchio will add a distinctive, stronger flavor. A cellophane bag of mixed greens (often called mesclun) is ideal for many uses, providing different colored, shaped, and flavored leaves for maximum impact.

Vegetables: Lots of vegetables, raw or cooked, are great in salads. Not only do they add extra nutrients, they also add huge visual appeal with their various bright colors. Classic raw ingredients include cucumber, carrot, tomato, onion, bean sprouts, bell peppers, celery, and avocado. However, cooked ingredients—added warm or cold—can make a great addition too. Try roasted peppers, squash, red onions, cherry tomatoes, cooked beets, lightly blanched broccoli, cauliflower, and green beans. Cold cooked new potatoes are a great addition to salads and can help transform a light accompaniment into a main meal.

Fruits: Fresh fruits such as pear, apple, grapes, peaches or nectarines, kiwi, oranges, grapefruit, and berries can make a great addition to savory salads, providing a sweet and juicy tang. Fruits can also be used as the base of dessert salads and are delicious in most combinations. Select a few different fruits with different flavors, textures, and colors—such as apple, orange, blueberry, pineapple, mango, or strawberry—and simply peel or slice into bite-size pieces and toss with a splash of fruit juice or dessert wine.

Beans, pasta & grains: Adding hearty pasta, beans, or grains to a salad can be a great way of boosting nutrients and turning a light salad into a substantial one. All three provide plenty of healthy carbohydrates for energy, but beans contain lots of fiber and protein too. Whole grains such as brown rice and bulgur wheat are a good source of fiber, while some such as quinoa are a powerhouse of nutrients containing protein as well.

Proteins: Egg, cheese, and tofu are all delicious in savory salads. They are good combined with salad greens, pasta, grains, or beans and are made even more delicious with the addition of salad vegetables, fruits, and herbs.

Green Salad & Ranch-Style Dressing

(V)

A simple green salad is the perfect accompaniment to most main dishes. This vegan version of the classic American dressing has a wonderful, creamy, tangy bite that shows off the texture and flavors of the salad perfectly. The dressing may be made in advance, as it keeps for up to a week in the refrigerator.

Serves 6

for the dressing
½ cup (125 g) silken tofu
4 tbsp. cider vinegar
2 garlic cloves, minced
2 tbsp. olive oil
1 tsp. Dijon mustard
1 tsp. maple syrup
2 tbsp. minced fresh flat-
    leaf parsley
½ tbsp. fresh oregano
¼ tbsp. fresh thyme
sea salt and white pepper
oat milk, if required

for the salad
1 head Boston or butter
    lettuce, torn into bite-
    size pieces
1 small head radicchio,
    torn into bite-size
    pieces
1 bunch arugula, tough
    stems removed
4 scallions, thinly sliced
1 cup (50 g) alfalfa
    sprouts

1 To make the dressing, put all the ingredients except the salt, pepper, and oat milk in a blender. Process until blended. Taste, season with salt and pepper, and add a little oat milk to thin, if needed. Cover and refrigerate.

2 To make the salad, wash, dry, and prepare the vegetables, and place in a serving bowl.

3 Just before serving, pour in enough dressing to lightly coat the salad, toss gently, then serve with additional dressing on the side.

WITH MUSTARD DRESSING
Prepare the dressing, using 1 tbsp. grainy mustard in place of the Dijon. Prepare the salad, adding 1 small cucumber, sliced; ½ red bell pepper, sliced; ½ yellow bell pepper, sliced; 2 tomatoes, sliced; and ½ cup (75 g) pitted small olives.

WITH MARINATED TOFU
Prepare the basic recipe, adding 8 oz. (22g g) prepared marinated or herbed tofu.

WITH GARBANZO BEANS
Prepare the basic recipe, adding 14 oz. (400 g) garbanzo beans.

WITH HAZELNUT DRESSING
Prepare the salad. Whisk together 4 tbsp. olive oil, 2 tbsp. cider vinegar, and 2 tsp. Dijon mustard. Stir in ¼ cup (25 g) roasted chopped hazelnuts, then season with sea salt and black pepper.

Avocado & Tomato Salad

The only fruit that contains more monosaturated fatty acids than the avocado is the olive. Avocados are also extremely high in potassium and are a significant source of vitamins, among which are the B-complex group, especially folic acid—important to those on a meat-free diet. They are also slow-burning and easy to digest. Oh yes, they are also delicious!

Serves 4

2 tbsp. pine nuts
2 avocados, peeled, pitted, and sliced
1 tbsp. lemon juice
3 ripe beefsteak tomatoes, roughly chopped
1 small red onion, finely sliced
8 radishes, trimmed and sliced
2 tbsp. chopped fresh basil

sea salt and black pepper
1 head Romaine lettuce, trimmed and roughly torn

for the dressing
3 tbsp. olive oil
1 tbsp. balsamic vinegar
1 small garlic clove, minced

1 Toast the pine nuts in a dry hot skillet until golden, set aside, and cool. Toss the sliced avocado in lemon juice to prevent it browning, then combine with the tomatoes, onions, and radishes. Season with salt and pepper.

2 Mix all the ingredients together for the dressing. Pour the dressing over the avocado–tomato mixture. Set aside for at least 30 minutes for the flavors to blend.

3 Line a salad bowl with the Romaine lettuce, gently add the avocado–tomato mixture, and serve garnished with the pine nuts.

WITH CILANTRO, LIME & JALAPEÑO
Prepare the basic recipe, using cilantro in place of the basil in the salad, and fresh lime juice in place of the balsamic vinegar in the dressing. Add ½ tbsp. finely chopped, pickled jalapeño to the salad.

WITH MINT, LEMON & POMEGRANATE
Prepare the basic recipe, using mint in place of the basil in the salad, and lemon juice in place of the balsamic vinegar in the dressing. Add the seeds of 1 pomegranate to the salad.

IN AVOCADO "BOATS"
Prepare the basic recipe, omitting the avocados when making the salad. Halve and pit the avocados without peeling. To serve, pile the salad into the avocado shells, omit the lettuce, garnish with a lemon wedge, and sprinkle with paprika.

WITH "MOZZARELLA"
Prepare the basic recipe, adding 8 oz. (225 g) thinly sliced dairy-free mozzarella-style cheese alternative to the salad ingredients.

GF   V
Use
non-dairy
yogurt and
milk

Big Green Salad with Green Goddess Dressing

Adding fennel to a green salad gives a delicious aniseed flavor, which is balanced out by the creamy avocado-based dressing. Never dress a green salad until the very last moment to keep all the leaves crisp. You can, however, prepare the salad a few hours ahead, cover and keep in the fridge until required.

Serves 4

¼ romaine lettuce, roughly torn into pieces
3½ oz. (100 g) mixed peppery salad leaves,
    roughly torn
3 scallions, thinly sliced
½ small fennel bulb, thinly sliced
2-in. (5-cm) piece cucumber, sliced
2 celery sticks, thinly sliced

for the green goddess dressing
½ avocado, peeled, pitted and flesh chopped
grated zest and juice of ½ lime
4 tbsp. Greek yogurt or non-dairy substitute
1 garlic clove, crushed
2 scallions, finely sliced
2 tbsp. chopped fresh cilantro

4fl oz. (125 ml) milk or non-dairy substitute
pinch of ground cumin
salt and freshly ground black pepper, to taste

1 In a serving bowl, toss all the salad ingredients together. Cover and chill until ready to serve.

2 Put all the dressing ingredients in a blender and purée until smooth. Taste and adjust the seasoning. Just before serving, drizzle the dressing over the salad. This dressing keeps well in the refrigerator and can be made in advance, too.

WITH CHARRED LITTLE GEMS
Cut 1 little gem lettuce per person in half lengthways, drizzle with 1 tsp. extra-virgin olive oil and season with salt and pepper. Heat a non-stick frying pan until very hot. Fry the lettuce for 30–60 seconds per side, until slightly charred. Serve at once with the dressing.

WITH PEA SHOOTS & SPINACH
Replace the salad with 3 oz. (75 g) frozen edamame beans, cooked then cooled under cold running water and tossed with 3 oz. (75 g) each of baby spinach leaves and pea shoots.

WITH TOMATO & CUCUMBER
In place of the salad, roughly chop 4 tomatoes and ¼ cucumber and combine with ½ small red pepper, finely sliced. For extra zing, add ½ small red chili, sliced (seeds left in for extra heat).

WITH BEANY LEMON DRESSING
In place of the dressing, drain 1 x 14 oz. (400 g) tin of cannellini beans and put in a blender with 1 chopped shallot and 4fl oz. (125 ml) water, then purée until smooth. Add the zest and juice of 1 lemon, 1 crushed garlic clove, 1 tbsp. tahini, 1 tsp. dried oregano, a pinch of chili powder, ½ tsp. each of superfine sugar and salt, and a grinding of pepper. Pulse to combine, adding a little more water as required to gain a good pouring consistency.

Warm Lentil Salad

Firm lentils such as brown and Puy lentils make the ideal base for salads as they retain their shape once cooked. The salad is great served warm or cold.

Serves 4

2½ cups (400 g) brown
   lentils
¼ cucumber
1 cup (200 g) small
   cherry tomatoes,
   quartered
5 radishes, cut in small
   sticks
2 carrots, finely diced
2 scallions, finely chopped
1 red onion, finely diced
1 tbsp. finely chopped
   fresh parsley

for the dressing
2 tbsp. safflower oil (or
   canola oil)
4 tbsp. apple cider
   vinegar
salt and freshly ground
   pepper
purslane (stems removed)
   and small salad leaves,
   to serve

1 Place the lentils in a large saucepan, cover with salted water, and bring to a boil. Turn heat to medium-low, cover, and simmer about 30–40 minutes or until tender. Drain well.

2 Peel the cucumber, halve lengthways, scrape out the seeds, and finely dice the flesh. In a large bowl, mix the cucumber with the lentils, tomatoes, radishes, carrots, scallions, and onion. Add the chopped parsley.

3 Make a dressing from the safflower oil, vinegar, salt, and pepper. Pour the dressing over the lentil salad and mix well. Serve the salad on plates on a bed of purslane and lettuce leaves.

WITH SPINACH
Prepare the basic recipe, tossing 2 handfuls of baby spinach leaves into the lentils with the parsley.

WITH NEW POTATOES
Prepare the basic recipe. Quarter 8 new potatoes and steam for about 10 minutes, or until tender. Add the potatoes to the salad with the tomatoes and other vegetables.

WITH HERBS
Prepare the basic recipe, replacing the tbsp. of parsley with 3 tbsp. roughly chopped fresh cilantro leaves and 2 tbsp. roughly chopped fresh parsley leaves.

WITH BROCCOLI
Prepare the basic recipe. Divide 8 oz. (226 g) broccoli into florets and steam for about 4 minutes until just tender. Toss into the salad with the tomatoes and other vegetables.

Montagnard Goat Cheese Salad

Serves 4

12¼ oz. (350 g) new
    potatoes, halved
3 tbsp. extra-virgin olive
    oil
2 small red onions, peeled
    and cut into wedges
5¼ oz. (150 g)
    mushrooms, sliced
5¼ oz. (150 g) goat
    cheese log

8 slices baguette, about
    ½-in. (1.5 cm) thick
1 tbsp. wholegrain
    mustard
1 tbsp. red wine vinegar
1 romaine lettuce, torn
    into pieces
salt and freshly ground
    black pepper

1   Preheat the oven to 400°F (200°C). Place the
    potatoes in a roasting tin, then toss with 1 tbsp.
    of the oil and a sprinkling of salt. Roast for 15
    minutes, then add the onion wedges, shaking
    the tin to glaze the onions in oil. Roast for
    another 25 minutes until the potatoes are
    golden brown and the onions have caramelized
    and softened. Leave to cool slightly.

2   Meanwhile, heat 1 tbsp. of olive oil in a
    medium frying pan and add the mushrooms.
    Cook for 4–5 minutes, stirring, until the
    mushrooms are tender.

3   About 15 minutes before the potatoes and
    onions are ready, remove the skin at each end
    of the goat cheese log and slice the log into
    eight. Place on top of the bread slices on a
    lined baking tray and transfer to the oven for
    10–12 minutes, until melted and just beginning
    to brown.

4   Meanwhile, make the dressing. Whisk the
    mustard, vinegar, and remaining oil with a
    splash of water. Season with salt and pepper to
    taste. To construct the salad, line four plates
    with lettuce, top with the potatoes, onions, and
    mushrooms, then drizzle over the dressing.
    Place two cheesy croutons on top of each
    mountain and serve while still warm.

WITH CHILI JAM
Make the salad as directed, omitting the cooked vegetables and
increasing the quantity of olive oil in the dressing to 2 tbsp. For
the chili jam, put 6 finely sliced red chilis in a small pan with
6 tbsp. red wine vinegar and 5 tbsp. of superfine sugar, bring to
the boil, then simmer until the liquid has thickened, about 10
minutes. Sprinkle 1 tbsp. chopped fresh mint leaves into the jam
and serve alongside the salad.

WITH WALNUTS & ORANGE MUSTARD DRESSING
Sprinkle 3 oz. (75 g) toasted walnuts over the lettuce and make
the dressing by combining 2 tbsp. olive oil, 1 tsp. each of Dijon
mustard and agave syrup, 1 tbsp. orange juice and a pinch of salt
and pepper. Pour over the salad and top with the goat cheese
croutons, omitting the cooked vegetables.

WITH BEETS & PEACHES
Make the salad as directed, omitting the cooked vegetables and
increasing the quantity of olive oil in the dressing to 2 tbsp. Peel,
stone and slice 2 small, ripe peaches, then slice 4 cooked baby
beets and arrange them over the lettuce. Top with the goat cheese
croutons.

Warm Potato Salad

(V)

Vegans can enjoy a creamy potato salad using either a purchased dairy-free mayonnaise or by making it from scratch. The mayonnaise for this recipe is also delicious in a baked potato, on a sandwich, or with your favorite salad ingredients.

Serves 6

for the mayonnaise
½ cup (125 ml) soy milk
4 tbsp. lemon juice
½ tsp. Dijon mustard
pinch paprika
approximately ¾ cup
(185 ml) mixed olive
oil and canola oil
sea salt

for the salad
1½ lbs. (750 g) small red-
skinned potatoes, diced
1 tbsp. chopped fresh dill
1 tbsp. snipped fresh
chives
1 small red onion, finely
chopped
sea salt and black pepper

1 To make the mayonnaise, place the soy milk, lemon juice, Dijon mustard, and paprika in a bowl. Whisk to combine or use a blender. Slowly add the oil in a thin stream, whisking constantly, until the mayonnaise is thick, then continue with the mixing for 1 minute longer.

2 Cook the potatoes in a pan of boiling salted water for 12–15 minutes until just tender. Drain the potatoes and tip into a large bowl. Set aside until just warm. Drizzle the mayonnaise over the potatoes and gently mix. Let stand for at least 15 minutes to allow the potatoes to absorb the flavors.

3 Stir the dill, chives, and red onion into the potatoes, then season to taste with salt and pepper. Serve immediately.

WITHOUT MAYONNAISE
Prepare the basic recipe, omitting the mayonnaise. Replace with a dressing made by combining 2 tbsp. olive oil, juice of 1 lemon, 2 tsp. wholegrain mustard, and salt and pepper to taste.

WITH MIXED POTATOES
Prepare the basic recipe, using a combination of mixed colors of small potatoes, with Peruvian (purple), small red, and small white.

GERMAN POTATO SALAD
Prepare the light potato salad variation above, adding 1 diced dill pickle with the dill and chives. Add 8 oz. (225 g) vegan "hotdog," which has been cooked, cooled, and sliced.

COLD POTATO SALAD
Prepare any of the potato salad recipes, but allow the potatoes and mayonnaise to cool completely before adding the dill and chives. Serve cold.

Pasta Salad with Blue Cheese & Grapes

Everyone needs a pasta salad in their repertoire, and this one is flavorsome and doesn't require a lot of prep. Serve as a meal in itself or alongside a light main course, and double up the quantities to take to parties. It's a great one for making on a Sunday for packed lunches throughout the week as it keeps in the fridge for a couple of days.

Serves 4 as a main, or 6 as a side dish

5¼ oz. (150 g) dried pasta shapes, such as farfalle, conchigliette or orecchiette
¼ cucumber, halved lengthways and chopped into small chunks
2 celery sticks, sliced
5 oz. (50 g) seedless red grapes, halved if large
2 scallions, trimmed and sliced

2 tbsp. chopped fresh chives
4½ oz. (140 g) crumbly blue cheese, such as Stilton
freshly ground black pepper

for the dijon vinaigrette
2 tbsp. extra-virgin olive oil
2 tsp. red wine vinegar
½ tsp. honey
½ tsp. Dijon mustard

1 Cook the pasta according to the package directions until just al dente. Run the pasta under cold water to stop the cooking process and remove the starches that will otherwise stick the pasta shapes together. Drain and pat dry with a tea towel, then transfer to a serving bowl.

2 Put all the vinaigrette ingredients in a lidded jar and shake to combine; alternatively, whisk all the ingredients together in a bowl. Pour over the pasta. Add the remaining ingredients, crumbling the blue cheese into the bowl. Season generously with black pepper and serve.

WITH ROASTED VEGETABLES
Cook the pasta as directed. Omit the vegetables from the main recipe. Cook a batch of roasted vegetables such as red peppers, red onion, butternut squash, and cherry tomatoes. Toss with the dressing and add 2 oz. (50 g) halved pitted black olives and 2 tbsp. toasted pine nuts.

WITH FETA & OLIVES
Cook the pasta as directed. Add ¼ tsp. dried oregano to the dressing and toss through the pasta. Replace the blue cheese with feta. Omit the grapes and add 1 diced romano red pepper, 3½ oz. (100 g) halved cherry tomatoes, and 2 oz. (50 g) pitted black olives. Replace the chives with chopped fresh basil.

WITH ARTICHOKE & PEA
Use 3½ oz. (100 g) cooked frozen peas, 5 oz. (50 g) jarred or deli artichokes, and 6 piquante peppers, both drained and roughly chopped. Omit the grapes and cucumber.

Tomato & Burrata Salad

Serves 2

3½ oz. (100 g) bag mixed salad leaves
11 oz. (300 g) ripe tomatoes, at room
   temperature, sliced
2 tbsp. fresh basil leaves, torn

2 tbsp. extra-virgin olive oil
2 tbsp. balsamic vinegar
1 ball of burrata, cut into quarters
salt and freshly ground black pepper

1   Divide the salad leaves between two plates. Top with the tomatoes and basil.

2   Drizzle over the oil and balsamic vinegar and season with salt and pepper to taste.

3   Top with the burrata and serve.

WITH FETA
Replace the burrata with 2 x 2 oz. (50 g) pieces of feta cheese. Brush with olive oil and place under a hot grill for 5 minutes until bubbling and just starting to turn golden brown. Drizzle ½ tsp. honey over each piece and sprinkle with thyme leaves. Serve at once over the tomato salad.

WITH ORANGE & MINT
Add one small orange, peeled, membrane removed and segmented, and 2 sliced scallions. Replace the basil with mint.

WITH AVOCADO & CORN
Add the diced flesh of 1 small avocado tossed in 1 tbsp. lime juice, and 4 tbsp. cooked corn kernels. Replace the basil with cilantro.

Spinach Salad

Serves 6

1 oz. (25 g) pine nuts
4 oz. (125 g) baby spinach, washed and dried
1½ oz. (40 g) sun-dried tomatoes packed in
   extra-virgin olive oil, chopped

1 small red onion, thinly sliced
1 avocado, peeled, pitted, and sliced
1 x 14-oz. (400-g) can garbanzo beans
16 cherry tomatoes, halved
3 oz. (75 g) whole pitted black olives

for the walnut vinaigrette
2 tbsp. freshly squeezed lemon juice
¼ tsp. sugar
½ tsp. Dijon mustard
sea salt and black pepper
4 tbsp. walnut oil

1   Toast the pine nuts in a dry hot skillet until golden, set aside, and cool.

2   Place the spinach in a salad bowl. Carefully toss in the remaining salad ingredients.

3   To make the vinaigrette, whisk together the lemon juice, sugar, mustard, and salt and pepper to taste in a medium bowl. Continue to whisk while slowly adding the walnut oil in a thin stream, to thicken.

4   Pour the dressing over the salad and toss gently, taking care not to break up the garbanzos and avocado.

WITH WILTED SPINACH
Prepare the basic recipe, but warm the vinaigrette in a small pan until hot, but not boiling. Pour over the salad and toss to wilt the spinach.

WITH CRISPY TOFU
Prepare the basic recipe. In a large skillet, heat 2 tbsp. oil over medium heat and add 1 block firm tofu, which has been squeezed, drained, and cubed. Cook, turning occasionally, until golden brown. Toss into the salad.

WITH TOASTED PECANS
Prepare the basic recipe, but roast 3 oz. (75 g) chopped pecans along with the pine nuts.

SPINACH SALAD WRAP
Prepare the basic recipe, and use it to fill 4 flour tortillas. Roll up tightly and fold in the ends. Cut tortillas in half and serve, either cold or heated in a microwave for 1½ minutes until warm.

Quick Pickled Carrots & Cauliflower

(GF) (V)

The addition of a few pickles to a lunchbox is a lovely thing. Try them in sandwiches and as a side dish with a cheese board or salad meal. This recipe is very adaptable and a great starting point to get you into pickling.

Makes 2 x 1 lb. 2 oz. (500 g) jars

8 oz. (225 g) carrots, sliced
8 oz. (225 g) cauliflower, broken into small florets
½ red onion, cut into semi-circular slices
3 garlic cloves, quartered
1 tsp.cilantro seeds
½ tsp. mustard seeds
¼ tsp. black peppercorns

2 small red chilis, cut in half lengthways
2 sprigs of fresh rosemary

for the pickling liquid
8 fl oz. (250 ml) white wine or cider vinegar
7 fl oz. (200 ml) water
1 tbsp. salt
2 tbsp. superfine sugar

1 Place all the ingredients for the pickling liquid in a saucepan and bring to a boil for 3 minutes, then remove from the heat and leave to cool to room temperature.

2 Meanwhile, pack the carrots, cauliflower and onions in layers in sterilized glass jars, adding the garlic and spices as you go—there should be sufficient to fill two 1 lb. 2 oz. (500 g) glass jars; if not, add a few more vegetables.

3 Carefully, pour the pickling liquid into the jars, pressing down the vegetables with a wooden spoon as you do to remove any air bubbles. Poke in the chilis and rosemary. The vegetables should all be submerged and there should be at least 2 in. (1.5 cm) between the top of the liquid and the lid of the jar. Put the lids on the jars and allow to cool.

4 The pickles can be eaten after a couple of hours but are best if left for at least 6 hours. They keep for up to 3 weeks in the fridge.

WITH BEETS
In place of the vegetables, wrap 2 lb 3 oz. (1 kg) beets, leaves removed, in foil and bake at 400°F (200°C) for 60–90 minutes until tender. When cool, slip off the skins and slice. Continue as directed, replacing the rosemary with a bay leaf.

WITH DILL
Make the pickling liquid as directed, adding 6 tbsp. chopped fresh dill as soon as the liquid is removed from the heat. In place of the vegetables, pack about 12 baby cucumbers into a 1¾ pint (1 liter) jar. Continue as directed, omitting the cilantro seeds, chili and rosemary.

WITH PICKLED CABBAGE
Replace the cilantro and mustard seeds, chili, and rosemary with 2 tbsp. caraway seeds; and the vegetables with half a head of red cabbage, thinly sliced. Pack into jars with a bay leaf.

Minted Watermelon & Feta Salad

(GF)

This surprising salad is delicious at lunchtime on a hot day—it's simultaneously cold, fresh, sharp and sweet. Greek feta cheese is traditionally made from sheep's milk, often combined with goat milk, so watch out for the lookalike versions made from cow's milk, which don't quite have the essential tangy-creamy taste of the real thing.

Serves 4

½ red onion
1–2 limes
1 lb 12 oz. (800 g) watermelon
5 oz. (50 g) feta cheese
4 tbsp. chopped fresh mint leaves

5 oz. (50 g) pitted black olives
4 tbsp. extra-virgin olive oil
freshly ground black pepper

1 Cut the onion into thin semi-circular slices, then place in a non-metallic bowl. Squeeze over sufficient lime juice to just cover. Leave to sit while preparing the salad—to pickle and to remove the bitter flavor of the onion.

2 Remove the skin from the watermelon, then remove the seeds. Cut into 1-in. (3 cm) chunks, then cut the feta into ¾-in. (2 cm) pieces and combine in a salad bowl. Add the mint and olives and drizzle with the olive oil.

3 Pour over the lime-mellowed onions and the lime juice. Season with black pepper, then toss everything very gently to prevent breaking up the feta—this is best done by hand. The salad will keep for a few hours before serving, if kept chilled.

WITH CUCUMBER
Make the salad as directed, omitting the feta cheese. Toss ½ cucumber, cut into chunks, through the salad; peel and seed the cucumber if the skin is hard and the seeds prominent.

WITH TOMATO
Make the salad as directed, omitting the feta cheese. Toss 1 lb 2 oz. (500 g) ripe, well-flavored tomatoes through the salad —a mixture of varieties, including yellow, red, and brown, looks particularly lovely.

WITH GREEN MELON & CHILI
Replace half the watermelon with cubed green melon, such as honeydew. Add 1 mild red chili, cut into thin rings (seeds left in for extra heat, or seeded for a milder flavor).

VIETNAMESE-STYLE WATERMELON SALAD
Make the salad as directed, omitting the feta cheese. Add 1 tbsp. rice vinegar, ½ tsp. freshly grated ginger, 2 tbsp. each of chopped fresh mint and basil. Garnish with crushed roasted peanuts.

Spring Rain Salad

Serves 6

for the dressing
1 tbsp. white miso
1 tbsp. hot water
1 shallot, minced
1 tbsp. minced pickled ginger

pinch wasabi, to taste
1 tbsp. rice vinegar
1 tbsp. soy sauce
4 fl oz. (125 ml) grapeseed oil or canola oil

for the salad
1½ oz. (40 g) dried harusame noodles, or cellophane noodles (bean thread noodles)
1 small cucumber, cut into very thin strips
½ carrot, cut into very thin strips
1 scallion, finely shredded

1   To make the dressing, mix the miso to a paste with the hot water, and whisk together with the shallot, ginger, wasabi, rice vinegar, and soy sauce. Slowly whisk in the oil in a thin stream, to thicken. Taste and adjust the seasoning, and add more wasabi, if desired.

2   Bring a saucepan of water to a boil and cook the noodles according to the package directions. Refresh in cold water and drain. Mix the noodles, cucumber, carrot, and scallion in a large salad bowl or in individual serving dishes.

3   Just before serving, pour the dressing over the salad and toss to mix.

WITH TOFU
Prepare the basic salad. Before serving, carefully slice 12-oz. (350-g) block silken tofu into small cubes and arrange them around the salad.

WITH ROOT VEGETABLES
Prepare the basic recipe, using 1 carrot, ½ daikon root, and 1 Japanese turnip (Hakurei) or regular turnip, all finely sliced, in place of the cucumber. Marinate the root vegetables in the dressing for at least 1 hour before combining with the other ingredients.

JAPANESE SPROUT SALAD
Prepare the basic recipe, using half the quantity of noodles and adding 2 cups bean sprouts. Sprinkle the finished salad with 1 tbsp. toasted sesame seeds.

Arugula & Peach Salad

Serves 4

2 oz. (50 g) pecans
2 small ripe peaches
1 tbsp. balsamic vinegar

3½ oz. (100 g) arugula leaves
4 tbsp. mustard and cress
1 tbsp. chia seeds

2 tbsp. virgin olive oil
salt and freshly ground black pepper

1   Dry roast the pecans in a single layer in a frying pan, watching constantly and shaking frequently for about 5 minutes, until they begin to brown. Set aside to cool.

2   Peel the peaches by placing them in a pan of boiling water for 10–20 seconds or until the skin splits. Remove with a slotted spoon and immediately run them under cold water to cool. The skin should peel away easily. Cut them in half, remove the stone and slice the flesh. Place in a salad bowl along with the vinegar and set aside for 10 minutes to marinate.

3   Add the arugula, mustard and cress, chia seeds and the pecans to the peaches and drizzle over the oil.

4   Toss gently, adding a little salt and pepper to taste.

WITH STRAWBERRY
Replace the peaches with 9 oz. (250 g) strawberries, hulled and cut into halves or quarters. If red peppercorns are available, crush a few and use these in place of the black pepper.

WITH FIG
Replace the peaches with 3 ripe figs; do not marinate. Drizzle ½ tbsp. balsamic vinegar over the salad along with 1 tbsp. pomegranate molasses in place of the olive oil and sprinkle with 2 tbsp. pomegranate seeds.

WITH PEAR
Replace the pecans with hazelnuts. Peel, core and slice a ripe pear, then toss in a serving bowl with 1 tbsp. lemon juice instead of vinegar; do not marinate. Continue with the salad as directed, adding 1 tsp. hazelnut oil instead of the olive oil.

WITH FENNEL & PEACH
Prepare the pecans and peaches. Use 1 little gem lettuce, torn into pieces, in place of the arugula and thinly slice 1 fennel bulb into the salad. Finish the salad as directed.

Cauliflower Rice with Spiced Walnuts

Cauliflower rice is a wonderful thing, full of nutrition and crunch and remarkably low in calories. If there is any cauliflower rice left over, freeze it in plastic containers and use in cooked dishes from frozen.

Serves 4 as a main, or 6 as a side dish

1 tbsp. sunflower oil
5 oz. (50 g) walnut halves
1 tsp. maple or agave syrup
1 tsp. ras-el-hanout or ½ tsp. each of cumin and chili powder
5 oz. (50 g) frozen peas
1 head cauliflower, cut into florets
1 red apple, thinly sliced

4 scallions, trimmed and sliced
2 celery sticks, sliced
½ small bunch each of fresh mint and parsley, chopped
2 ripe but firm avocados, peeled, pitted and cut into chunks
salt and freshly ground black pepper, to taste

for the dressing
4 tbsp. extra-virgin olive oil
4 tbsp. water
2 tbsp. wholegrain mustard
2 tbsp. maple or agave syrup
grated zest and juice of 1 lemon

1 Warm the oil in a frying pan over a medium–high heat. Add the walnuts and sprinkle over the maple or agave syrup and spices, and season with salt and pepper. Cook in a single layer, watching constantly and shaking frequently until the walnuts begin to brown, about 5 minutes; let cool.

2 Meanwhile, cook the frozen peas in boiling water for 3 minutes. Drain, then cool in cold water and drain again.

3 Rice the cauliflower by pulsing it in a food processor. Do not overfill the processor—fill the bowl to about one-third full and process in batches, transferring each batch of rice to a serving bowl as you work. Toss in the walnuts, peas and the remaining salad ingredients, and season to taste.

4 Put all the dressing ingredients in a lidded jar with a little salt and pepper, and shake to combine; alternatively, whisk together in a bowl. Pour over the salad and toss before serving.

WITH BROCCOLI
Substitute a small head of broccoli for half of the cauliflower. This makes the salad a lovely green color, so add 2 oz. (50 g) pomegranate seeds to provide contrast.

WITH DRIED FRUIT
Omit the apple and replace with 3 oz. (75 g) mixed dried fruit (sultanas, dried cranberries, currants, cherries).

WITH TOMATO
Omit the apple and replace with 3 oz. (75 g) mixed small tomatoes, quartered or sliced. Replace the parsley with basil.

WITH GARBANZO BEANS
Add 1 x 14 oz. (400 g) can drained garbanzo beans instead of the walnuts. Replace the parsley with cilantro.

Grilled Halloumi, Pomegranate, Kale & Pearl Couscous Salad

This is a great base recipe for swapping out the grains—it works just as well with spelt, freekeh, pearl barley or even brown rice. And for a satisfying side salad, simply omit the halloumi.

Serves 4

½ red onion, finely sliced
2 tbsp. white wine vinegar
½ tsp. superfine sugar
5 tbsp. olive oil
6 oz. (175 g) pearl couscous

7 oz. (200 g) chopped kale
5 oz. (50 g) cherry tomatoes, halved
¼ cucumber, chopped
4 tbsp. chopped fresh mint leaves
4 tbsp. chopped fresh parsley

seeds of ½ pomegranate
2 tbsp. pomegranate molasses
9 oz. (250 g) halloumi, cut into (½-in.)
  1 cm slices
salt and freshly ground black pepper

1 Place the onion, vinegar and sugar in a small bowl and set aside to pickle while you prepare the couscous. Heat 1 tbsp. of the olive oil in a saucepan and add the pearl couscous. Fry for a couple of minutes until it smells toasted, then cover with salted water, bring to a boil, and simmer for about 6–8 minutes, until it has swollen and is soft and translucent. Drain, then transfer to a serving bowl to cool.

2 Meanwhile, pour a kettle of boiling water over the kale in a saucepan and leave it to sit for 2 minutes. Drain, refresh the kale under cold running water, then drain again. Gently mix all the remaining ingredients, except the halloumi, into the couscous. Season to taste with salt and pepper, remembering halloumi is very salty; set aside while you fry the halloumi.

3 Heat 2 tbsp. of olive oil in a frying pan and add as many of the halloumi slices as will comfortably fit in one layer. Fry for a few minutes without moving around the pan until golden brown on the first side, then turn gently and fry the other side. Keep the cooked slices warm while cooking a second batch in the remaining oil. Stir the pickled onions into the salad, top with the halloumi, and serve.

WITHOUT HALLOUMI
Use 1 x 14 oz (400 g) can of kidney beans, drained and rinsed, in place of the halloumi. Substitute the chopped flesh of 1 avocado tossed in ½ tbsp. lime juice for the kale. Add ¼ tsp. ground cumin to the pickling onions.

WITH TOFU
Substitute tofu for the halloumi. Cut 7 oz. (200 g) drained tofu into ¼-in. (5-mm) slices. Prepare a marinade of 6 tbsp. nutritional yeast, 4 tbsp. boiling water, 1 tbsp. each of onion powder, ground paprika, and salt, ½ tsp. ground turmeric and a good grinding of black pepper. Marinade the tofu for at least 2 hours, or overnight, basting occasionally.

WITH BUCKWHEAT
Substitute 5 oz. (50 g) toasted buckwheat (kasha) for the couscous. Rinse the buckwheat, then cover in salted water, bring to a boil and simmer for 15–20 minutes, until tender.

WITH WATERCRESS
Substitute 3 oz. (75 g) watercress or other peppery leaves for the kale.

Tangy Citrus-Dill Dressing

Makes 7 fl oz. (200 ml)

2 small garlic cloves, peeled
¾-in. (2-cm) piece of fresh root
ginger, peeled

few sprigs of fresh dill
3½ fl oz. (100 ml) lemon juice
3½ fl oz. (100 ml) lime juice

2 tbsp. maple or agave syrup
1 tbsp. Dijon mustard
salt and freshly ground black pepper, to taste

1 Put all the ingredients in a blender and process until smooth; alternatively, if making by hand, crush the garlic, grate the ginger and finely chop the dill.

2 Whisk into the remaining ingredients. Whichever method is used, taste and adjust the mustard, salt and pepper to suit. If the salad dressing is too sharp, add a little water to thin. The dressing will keep for several days in the fridge.

WITH POPPYSEEDS
Follow the base recipe as directed, using 8 fl oz. (250 ml) lemon juice instead of the lime juice. Stir 1 tbsp. poppy seeds in to the finished dressing.

WITH ORANGE & ZA'ATAR
Follow the base recipe as directed, using orange juice instead of lime juice and omitting the dill. Instead, stir 1 tsp. za'atar into the finished dressing.

WITH CILANTRO & YOGURT
Blend together 8 fl oz. (250 ml) dairy-free yogurt; 2 tbsp. white wine vinegar; 1 tbsp. lemon juice; 1 tsp. Dijon mustard; 1 garlic clove; a pinch of chili flakes; a few sprigs of fresh cilantro; a pinch of soft brown sugar; and salt and pepper to taste.

WITH GINGER
Blend together 1 small garlic clove; ¾-in. (2 cm) piece of fresh root ginger; 3 fl oz. (75 ml) rice wine vinegar; 2 tbsp. light soy sauce; 1 tsp. soft brown sugar; and sesame oil and salt and pepper to taste.

Creamy Cashew "Mayonnaise"

Makes 10 fl oz. (300 ml)

4 oz. (125 g) cashew nuts
2 pitted Medjool dates
2 tbsp. lemon juice

4 tbsp. almond milk
4–6 tbsp. water
1 tsp. cider vinegar

½ tsp. Dijon mustard
½ tsp.salt
2–4 drops hot chili sauce, or to taste

1 Soak the cashew nuts in water for at least 2 hours, then drain. Cut the dates in half and cover in boiling water for 10 minutes, then drain.

2 Place all the ingredients in a blender or food processor and process until smooth and creamy. Taste and adjust the seasonings to suit. Refrigerate for at least an hour before serving.

WITH CHIPOTLE
Make the mayonnaise as directed, replacing the hot sauce with 2 tbsp. spicy chipotle chili paste, 1 crushed garlic clove, 2 tsp. lime juice and 1 tsp. tomato ketchup.

CURRIED "MAYONNAISE"
Make the mayonnaise as directed, omitting the hot sauce and replacing it with 2 tsp. curry powder, 1 tbsp. lime juice, 1 tsp. mango chutney, and cayenne pepper, to taste.

WITH ROASTED GARLIC
Peel the papery layers from the outside of a head of garlic and cut ¼ in. (5 mm) from the top to expose the cloves. Place in a small ovenproof dish, drizzle with oil and roast at 350°F (180°C) for 30 minutes, until browned and soft. Cool and remove the individual cloves and squeeze out the roasted garlic. Mash with a fork, then mix into the mayonnaise.

Quick Side Slaw

(V)

A good slaw competes with a well-dressed green salad as the most versatile salad to have in your repertoire. It's speedy to prepare, especially if you use a mandoline, and goes well alongside a beanburger or risotto, as well as being a welcome addition to any array of mixed salads. Add falafels and you have the perfect nutritious lunch.

Serves 4

9 oz. (250 g) red and/or white cabbage, thinly sliced
½ small red onion, thinly sliced
1 carrot, coarsely grated
½ red pepper, thinly sliced
4 radishes, thinly sliced
2 tbsp. chopped fresh parsley

for the olive & lemon dressing
2 tbsp. extra-virgin olive oil
1 tbsp. lemon juice
1 garlic clove, crushed
½ tsp. Dijon mustard
salt and freshly ground black pepper, to taste

1 Combine all the salad ingredients in a serving bowl.

2 Put all the dressing ingredients in a lidded jar and shake to combine; alternatively, whisk all the ingredients together in a bowl. Pour over the salad and toss to combine.

WITH MISO & KALE
Use kale in place of cabbage and add 3½ oz. (100 g) beansprouts. Make a dressing as directed, adding 1 tbsp. miso paste and a pinch of chili flakes.

WITH ROASTED SEEDS
Make the slaw as directed, and top with a handful of roasted mixed seeds.

WITH PINEAPPLE
Add 5 oz. (50 g) thinly sliced fresh pineapple flesh to the salad. Alternatively, use the segments of an orange.

WITH BEET & CARROT
Make the slaw using 1 raw beet, 2 carrots and 1 sharp dessert apple, peeled and coarsely grated, instead of the vegetables listed in the main recipe. Make the dressing as directed, adding 1 tbsp. toasted sesame seeds.

Fattoush

(V)

This is a Middle Eastern version of the tomato and bread salad often called panzanella. It's a good way to use up leftover pittas, which are toasted lightly to keep them crisp, but be sure to use very ripe, juicy tomatoes by way of contrast.

Serves 4

2 pitta breads
2 tbsp. extra-virgin olive oil
3 ripe tomatoes, cut into small chunks
¼ cucumber, cut into small chunks
3 scallions, sliced
2 radishes, sliced
1 little gem lettuce, torn
4 tbsp. chopped fresh parsley

4 tbsp. chopped fresh mint leaves
salt

for the sumac dressing
1 tsp. sumac, soaked in 2 tsp. warm water
  for 15 minutes, plus extra to garnish
2 tbsp. fresh lemon juice
1 tbsp. pomegranate molasses

1 small garlic clove, crushed
¼ tsp. ground cinnamon
pinch of ground allspice
3 tbsp. extra-virgin olive oil

1 For the dressing, put the sumac and its soaking water in a lidded jar along with all the other ingredients, plus salt to taste, and shake to combine; alternatively, whisk together.

2 Toast the pitta breads and allow to cool, then tear into bite-sized pieces. Place the pitta pieces in a small bowl, pour over the oil and a sprinkling of salt, and toss to combine.

3 When ready to serve, put all the remaining salad ingredients in a serving bowl and pour over about two-thirds of the dressing, gently mixing and adding more if required. Add the pittas and toss through gently. Garnish with sumac and serve at once, while the pittas remain crisp.

PANZANELLA
Use 5 oz. (50 g) stale bread such as ciabatta or sourdough in place of pitta. Tear into pieces and leave in a warm place for about 30 minutes to dry out, or lightly toast it. Combine 3 tbsp. extra-virgin olive oil, ½ tbsp. red wine vinegar and a little salt and pepper to make a dressing as an alternative to the sumac dressing. Make the salad as directed, but leave it to rest to enable the bread to absorb the juices. Use 2 tbsp. chopped fresh basil instead of the herbs and add 5 oz. (50 g) black olives.

WITH PEPPERS
Drain 3½ oz. (100 g) jarred grilled peppers of their oil and chop into pieces. Add to the fattoush (or panzanella above) with all the other ingredients.

WITH "BUTTERMILK" PITTA
Put the toasted pitta pieces in 10 fl oz. (300 ml) non-dairy milk instead of oil and set aside for 10 minutes to infuse. Add to the salad with all the other ingredients.

WITH "BLUE CHEESE" DRESSING
Make the salad as directed, but omit the dressing and instead whisk together 4 tbsp. vegan mayonnaise (see page 58), 2 tbsp. non-dairy milk, 1 tsp. lemon juice, and 2 oz. (50 g) vegan blue cheese alternative, and salt and pepper to taste.

Use tamari
instead of
soy sauce

Spiralized Salad with Cashew Nuts & Thai Dressing

If you don't have a spiralizer you could use a mandoline or simply cut the zucchini and carrots into matchsticks. This is a great crowd-pleaser—simply double up the ingredients!

Serves 3–4 as a main, or 6 as a side dish

2 zucchini
1 carrot, peeled
5 oz. (50 g) celeriac, peeled
3½ oz. (100 g) cashew nuts
½ green pepper, finely chopped
½ red pepper, finely chopped
½ red onion, finely chopped

2 oz. (50 g) baby spinach
2 oz. (50 g) mangetout
salt

for the dressing
1½ tbsp. rice vinegar
1 tbsp. soy sauce or tamari

¾ tbsp. lime juice
½–1 tbsp. maple or agave syrup, to taste
pinch of chili flakes
½ tsp. toasted sesame oil

1 Spiralize the zucchini, toss with a little salt and leave in a colander for 20 minutes to allow the excess water to drain. Spiralize the carrots and celeriac and place in a serving bowl.

2 Toast the cashew nuts in a dry frying pan over a medium heat, tossing frequently, for 3–4 minutes or until they have browned all over and smell nutty. Transfer to a plate to cool.

3 Add the peppers and onions to the serving bowl. Put the spinach on a chopping board in a thick bundle and cut it into rough slices, then add to the bowl with the mangetout. Dry the zucchini with kitchen towel and add to the bowl, then carefully mix everything together.

4 Put all the dressing ingredients in a lidded jar and shake to combine; alternatively, whisk together in a bowl. Taste and adjust the sweetness, if necessary. Just before serving, add the cashew nuts to the bowl and pour the dressing over the salad, tossing lightly to coat.

WITH TOFU
Slice 12 oz. (350 g) tofu and place on a baking tray. Bake at 400°F (200°C) for about 25 minutes until golden brown. Toss through the prepared salad, omitting the cashew nuts if liked.

WITH SATAY DRESSING
Combine 4 tbsp. crunchy peanut butter, 2 tbsp. soy sauce or tamari, 1 tbsp. rice vinegar, ½ tbsp. maple or agave syrup, 2 crushed garlic cloves, 1 tsp. toasted sesame oil, and ¼ tsp. fresh grated ginger to create a dressing. Thin to a pouring consistency with water or coconut water and use in place of the original dressing. Omit the cashew nuts.

WITH TAHINI DRESSING
Make a dressing by combining 2 tbsp. each of tahini and lemon juice, 1 tbsp. olive oil, ½ tbsp. agave syrup, ¼ tsp. ground turmeric, and a pinch of salt and freshly ground black pepper. Thin to a pouring consistency with a little water and use to dress the salad.

WITH MUSTARD DRESSING
Make the mustard dressing on page 55 and use it in place of the original dressing. Season with salt and black pepper.

Quinoa with Rosemary & Bell Peppers

(V)

Highly nutritious and one of the only grains that constitute a whole protein, quinoa has been eaten for thousands of years. It was cultivated by the ancient Incas.

Serves 4

14 oz. (400 g) quinoa
2 red bell peppers, diced
1 large can corn kernels, drained
2 scallions, sliced in thin rings
juice of ½ lemon
1 tsp. agave syrup
3 tbsp. grapeseed oil (or canola oil)

2 tbsp. wine vinegar
2 tbsp. chopped fresh rosemary
½ tsp. dried cilantro
½ tsp. fennel seeds
salt and freshly ground pepper

1 Cook the quinoa in salted water over low heat for about 15 minutes. Drain. Toss the quinoa with the diced bell pepper, sweet corn, scallion rings, lemon juice, agave, oil, vinegar, rosemary, cilantro, and fennel seeds.

2 Taste, season with salt and pepper as needed. Chill for 30 minutes and check the seasoning before serving.

WITH BULGUR WHEAT
Prepare the basic recipe, using cooked bulgur wheat in place of the quinoa.

WITH "HALLOUMI"
Cut 8 oz. (225 g) vegan halloumi cheese substitute into thick slices, then broil on both sides until golden. Toss into the salad just before serving.

WITH COUSCOUS
Prepare the basic recipe, using prepared couscous in place of the quinoa. Fluff up the grains before tossing with the other ingredients.

WITH BORLOTTI BEANS
Prepare the basic recipe, adding 1 x 14 oz. (400 g) can borlotti beans, drained, to the salad.

(GF) (V)

Green Bean & Chickpea Salad with Cherry Tomatoes

This brightly colored salad is packed with healthy, nutritious ingredients and makes a great vegan lunch or supper, but is also good served as an accompaniment at a barbecue.

Serves 2

3½ oz. (100 g) green
  beans
7 oz. (200 g) canned
  garbanzo, drained and
  rinsed
3½ oz. (100 g) halved
  cherry tomatoes

for the dressing
3 tbsp. white wine vinegar
4 tbsp. olive oil
salt and freshly ground
  pepper
3 tbsp. finely chopped
  fresh basil
1 red onion, diced

1 Wash, trim, and halve the green beans and cook in boiling, salted water until tender, about 6–10 minutes. Drain, refresh in cold water, and drain well. Put the beans, garbanzo, and tomatoes in a serving bowl.

1 To make the dressing, mix the vinegar with the olive oil, salt, and pepper. Stir in the basil and onion and check the seasoning. Mix with the beans, garbanzo, and tomatoes, and let stand for a while before serving.

WITH BUTTER BEANS
Prepare the basic recipe, replacing the garbanzo with butter beans.

WITH LEMON DRESSING
Prepare the basic recipe, adding 1 tsp. lemon zest to the dressing.

WITH SNOW PEAS
Prepare the basic recipe, using snow peas in place of the green beans. Cook them for 2 minutes only, then refresh in cold water.

WITH THYME DRESSING
Prepare the basic recipe, replacing the basil with 1 tsp. fresh thyme leaves.

Pear & Endive Salad with Caramelized Cashews

(V)

Belgian endive has a bright, tangy flavor, which is balanced by the sweetness of the pear and the crispy, caramelized cashews in this salad.

Serves 4

for the cashews
3 oz. (75 g) cashews
2 tsp. vegetable oil
sea salt
4 tbsp. maple or agave syrup

for the salad
4 heads Belgian endive
2 ripe pears, unpeeled

for the dressing
2 tbsp. white wine vinegar
1 tsp. Dijon mustard
4 tbsp. olive oil
salt, to taste

1 Line a plate with parchment paper. Preheat a heavy-bottomed pan over a low-medium heat, then toast the cashews for about 5 minutes, tossing them frequently.

2 Sprinkle the vegetable oil and a little salt over the cashews, and toss to coat. Add the maple or agave syrup, continue to toss for about 30 seconds, until the syrup begins to bubble. Transfer to the parchment paper and allow to cool completely. Break apart.

3 Separate some large leaves of Belgian endive and arrange them around each individual serving plate in a star pattern. Chop the remaining endive and place in the center of the dish.

4 Just before serving, combine all the dressing ingredients in a small bowl. Chop the pears and toss with a little of the salad dressing to prevent the pears from browning, then arrange them over the endive leaves. Sprinkle caramelized cashews over each serving.

WITH ROASTED PEAR
Prepare the basic recipe, but core the pears and cut into eighths. Place on parchment paper in an ovenproof dish. Brush or spray with sunflower oil and roast in the oven at 450°F (230°C) for about 10 minutes, until lightly caramelized. Allow to cool before making the salad.

WITH SPINACH
Prepare the basic recipe, using only 3 heads of endive. Do not fan the endive leaves on the plate; instead, line each plate with baby spinach leaves (1 package will be sufficient).

WITH ORANGE
Prepare the basic recipe, using 2 segmented oranges in place of the pears. Use 1 tbsp. orange juice and 1 tbsp. lemon juice in place of the vinegar in the dressing.

WITH PEACH
Prepare the basic recipe, using 2 large ripe, sliced peaches in place of the pears.

Warm Puy Lentil Salad with Charred Squash & Beets

(GF) (V)

This standard method of cooking Puy lentils is the same for most dishes using lentils, hot or cold. Make double the quantity you need, then bag them up when cold and freeze for the next time you need them.

Serves 4 as a main, or 6 as a side dish

½ butternut squash, peeled, seeded and diced
3 tbsp. extra-virgin olive oil
1 tsp. dried thyme
2 beets, peeled and diced

1 red onion, chopped
1 garlic clove, crushed
7 oz. (200 g) Puy lentils, rinsed
1 tsp. vegetable stock powder
1 tbsp. balsamic vinegar

1 tsp. wholegrain mustard
4 tbsp. chopped fresh parsley
2 tbsp. chopped fresh chives
2 tbsp. toasted pumpkin seeds
salt and freshly ground black pepper

1 Preheat the oven to 400°F (200°C). Place the butternut squash in a baking dish, toss with 2 tbsp. of olive oil and sprinkle with half the dried thyme and a little salt and pepper. Repeat with the beets (this is cooked separately to prevent the colors bleeding). Roast for about 30 minutes until soft and the squash is just blackening at the edges.

2 Meanwhile, heat 1 tbsp. of the oil in a large saucepan, add the onions and cook for 5–7 minutes, stirring occasionally, until softened and translucent. Add the garlic and cook for a further minute. Add the lentils and sufficient water to cover, then whisk in the stock powder with a fork. Bring to a boil, cover, and simmer for about 20 minutes, until tender. Drain, then place in a serving bowl.

3 While the lentils are cooking, mix together the remaining olive oil with the balsamic vinegar and mustard. Pour over the hot lentils and toss together.

4 Mix the parsley and chives through the lentils, then add the squash and beets and toss gently. Serve the salad warm, sprinkled with the pumpkin seeds. Alternatively, make the salad in advance and serve cold.

CHEAT'S PUY LENTIL SALAD
Use 2 x 14 oz. (400 g) tins of Puy lentils, drained and rinsed. Instead of the vegetables suggested, use a 14 oz. (400 g) pack of prepared vegetables for roasting. Add 1 garlic clove to the roasting vegetables and, when cooked, squeeze the garlic paste into the olive oil dressing along with 1 tbsp. soy sauce or tamari.

WITH VEGAN CHEESE
Sprinkle 3½ oz. (100 g) grated vegan cheese over the finished salad.

WITH CAPERS & OLIVES
Make the lentils as directed. Omit the roasted vegetables and mustard. Add 5 oz. (50 g) cherry tomato halves, 3½ oz. (100 g) pitted black olives, 1 small diced red onion and 3 tbsp. drained capers to the lentils.

CHAPTER 3
Healthy Soups

Homemade soups are simple to prepare, highly nutritious, economical, and the perfect way to make the most of seasonal vegetables. This chapter includes soups that can be treated as a main meal as well as lighter soups for use as a starter or quick lunch. There are ideas for all seasons and the recipes reflect a number of different culinary traditions. Whichever you choose, always make plenty and freeze in portions for emergency meals or packed lunches.

DIFFERENT TYPES OF SOUP

The bulk of soups are cooked but here you will also find uncooked soups, such as the gazpachos on pages 72 and 73, for which uncooked ingredients are blended together to make a smooth soup. Soups may be light and clear, such as stock or consommé, rich and creamy, thick and substantial, or chunky and stew-like. Although they are usually savory, there are also a few sweet soups, including those made with melon, cherry, or pear. Sweet soups are generally served in small quantities.

There are many types of soup and an almost infinite number of combinations of ingredients. The flavorings give each soup its own distinctive character. In their wonderful variety, soups can be eaten at almost any time of day, at any time of year. In Asia, they are often served for breakfast. Lighter soups made from vegetables can make a healthy snack between meals, while a more substantial soup can make a sustaining meal in a bowl. Soup is one of the classic first courses on Western menus, served before the main course. It is also perfect for a light lunch or even as a late-night snack before bed. In winter, soups can be fabulous warmers—warding off the seasonal chills—while in summer, chilled soups can be gloriously refreshing.

Wholesome and comforting, plain or complex, sophisticated or simple, whatever kind of soup you're looking for, you're sure to find it here. Packed with delicious recipes and inspiring serving suggestions, this chapter proves that there really is a soup for every occasion.

SERVING SOUP

There are hundreds of different ways to serve soup, including when and how to present it. Soup can be served on its own, simply ladled into a bowl, or accompaniments, garnishes and toppings can be added to transform a plain soup into something extraordinary. A cheeseboard, perhaps with a small selection of cheese and some grapes or celery, is an excellent choice for complementing soup and bread, making a delicious light, but satisfying, meal.

Chunks, wedges or slices of bread are probably the simplest of all accompaniments. There is plenty of choice, including bought or home-made. Lightly bake a loaf of bread, ready to heat it in the oven while the soup cooks. This is a clever choice as it gives the impression that the bread is freshly baked with none of the effort of making a loaf at the same time as making soup. Try different types of bread, include crusty baguettes, wholegrain loaves, Italian ciabatta, flavored focaccia, wholesome rye breads (such as pumpernickel), and individual rolls. More unusual choices include savory scones, wedges of warm naan bread, or pitta bread. You may want to serve the bread plain or with butter for spreading.

Bread can be plain or toasted. Small slices of toasted bread, such as baguette, ciabatta, or brioche can be topped to make bruschetta or crostini. These delicious accompaniments can be served on the side or floated on top of the soup as a sophisticated garnish. Garlic bread is another great accompaniment that can be made simply by splitting a baguette or ciabatta, spreading the slices with garlic butter, wrapping in foil and heating in the oven until hot and crisp.

VEGETABLE STOCK FOR SOUPS

A good stock is the essential base for almost every soup. This home-made stock can be frozen, so it is worth making a large batch and freezing it in smaller quantities, ready for thawing and using in the recipes that follow.

2 onions, roughly chopped
2 carrots, sliced
2 celery sticks, roughly chopped
1 bay leaf
2 sprigs fresh thyme
4 fresh parsley stalks
1 tsp black peppercorns
½ tsp salt
3 pints (1.7 liters) water

Makes about 2 pints (1.2 liters)

Put all the ingredients in a saucepan and bring to a boil. Reduce the heat and simmer for about 1 hour, skimming off any scum that rises to the surface. Strain and leave to cool, then chill or freeze until ready to use.

Gazpacho

(GF) (V)

A quick and easy version of the chilled classic Spanish soup. If you prepare the vegetables and herbs in advance, and keep them in an airtight container in the refrigerator, the soup can be put together in a minute, just before serving. Gazpacho looks particularly impressive served over ice cubes in a glass dish.

Serves 4–6

2 large garlic cloves
1 large onion, roughly chopped
1 celery stalk, roughly chopped
1 x 14-oz. (400-g) can whole or chopped tomatoes
4 tbsp. olive oil
1 tbsp. red wine vinegar
sea salt and black pepper

1 cucumber, peeled, seeded, and finely chopped
1 small red bell pepper, seeded and finely chopped
1 tbsp. chopped fresh mint
1 tbsp. chopped fresh parsley
lemon wedges, to serve

1 Turn on the food processor and, with the motor running, drop in the garlic to mince. Add the onion, celery, tomatoes with juice, olive oil, vinegar, and salt and pepper to taste. Blend until smooth. Refrigerate.

2 Just before serving, chop the cucumber, bell pepper, mint, and parsley. Stir into the tomato soup and serve with a slice of lemon on the side.

WITH CHUNKY TOMATOES
Prepare the basic recipe, but omit the tomatoes from the initial blending process. Use canned chopped tomatoes and stir them into the blended ingredients.

WITH SPICY SALSA
Prepare the basic recipe. Make salsa by combining 3½ oz. (100 g) chopped arugula, 1 very finely chopped jalapeño pepper, a pinch of sea salt, and 3 tbsp. olive oil. Drizzle the salsa onto the center of the gazpacho just before serving.

WITH CILANTRO & CHILI
Prepare the basic recipe, but use 2 tbsp. cilantro in place of mint and parsley and add 1 finely chopped jalapeño chili, ½ tsp. cumin, and ¼ tsp. Tabasco. Serve with lime wedges instead of lemon wedges.

WITH VODKA
Prepare the basic recipe, adding 2–3 fl oz. (50–75 ml) vodka, or to taste.

Mango Gazpacho

(GF) (V)

Cold fruit soups come into their own on a hot day as they are brilliantly refreshing. This is a sweet and savory soup, but if you find that a little too challenging as a concept, try the sweet mango variation first and graduate to the spicy. It's a nice touch to freeze some orange juice in ice cube trays to pop into the soup when serving.

Serves 4

2 ripe mangos (about 12 oz./350 g each)
2 garlic cloves, crushed
12¾ fl oz. (375 ml) orange juice
3 tbsp. lime juice
⅔ cucumber, peeled and if the skin is thick, finely diced
1 small red pepper, finely chopped

2 scallions, finely chopped
1 small jalapeño or other mild chili, deseeded and finely chopped
2 tbsp. chopped fresh cilantro
salt and freshly ground white pepper

1 Place the mango flesh, garlic, half the orange juice and the lime juice in a bowl and purée with a hand-held blender, or process in batches in a blender. If you want a really smooth gazpacho base, sieve the purée into a serving bowl.

2 Stir all the remaining ingredients into the soup, seasoning to taste with salt and white pepper. Refrigerate for at least 2 hours, or up to 24 hours, before serving; it must be very cold. If liked, when serving, add a few ice cubes or frozen orange cubes to the soup.

WITH SWEET MANGO
Make the soup by puréeing the mango and 4 fl oz. (120 ml) orange juice; sieve the purée, if liked. Stir in the lime juice, a generous pinch each of ground ginger and cinnamon, 2 tbsp. syrup from a jar of stem ginger, and the remaining 14 fl oz. (120 ml) orange juice. Cover and refrigerate, then garnish with chopped fresh mint leaves and finely chopped stem ginger. Omit the savory ingredients.

WITH CANTALOUPE MELON
Replace the mango with 12 oz. (350 g) fresh or frozen cantaloupe melon.

MANGO SMOOTHIE
Omit the garlic, place all the remaining ingredients in a heavy-duty blender and purée in batches, adding 2 ice cubes with each. Add more orange juice to obtain the desired consistency.

Borscht

Use
non-dairy
yogurt

This simple classic always seems sophisticated, although its ingredients are inexpensive and easily available. The original specifies a rich beef stock, so in this recipe nutritional yeast or yeast extract is used in addition to the vegetable stock to add that missing 'oomph'.

Serves 4 as a main, or 6 as a starter

1 tbsp. olive or sunflower oil
1 onion, chopped
2 pints (1.2 liters) vegetable stock
1 lb 2 oz. (500 g) beets, peeled and chopped
1 small potato, chopped

3 tbsp. cider vinegar
1 tbsp. nutritional yeast or 1 tsp. yeast extract
salt and freshly ground black pepper
1 bay leaf

grated nutmeg, to taste
soured cream, natural yogurt or non-dairy substitute, to serve
chopped fresh dill or parsley, to garnish

1 Heat the oil in a large saucepan and add the onion. Cook, stirring frequently, for 5–7 minutes until soft and translucent. Pour the stock into the pan, then add the remaining soup ingredients, seasoning to taste with salt, pepper and a few gratings of nutmeg. Bring to a boil over a high heat, then reduce the heat, cover and simmer for about 30 minutes, until the vegetables are very soft.

2 Remove the bay leaf, then purée the soup with a hand-held blender, or process in batches in a blender. Add a little more stock or water if you prefer a thinner soup. Serve with a swirl of soured cream, natural yogurt or soy yogurt, and a garnish of fresh dill or parsley.

WITH RED CABBAGE
Sweat the onions as directed, then add 1 tsp. caraway seeds and cook for a further minute. Proceed with the soup, using 12 oz. (350 g) beet and 7 oz. (200 g) red cabbage. This version of borscht is not puréed but served chunky.

WITH WILD MUSHROOMS
Soak 4 dried wild mushrooms in sufficient cold water to cover for 30 minutes. Roughly chop, then add to the soup with the other vegetables. Pour the mushroom soaking water into the soup, straining through a sieve lined with kitchen towel and reducing the stock by the equivalent amount. Use a pinch of ground allspice in place of the nutmeg.

WITH LENTILS
To add protein to the borscht, add 2 oz. (50 g) rinsed red or yellow lentils with the vegetables. Yellow lentils can take a little longer to cook, so add an extra 5 minutes to the cooking time, if required. Serve puréed or chunky.

WITH VODKA
Make the borscht as directed, adding a little more liquid to create a thinner soup. Leave to cool, then chill. Serve with a shot of iced vodka, added at the table for a bit of drama.

Quick Minted Pea Soup

(GF) (V)

Serves 2

2 tbsp. olive oil
2 scallions, sliced
8 oz. (250 g) frozen peas

14 fl oz. (400 ml) vegetable stock
pinch of sugar
squeeze of lemon juice

salt and freshly ground black pepper
1 tbsp. chopped fresh mint, to garnish

1. Heat the butter or oil in a saucepan and add the scallions. Cook over a gentle heat for about 3 minutes until soft. Add the peas, stock and a pinch of sugar, bring to a boil, then reduce the heat, cover and simmer for 10 minutes.

2. Purée the soup using a hand-held blender, or process in batches in a blender, then add the lemon juice and season to taste. Serve garnished with chopped mint.

WITH "CREAM"
Ladle the soup into bowls and swirl 2 tbsp. non-dairy cream into each one.

WITH SPINACH
Replace half the peas with 3½ oz. (100 g) baby spinach, stir with a wooden spoon until the spinach has wilted into the stock, then proceed as directed. Add cream, as above, if desired.

WITH CORN
Make the soup using 5 oz. (150 g) frozen peas. Once the soup is puréed, return to the pan and add 3½ oz. (100 g) frozen or tinned corn. Cook for a few minutes until tender before serving.

WITH CHILI & SPICES
Add ½ sliced green chili to the pan with the scallions. Once soft, add 1 tsp. ground cilantro and a pinch each of ground cumin and ground ginger and cook for 1 minute.

Roasted Pepper Soup

(GF) (V)

Serves: 4

5 red peppers
6 large, ripe tomatoes, halved
2 red onions, skinned and quartered
2 garlic cloves, peeled

1 tbsp. extra-virgin olive oil
1 tbsp. balsamic vinegar
1 tsp. sugar
pinch sea salt

pinch black pepper
1 tbsp. fresh basil, chopped
1½ pints (900 ml) vegetable stock
wholegrain bread, to serve

1. Preheat the oven to 350°F (180°C). Place the peppers, tomatoes, onions and garlic in a roasting tin, drizzle with the olive oil and balsamic vinegar, sugar, salt, and black pepper.

2. Sprinkle the basil over the vegetables and roast for 30 to 40 minutes until they are starting to char at the edges.

3. Remove the roasting tin from the oven, and carefully tip the contents into a large saucepan, add the stock and bring to a boil. Simmer gently for 20 minutes, transfer to a liquidizer and purée until smooth. Check the seasoning and serve with crusty wholegrain bread.

WITH BUTTER BEANS & OREGANO
Replace the fresh basil with oregano. To serve, warm through 3 oz. (75 g) cooked butter beans and serve in the center of the soup with a little chopped oregano.

WITH WILD RICE & SPIRULINA
Cook 3½ oz. (100 g) wild rice, mix with 1 tsp. spirulina powder and a good pinch of cajun seasoning. Serve on the soup.

WITH SPELT MACARONI
Cook 3½ oz. (100 g) spelt macaroni, share it between the bowls, pour over the soup and finish with shredded vegan cheese.

WITH TOASTED SEEDS
Serve the soup topped with toasted golden linseeds.

Minestrone

(V)

Long cooking time is the key to this wonderful, heady minestrone. The soup matures with time, so it is best made the day ahead. Don't be off put by the quantity of olive oil; treat it as a flavoring.

Serves 6–8

½ cup (125 ml) olive oil
2 medium onions, chopped
2 carrots, chopped
2 stalks celery, sliced
1 cup (125 g) sliced green
   beans
3 medium zucchini,
   chopped
3 cups (200 g) shredded
   cabbage
8 cups (2 liters) vegetable
   stock (see page 71)

1 cup (200 g) chopped
   canned tomatoes
2 tbsp. nutritional yeast
1 tsp. dried oregano
½ tsp. dried basil
sea salt and black pepper
1 x 14-oz. (400-g) can
   white beans
1 cup (125 g) orzo or
   other tiny pasta

1 Heat the oil in a saucepan, then add the onions and cook, stirring frequently for about 8 minutes until golden. Stir in each of the other vegetables in turn, cooking each one for 3 minutes before adding the next.

2 Add the stock, tomatoes, yeast, oregano, and basil. Season to taste with salt and pepper. Bring to a boil, then reduce the heat to very low, cover, and simmer for 2 hours. If making in advance, chill.

3 Reheat if required. Add the beans and orzo and cook for 15 minutes before serving.

WITH TOFU
Prepare the basic recipe, omitting the pasta. Press 6 oz. (175 g) tofu well, drain, then cube and toss in 2 tbsp. soy sauce. Place in a baking dish and cook at 375°F (190°C) for 10 minutes, toss gently, then bake for 5 more minutes. Add cubes to the soup with the white beans.

WITH BARLEY
Prepare the basic recipe, omitting the pasta. Dry roast 1 cup (200 g) barley in a heavy-based pan for 3–4 minutes, stirring constantly. Add to the soup with the stock.

WIHOUT PASTA
Prepare the basic recipe, omitting the pasta. Purée the soup using an immersion blender or in a food processor.

WITH "CREAM"
Prepare the basic recipe, omitting the pasta and using 6 cups (1 liter) vegetable stock and 2 cups (450 ml) soy milk. Purée the cooked soup with an immersion blender or in a food processor. Stir in ½ cup (125 ml) soy cream and heat through just before serving.

Turmeric Squash Soup

(GF) (V)

Turmeric is an essential component of Ayurvedic and other traditional medicines, where it is valued for its active ingredient, curcumin, an anti-inflammatory and antioxidant.

Serves 4

1 tbsp. plus 1 tsp. coconut or sunflower oil
1 onion, diced
1 garlic clove, crushed
¾-in. (2-cm) piece of fresh root ginger, peeled and grated
1 bay leaf

1 small cinnamon stick
2¼ tsp. ground turmeric
1 butternut or similar winter squash (about 2 lb 3 oz./1 kg), peeled, seeded (seeds retained for toasting, optional) and chopped into 1-in. (2½–cm) chunks

1 carrot, sliced
2 celery sticks, sliced
1¼ pints (750 ml) vegetable stock
2 fl oz. (50 ml) coconut milk
salt and freshly ground black pepper

1 Preheat the oven to 375°F (190°C), if using the toasted seeds. Heat 1 tbsp. of the oil in a large saucepan and add the onion. Cook, stirring frequently, for 5–7 minutes until soft and translucent. Add the garlic, ginger, bay leaf, cinnamon stick, 2 tsp. of turmeric, and ½ tsp. of black pepper and cook for 1 minute longer.

2 Add the squash, carrots and celery to the pan and stir to coat in the oils. Cover with the stock and bring to a boil, then reduce the heat, cover and simmer for 20–25 minutes, until the vegetables are very tender. Stir in the coconut milk and heat for 1 minute. Remove the bay leaf and cinnamon stick.

3 Meanwhile, put the reserved squash seeds on a small baking tray and toss in the remaining tsp. of oil and ¼ tsp. each of turmeric, black pepper and salt. Cook in the oven for 8–10 minutes until golden brown and crispy.

4 Purée the soup using a hand-held blender, or process in batches in a blender. Taste and add salt if required (depending on the stock), and adjust the pepper to suit. Ladle into bowls and serve garnished with the crispy seeds, if using.

WITH LENTILS
Use a small butternut squash (about 1 lb 11 oz./750 g) and add 3½ oz. (100 g) rinsed lentils to the pan with the squash.

WITHOUT TURMERIC & COCONUT
Omit the ginger, turmeric and coconut milk. Add 2 tbsp. tomato purée and 1 tsp. dried mixed herbs with the stock. If making the toasted seeds, omit the turmeric and sprinkle with a little salt.

TURMERIC SQUASH CURRY
Make the soup as directed, adding 1 sliced green chili with the ginger, and using only sufficient water to just cover the squash. Serve the resulting curry over rice.

SQUASH LAKSA
Make the soup as directed, adding ½ sliced red chili and 1 stick of lemongrass with the ginger. Reduce the turmeric to ½ tsp. and the pepper to ¼ tsp, and add ½ sliced red bell pepper with the butternut squash. While the soup is cooking, soak 1 oz. (25 g) dried rice noodles in water for 10 minutes. When the vegetables are tender, remove half of them to a bowl using a slotted spoon; discard the lemongrass. Purée and finish the soup as directed, adding the reserved vegetables, the drained rice noodles and a squeeze of lime to each soup bowl.

Corn & Jalapeño Chowder

GF V

Served with hot crusty bread, and perhaps with some Mushroom Herb Pâté (page 110), this soup makes a rich, delicious, well-balanced meal.

Serves 4–6

4 large corn cobs, shucked and silks discarded (or 4 cups/500 g frozen corn)
2 tbsp. sunflower oil
1 large white onion, chopped

2 medium potatoes, chopped
1–2 jalapeño chilis, chopped
2 cups (500 ml) soy milk
1 vegetarian stock cube
sea salt and black pepper
chopped fresh parsley, to garnish

1 If using fresh corn, put the corn cobs in a large saucepan in boiling water and simmer for 10–12 minutes until tender. Cool, reserving the cooking liquor. Using a sharp knife, remove the corn kernels.

2 Heat the oil in a saucepan, then add the onion and cook for 5–7 minutes over medium-high heat until soft. Stir in the potatoes and the jalapeño, to taste, and cook for 3 minutes more. Add 14 fl oz. (400 ml) of strained reserved corn cooking liquor or water, the soy milk, stock, and corn. Season to taste with salt and pepper. Bring to a boil, then reduce the heat and simmer for 15 minutes, or until the potatoes are tender but still retaining their shape. Serve garnished with chopped parsley.

WITH SWEET POTATO
Prepare the basic recipe, using sweet potato in place of the potato.

WITH CAULIFLOWER
Prepare the basic recipe, using only 2 corn cobs or 2 cups (250 g) of frozen corn and 1 potato. Add half a head of cauliflower, cut into half florets, with the corn.

WITH ROASTED CORN
Prepare the basic recipe, but cook the corn in water for only 5 minutes, remove, and pat dry. Lightly oil the corn cobs with a little sunflower oil and place under a broiler or on the grill. Cook for 3–5 minutes or until the kernels are just beginning to char, then continue to turn until the whole cob is roasted.

WITH KALE & BUTTERNUT SQUASH
Prepare the basic recipe, using only 2 corn cobs or 2 cups (250 g) of frozen corn and omitting the potatoes. Roast 1 small, peeled and chopped butternut squash tossed in a little oil at 350°F (180°C) for 30 minutes or until lightly caramelized, then add to the soup with the corn. Cook for 10 minutes, then add 2 cups (150 g) shredded kale and cook for 5 minutes.

Caribbean Bean & Rice Soup

(V)

The combination of tomato and coconut gives this soup a hint of sunshine even on the coldest of days.

Serves 2 generously

1 tbsp. sunflower oil
1 medium onion, chopped
2 garlic cloves, minced
2 stalks celery, chopped
2 carrots, chopped
1 small green bell pepper, seeded and chopped
1 small red bell pepper, seeded and chopped
2 bay leaves
2 tsp. paprika
3 cups (750 ml) tomato juice
4 tbsp. tomato paste
2 tsp. dried thyme

3 cups (750 ml) vegetable stock (see page 71)
1 x 14-oz. (400-g) can coconut milk
½ cup (90 g) long-grain rice
1 x 14-oz. (400-g) can red kidney beans
sea salt and black pepper

for the croutons
3 cups (125 g) day-old bread cubes
2 tbsp. olive oil
2 tsp. paprika
½ tsp. dried thyme

1 Heat the oil in a large saucepan, then add the onion and cook over medium-high heat for 5–7 minutes until the onion is soft. Add the minced garlic, celery, carrots, green and red bell peppers, bay leaves, and paprika, and continue to cook for another 5 minutes. Stir in the tomato juice, tomato paste, and thyme leaves, then cook for 5 minutes.

2 Add the stock, coconut milk, and rice. Bring to a boil, reduce the heat, cover, and simmer for 30 minutes. Add the kidney beans and cook for another 15 minutes. Remove the bay leaves and season to taste with salt and pepper before serving garnished with croutons.

3 To make the croutons, toss the cubes of stale bread with the olive oil, paprika, and thyme. Spread in a single layer on a baking sheet, and bake at 375°F (190°C) for 4–5 minutes until golden brown.

WITH BLACK BEANS
Prepare the basic recipe, using canned black beans in place of the kidney beans.

WITH CURRIED BEANS
Prepare the basic recipe, using 1–2 tbsp. medium curry powder in place of the paprika and thyme. Omit the croutons and serve with flat bread.

WITH WILD RICE
Prepare the basic recipe, using wild rice in place of the long-grain rice.

WITH VEGAN SAUSAGES
Prepare the basic recipe, using smoked paprika in place of paprika and adding ½ tsp. oregano, 1 tsp. cumin, and a pinch of cayenne pepper. Slice 8 oz. (225 g) vegan sausages into the soup 15 minutes before the end of cooking. Smoked or spicy sausage varieties would be the best choice.

Fresh Tomato & Basil Soup

(GF) (V)

A perennial favorite, the flavor of this particular version of the soup is
enhanced by slowly cooking the tomatoes in garlic-infused oil.

Serves 4–6

1½ lbs. (750 g) large ripe tomatoes
6 tbsp. olive oil
6 garlic cloves
1 medium onion, chopped
2 bay leaves

1 small potato, chopped
4 cups (1 liter) vegetable stock
   (see page 71)
sea salt and white pepper
2 tbsp. tomato paste (optional)

2 tbsp. chopped fresh basil
   or 2 tsp. dried basil
4 tsp. vegan pesto (see page 156) or
   chopped fresh basil, to garnish

1 Peel the tomatoes by immersing in boiling
water for 10 seconds, refreshing in cold water,
then slipping off the skins. Slice the tomatoes
into quarters and remove the seeds.

2 In a saucepan, heat the olive oil, then add the
garlic cloves. Cook cloves until golden brown,
remove from the pan, and discard. Cook the
onion in the flavored oil for about 5–7 minutes
until soft. Add the tomatoes and bay leaves,
reduce the heat, and allow to simmer, stirring
occasionally, for 15–20 minutes or until the oil
separates into small pools and the liquid has
thickened.

3 Stir in the chopped potatoes and coat in the
rich sauce, cook for 2 minutes. Add the stock,
bring to a boil, then cover and simmer for
15 minutes. Taste and season with salt and
pepper, then, depending on the depth of flavor
and the ripeness of the tomatoes, add tomato
paste, if desired.

4 Remove the bay leaves, add the fresh or
dried basil, then blend the soup in the pan
with an immersion blender or transfer to a
food processor. Reheat the soup to serving
temperature. Serve garnished with pesto
or basil.

WITH "CREAM"
Prepare the basic recipe, using 2 cups (450 ml) stock and
2 cups (450 ml) soy milk instead of 4 cups (1 liter) stock. Serve
with a swirl of soy cream in place of pesto or basil.

WITH CANNED TOMATOES
Prepare the basic recipe, but use 1 x 28-oz. (800-g) can chopped
tomatoes, with juice, instead of fresh tomatoes. Cook in the
flavored oil for 5 minutes.

WITH RED PEPPER
Prepare the basic recipe, omitting the basil and adding 2 seeded
and sliced red bell peppers and 1 tsp. paprika with the stock.
Purée as instructed or leave chunky as desired. Serve garnished
with basil in place of pesto.

WITH ORANGE
Prepare the basic recipe, omitting the basil and adding the zest
and juice of 2 oranges and 1 tsp. nutmeg with the stock. Use
cilantro to garnish in place of basil or pesto.

WITH MINT
Prepare the basic recipe, using chopped fresh mint in place of
the basil. Add 1 tbsp. lemon juice to the finished soup. Use mint
to garnish.

Leek & Potato Soup

Serves 4–6

2 tbsp. sunflower oil
3 large leeks, chopped
2 garlic cloves, minced
3 medium potatoes, chopped

4 cups (1 liter) vegetable stock (see page 71)
1 bay leaf
sea salt and black pepper
2 cups (450 ml) rice or oat milk

1 tsp. dried dill
½ cup (120 ml) soy cream
ground nutmeg, to garnish

1 Heat the oil in a saucepan, then add the leeks and garlic, cover, and cook over a low heat for 5 minutes, stirring occasionally to avoid the leeks scorching, which will produce a bitter flavor. Add the potatoes, stock, and bay leaf, and season to taste with salt and plenty of black pepper. Bring to a boil, reduce the heat, then cover and simmer for about 30 minutes or until the potatoes are tender.

2 Remove the bay leaf and blend the soup in the pan with an immersion blender or in a food processor until smooth. Add the rice or oat milk, dill, and soy cream. Heat through for 5 minutes and serve garnished with nutmeg.

VICHYSSOISE
Prepare the basic recipe, let cool, then pass through a mesh strainer to ensure the soup is absolutely smooth. Chill in the refrigerator before serving.

CREAMY POTATO SOUP
Prepare the basic recipe, replacing the leeks with 1 large yellow onion. When the onion has softened, add 1½ tbsp. celery seeds, 1 tbsp. caraway seeds, and 1 tbsp. cumin seeds, and cook for 1 minute. Use soy milk in place of rice or oat milk.

WITH GARLIC
Preheat oven to 400°F (200°C). Place 6 unpeeled garlic cloves in a small baking dish and drizzle with olive oil. Bake for 20 minutes, until the outside is lightly browned and the garlic cloves are soft. When cool enough to touch, squeeze each clove to extract the softened garlic. Stir garlic pulp into the soup at the same time as the stock. Prepare the creamy potato soup recipe above.

Quinoa Bean Soup

Serves 2

1 tbsp. olive or sunflower oil
1 leek, trimmed and sliced
1 carrot, sliced
1½ pint (900 ml) vegetable stock (see page 71)

1 tsp. tomato purée
1 x 14-oz. (400-g) can cannellini or other small beans
2 oz. (50 g) quinoa
salt and freshly ground black pepper

1 Heat the oil in a large saucepan and add the leeks and carrots. Cook, stirring frequently, for 4 minutes.

2 Pour the stock into the pan, then add the remaining ingredients, seasoning to taste with salt and pepper. Bring to a boil over a high heat, then reduce the heat, cover and simmer for 15–20 minutes, until the vegetables and quinoa are tender. Taste and adjust the seasoning before serving.

WITH ORZO
Replace the quinoa with 4 tbsp. orzo or other small pasta. Cook the soup ingredients in the stock for 4 minutes, then add the pasta and cook for another 5–6 minutes, until the orzo and vegetables are tender.

WITH CORN
Replace the beans with 1 x 5½ oz. (165 g) can corn kernels. Cook the soup ingredients in the stock for 7 minutes, then add the corn and cook for another 2–3 minutes, until the quinoa and vegetables are tender.

WITH PESTO
Prepare the soup as directed, omitting the carrot and replacing the tomato purée with 1 tbsp. vegan pesto (see page 156). Cook the soup ingredients in the stock for 4 minutes, then add 2 oz. (50 g) each chopped fresh or frozen green beans and peas and continue to cook until the quinoa and vegetables are tender.

Ribollita

Ⓥ

This is a version of the big, filling Italian labourers' soup, with lots of vegetables, thickened with leftover bread.

Serves 4 as a main, or 6 as a starter

5 tbsp. olive oil
1 small onion, chopped
1 carrot, chopped
1 celery stick, chopped
2 cloves garlic, crushed
1 x 14-oz. (400-g) can chopped tomatoes
2 pints (1.2 liters) vegetable stock (see page 71)
½ tsp. crushed chili flakes
1 bay leaf
1 sprig of fresh rosemary
1 sprig of fresh thyme
1 x 14-oz. (400-g) can borlotti or cannellini beans
12 oz. (350 g) chopped kale
4 large, thick slices wholemeal or sourdough bread
salt and freshly ground black pepper
freshly grated vegan Parmesan-style cheese

1 Heat 2 tbsp. of the oil in a large saucepan, then add the onion, carrot, celery and garlic and cook, stirring occasionally, for 6–8 minutes until the vegetables are soft. Add the tomatoes, stock, chili flakes, bay leaf, rosemary and thyme and season with salt and pepper. Bring to a boil, then reduce the heat, cover and simmer for 20 minutes, stirring occasionally. Remove the bay leaf, rosemary and thyme and stir in the beans and kale. Simmer until the kale is tender, about 8–10 minutes, then taste and adjust the seasoning.

2 For a traditional bread-thickened soup, tear the bread into pieces and add to the soup, simmering for about 10 minutes until the bread has broken apart and the soup is thick. Alternatively, toast the bread and place it in the base of each serving bowl, then ladle over the soup. Either way, drizzle the remaining olive oil and a few gratings of Parmesan over each bowl before serving.

WITH GARBANZO BEANS
Once the onion has cooked, add 1 tsp. ground cumin and fry for 1 minute. Add 1 cinnamon stick with the bay leaf and remove at the same time. Replace the beans with a 14 oz. (400 g) can of garbanzo beans. Stir 2 tbsp. lemon juice into the finished soup and garnish with fresh cilantro. Omit the bread and cheese.

WITH SPLIT PEAS
Once the onion has cooked, add 1 tsp. medium curry powder (or more to taste) and fry for 1 minute. Increase the chili flakes to 1 tsp. Add 8 oz. (225 g) yellow split peas with the stock and cook for 35–40 minutes, or until the peas are tender. Stir 2 tbsp. lemon juice into the finished soup. Omit the bread and cheese.

WITH BLACK BEANS
Follow the base recipe as directed, using a 14 oz. (400 g) can of black beans in place of the borlotti/cannellini. Replace the chili flakes with 1 chopped jalapeño or other mild green chili with seeds, and 1 tsp. ground cumin. Omit the cheese and drizzle of oil and top instead with soured cream and chopped fresh cilantro. This is good with or without bread.

Roasted Carrot & Parsnip Soup with Parsnip Crisps

(GF) (V)

The parsnip crisps in this recipe are great for serving with a number of soups, and make a nutritious snack on their own, too.

Serves 4

1 lb 2 oz. (500 g) carrots, cut into 1-in. (3-cm) slices
1 lb 2 oz. (500 g) parsnips, cut into 1-in. (3-cm) slices
1 onion, cut into wedges
3 garlic cloves, unpeeled

2 tbsp. olive oil
1 tsp. ground cilantro
1¾ pints (1 liter) vegetable stock (see page 71)
freshly ground black pepper
2 tbsp. chopped fresh cilantro, to garnish

for the parsnip crisps
1 parsnip, scrubbed
½ tsp. sunflower oil
¼ tsp. ground cumin
salt

1 Preheat the oven to 400°F (200°C). Place the carrots, parsnips, onion and garlic into a roasting tin and toss with the olive oil and black pepper. Roast for about 40 minutes, until just caramelized. Sprinkle over the ground cilantro and cook for a further minute.

2 To make the parsnip crisps, finely slice the parsnip with a mandoline or sharp knife and pat dry with a clean tea towel. Place in a small bowl, toss with the oil and sprinkle with cumin and a little salt. Arrange in a single layer on a baking tray and cook for 20–25 minutes until golden brown, turning often. Transfer to a wire rack, pat off the excess oil with kitchen towel and set aside to cool.

3 Put the stock into a large saucepan and bring to a boil. Once the vegetables are cooked, squeeze the roasted garlic pulp from its skin and add to the pan. Add the roasted vegetables to the stock and cook the soup for 10–15 minutes to allow the flavors to meld.

4 Purée the soup with a hand-held blender, or process in batches in a blender. Add a little more stock or water if you prefer a thinner soup. Pour the soup into bowls, garnish with fresh cilantro and serve with the parsnip crisps.

WITH TURMERIC & GINGER
Cook the soup as directed, but instead of the ground cilantro, add 1 tbsp. grated fresh root ginger, 2 tsp. ground turmeric and 1 bay leaf, and cook for 1 minute. Remove the bay leaf before blending. Serve with or without the parsnip crisps.

WITH CITRUS
Cook the soup as directed, using 2 lb 3 oz. (1 kg) carrots and omitting the parsnips. Add 3 strips of orange rind to the cold stock and heat through; remove the rind just before blending. Add the juice of 1 orange and the juice of ½ lime to the puréed soup. Omit the parsnip crisps and serve garnished with fresh mint.

WITH CARROT TOP PESTO
Make a vegan pesto following the instructions on page 156, substituting carrot tops for the kale. Drizzle over the finished soup. Omit the parsnip crisps.

WITH CARROT & SWEET POTATO
Cook the soup as directed, substituting 1 lb 2 oz. (500 g) sweet potato for the parsnips. For a creamy soup, add 3½ fl oz. (100 ml) coconut milk or soy cream. Serve with the parsnip crisps.

Zucchini & Pea Soup with Lemon Oil

(GF) (V)

This summer soup is equally delicious served hot, at room temperature or chilled. The lemon oil adds an extra flavor dimension, but may be omitted to cut calories.

Serves: 4

2 tbsp. rapeseed oil
2 onions, chopped
2 celery stalks, chopped
3 medium zucchini, thickly sliced
8 oz. (225 g) shelled peas, fresh or frozen
2 garlic cloves, minced
salt and black pepper

grated zest and juice of 1 lemon
½ oz. (15 g) chopped fresh parsley
1½ pints (900 ml) vegetable stock (see page 71)

1   Cook the onions and celery gently in 1 tbsp. of the oil in a large saucepan until softened, stirring occasionally. Add the zucchini, peas, garlic and black pepper, and cook for 5 minutes. Stir in half the lemon zest and juice, half the parsley and all the stock. Bring to a boil. Simmer for 15 minutes until the vegetables are soft.

1   Meanwhile, make the lemon oil by combining the remaining lemon zest and juice with the remaining oil. Add a little salt to taste. Set aside.

1   Purée soup until smooth. Season with salt and pepper. Stir in the remaining parsley and serve drizzled with the lemon oil.

WITH PESTO
Omit the garlic, lemon zest and juice, parsley and lemon oil garnish. Add 2 tbsp. vegan pesto (see page 156) just before blending.

WITH SCALLIONS
Use the white parts of 3 medium scallions instead of the zucchini. After blending, add 2½ oz. (60 g) vegan cream substitute. Reheat. Omit the lemon oil.

WITH HARICOT BEANS
Chop the zucchini into small chunks. Omit the lemon oil. Blend only one third of the soup and return to the pan. Add 15 oz. (425 g) haricot beans and heat through.

WITH MINT
Follow the basic recipe, using ½ oz. (15 g) mint leaves instead of parsley. Serve with or without the lemon oil.

Tortilla Soup

GF
Use corn tortillas

V
Use vegan cheese

It's the toppings that make this soup so exciting to eat—the creamy avocado contrasting with the crispy fried tortilla. Serve the toppings in large sharing bowls, Mexican-style.

Serves 4

1 tbsp. sunflower oil
1 onion, chopped
2 garlic cloves, crushed
1 tsp. chili powder
1 tsp. smoked paprika
1 tsp. ground cumin
1¼ pints (750 ml) vegetable stock (see page 71)
1 lb. (450 g) ripe tomatoes, peeled and chopped
1 green pepper, chopped
1 tsp. dried oregano
1 x 14-oz. (400-g) can black beans, drained and rinsed

kernels from 2 large corn cobs
5 oz. (150 g) chard, cut into thin strips
salt

for the toppings
2 small corn or flour tortillas
1½ tbsp. sunflower oil
1 avocado, sliced
2 oz. (50 g) crumbled Wensleydale, feta or vegan cheese
2 tbsp. chopped fresh cilantro
1 lime, cut into wedges

1 Heat the oil in a large saucepan and add the onion. Cook, stirring frequently, for 5–7 minutes until soft and translucent. Add the garlic, chili powder, smoked paprika and cumin and cook for a further minute. Pour the stock into the pan, then add the tomatoes, peppers and oregano and season to taste with salt. Bring to a boil over a high heat, then reduce the heat, cover and simmer for 15 minutes. Add the beans, corn and chard and continue to cook until the vegetables are just cooked through, about 5 minutes.

2 Meanwhile, for the toppings, slice the tortillas into 2-in. (5-cm) strips and place in a bowl. Drizzle with the oil and toss to coat. Place on a foil-lined grill tray and grill under a moderate heat until crisp and golden, or fry in a pan—either way watch carefully as they burn quickly.

3 Taste and adjust the seasoning in the soup. Serve with the toppings and a wedge of lime to be squeezed into the soup.

WITH CHIPOTLE
Replace the chili powder with 1–2 tbsp. chipotles en adobo or chipotle sauce. Be cautious, as you can always add more of this fiery chili at the end when adjusting the seasoning.

WITH PASILLA
Take 4 dried pasilla chilies and cut into 1-in. (3-cm) pieces with kitchen scissors. Heat 2 tsp. oil in a small frying pan and toast the chilies for 3–5 seconds, no more, then remove to kitchen towel to drain. Soak one-third of the chilies in boiling water for 30 minutes. Drain, then purée with 1 ladleful of the soup taken before the beans are added, then return to the pan. Finish the soup as directed. Serve the remaining fried pasillas as a topping.

QUICK TORTILLA SOUP
Use 1 x 14 oz. (400 g) can of tomatoes and 5½ oz. (165 g) canned or frozen corn in place of the fresh ingredients, and replace the tortillas with plain tortilla chips.

CREAMY TORTILLA SOUP
Tear 2 tortillas into pieces, add to the soup with the tomatoes; omit the corn. Cool slightly, then purée the soup. Add a squeeze of lime to taste, and serve with the toppings.

Miso Soup

(GF) (V)
Use tamari
instead of
soy sauce

A Japanese staple, this soup has a rich taste
and is quick and easy to make. And, it is so,
so much better than the packaged variety.
Wakame is a tender sea vegetable that expands
seven times during soaking. Do not be tempted
to use dashi (Japanese stock), as it may contain
dried sardines.

Serves 3–4

1 x 2-in. (5-cm) piece
  wakame
4 cups (1 liter) water
1 medium onion, finely
  chopped
1 large carrot, finely
  chopped

2 tbsp. miso, dissolved in
  2 tbsp. water
1 tbsp. mirin (sweet rice
  wine) (optional)
1 tbsp. soy sauce or
  tamari
chopped fresh parsley, to
  garnish

1 Soak the wakame in 1 cup of water for
10 minutes; drain. Remove the central rib and
cut into small pieces. In a saucepan, boil the
remaining water and add the onions, carrots,
and wakame pieces. Reduce the heat and
simmer for 5 minutes; the vegetables should be
just cooked.

2 Remove from the heat and add the dissolved
miso, mirin, and soy sauce. Do not reboil,
because this spoils the flavor of the miso. Serve
garnished with parsley.

WITH GINGER & SPINACH
Prepare the basic recipe, omitting the wakame. Add 2 tsp.
minced gingerroot with the onion and carrots, cook for
3 minutes, then add 2 cups (125 g) chopped spinach and cook
for 2 minutes until wilted. Remove from heat and finish as for
the basic recipe.

WITH ASPARAGUS
Prepare the basic recipe, omitting wakame. Add 4 asparagus
spears, finely sliced on the diagonal, at the same time as
the carrot.

WITH BOK CHOY & TOFU
Prepare the basic recipe, omitting wakame. Cook the carrots
for 2 minutes, then add 1 head shredded bok choy and cook
for another 3 minutes. Add 1 cup cubed silken tofu with the
miso paste.

WITH OYSTER MUSHROOM
Prepare the basic recipe, omitting the wakame. Add 1 cup (75 g)
sliced oyster mushrooms at the same time as the carrot.

Tom Yum Soup

GF · V
Use tamari
instead of
soy sauce

This fragrant vegan version of the classic Thai soup is very light but highly nutritious. The key to success lies in the balance between sweetness, spiciness, and sourness, so do taste and adjust the seasoning before serving.

Serves 6–8

4 cups (1 liter) vegetable stock (see page 71)
2 stalks lemongrass, white part only, minced
1 x 2-in. (5-cm) piece gingerroot, peeled and chopped into thin strips
1–2 fresh red chilis, seeded and chopped
6 kaffir lime leaves
juice of 1 lime
1 tsp. tamarind paste
1 cup (250 ml) coconut milk

3–4 tbsp. soy sauce or tamari
1–2 tsp. palm or brown sugar
chili sauce (optional)
1 cups (75 g) sliced mixed mushrooms (e.g., white, shiitake, enoki, straw, or portabello)
2 heads bok choy, chopped
8 cherry tomatoes, halved
1 x 12-oz. (350-g) package silken tofu, chopped
whole fresh cilantro leaves, to garnish

1 Put the first seven ingredients in a large saucepan and bring to a boil. Reduce the heat, cover, and simmer for 15 minutes. Strain and return liquid to the pan.

2 Stir in the coconut milk, then season to taste with soy sauce, sugar, and chili sauce, if using, to achieve a tangy, sweet-sour flavor to your liking. Add the mushrooms and cook for 5 minutes, or until soft. Add the bok choy and tomatoes, and cook for 2 minutes. Gently add the tofu and heat through. Serve garnished with cilantro leaves.

WITH GALANGAL
Prepare the basic recipe, adding a 2-in. (5-cm) piece of galangal, chopped, with the other aromatics to the stock.

WITH BROCCOLI
Prepare the basic recipe, omitting the bok choy. Add 1 head broccoli, cut into florets, with the mushrooms.

WITH SNOW PEAS
Prepare the basic recipe, using only 1 head bok choy and adding 1 cup (125 g) fresh snow peas.

WITH RED CURRY PASTE
Prepare the basic recipe, omitting tamarind paste and chili sauce and use only 3 kaffir lime leaves and 1 tbsp. lime juice. Flavor with 1–2 tbsp. red Thai curry paste prior to adjusting the seasonings.

GF V

Coconut, Zucchini & Mushroom Soup

Zucchinis have such a mild taste that they need a robust partner, and the earthy umami flavor of mushrooms is perfect.

Serves 4 as a main, or 6 as a starter

2 tbsp. coconut or olive oil
1 large onion, chopped
1 celery stick, sliced
2 garlic cloves, crushed
1 small green chili, thinly sliced
2 sprigs of fresh thyme

1 bay leaf
9 oz. (250 g) chestnut or portobello
    mushrooms, sliced
2 medium zucchini, sliced
1¾ pints (1 liter) vegetable stock
    (see page 71)

2 oz. (50 g) spinach, torn
1 x 14-oz. (400-g) can coconut milk
grated zest and juice of 1 lemon
salt and freshly ground black pepper

1 Heat the coconut or olive oil in a large saucepan and add the onion and celery. Cook, stirring frequently, for 5–7 minutes until soft and translucent. Add the garlic, chili, thyme and bay leaf, then cook for 1 minute longer.

2 Add the mushrooms and cook for 5 minutes, or until tender, then remove a few of the mushrooms to use as a topping and set aside. Add the zucchinis to the pan and cook, stirring frequently, for about 5 minutes. Reserve a few zucchini slices for the topping, too.

3 Pour the stock into the pan with a little salt and pepper and bring to a boil over a high heat, then reduce the heat, cover and simmer for about 10 minutes, until the vegetables are very tender. Add the spinach for a few minutes to wilt. Stir in the coconut milk and the lemon zest and juice, and season to taste with salt and pepper.

4 Remove the thyme and bay leaf, then purée the soup using a hand-held blender, or process in batches in a blender. Taste and adjust the seasoning and ladle into bowls, topped with the reserved mushrooms and zucchinis.

WITHOUT COCONUT & ZUCCHINI
Increase the quantity of mushrooms to 1 lb 2 oz. (500 g) and omit the zucchini, spinach and lemon juice and zest. Add 1 potato, cut into small cubes, with the stock. Replace the coconut milk with 7 fl oz. (200 ml) non-dairy cream.

WITH THAI SPICES
Add 1–2 tbsp. green Thai curry paste in place of the chili. These pastes vary considerably in strength, so better to err on the side of caution and taste the soup once it has been cooked and add a little more before serving.

WITH BROCCOLI
Replace the zucchinis with broccoli florets, reserving a few florets for the topping.

WITH CAULIFLOWER & BROCCOLI
Use a total of 1 lb 5 oz. (600 g) broccoli and cauliflower and omit the mushrooms, spinach, zucchinis and lemons. Make the soup as directed without reserving vegetables for the topping. Replace the coconut milk with 7 fl oz. (200 ml) crème fraîche and garnish the soup with shredded vegan cheese.

Ten-minute Noodle Soup

GF
Use rice noodles,
and tamari instead
of soy sauce

The stock in this soup is exposed, so using the best quality is particularly important. Similarly, not all soy sauces are the same, and some people prefer the Japanese tamari soy sauce, which is generally thicker and less salted.

Serves 2

1¼ pint (750 ml) vegetable stock (see page 71)
1½ tbsp. soy sauce or tamari
few gratings of fresh root ginger or a pinch of ground ginger
10 oz. (300 g) straight-to-wok ribbon noodles

few drops of hot chili sauce, to taste
7 oz. (200 g) baby stir-fry vegetables, or a combination of thinly sliced cabbage, carrot, zucchini, spinach, mangetout and mushrooms

1 Pour the stock into a medium saucepan and bring to a boil. Add the soy sauce, ginger, hot sauce and the noodles. Reduce the heat and simmer for a few minutes to separate the noodles, easing them apart with a fork.

2 Add most of the vegetables in the pack, leaving any leafy vegetables and scallions aside. Cook for 2 minutes, then add the reserved vegetables. Simmer for a further minute and ladle into bowls to serve.

WITH TOFU
Add 1 x 5½ oz. (165 g) packet marinated ready-to-eat tofu pieces with the leafy vegetables.

WITH EGG "NOODLES"
Omit the noodles. Lightly beat 1 egg in a bowl. Mix 1 tsp cornflour into 1 tbsp water until smooth, add 1 tbsp of the hot stock and mix. Pour in the hot cornflour and stir while the soup thickens slightly. Just before serving, drizzle the egg in a thin stream into the soup—it will cook instantly into fine "noodles".

WITH WAKAME SEAWEED
Omit the noodles. Add 3 tbsp. dried wakame to the soup once it has come to the boil and simmer for 2 minutes. For the vegetables, simply add 5 oz. (150 g) mixed baby sweetcorn and mangetout and simmer for a further 3 minutes until cooked but still crunchy.

Black Bean Soup

(GF) (V)

This is a fantastic soup for a cold day when the warming flavors of the spices work their magic. Some of the soup is puréed after cooking to produce a thickly textured soup, but you can omit this step if time is short.

Serves 6–8

2 cups (350 g) black beans, soaked in cold water overnight or at least 5 hours (or 3 x 14-oz./400-g cans black beans)
6 tbsp. olive oil
2 medium white onions, finely chopped
3 garlic cloves, minced
1 carrot, chopped
1–2 fresh red chilis, chopped
2 tsp. ground cumin
¼ tsp. smoked paprika

2 bay leaves
4 cups (1 liter) vegetable stock (see page 71)
1 x 14-oz. (400-g) can whole tomatoes
small bunch of fresh thyme, stalks removed
sea salt and freshly ground pepper

for garnish
1 small red onion, sliced
chopped fresh cilantro
juice of 1 lime

1 For dried beans only, drain the beans and put them in a saucepan with 5 cups of water over a high heat. Bring to a boil and boil rapidly for 10 minutes, then reduce heat and simmer for 1¼ to 1½ hours until soft. Drain.

2 Heat the oil in a saucepan, then add the onion and cook over medium-high heat for 5–7 minutes or until the onion is soft. Add the minced garlic, carrot, chilis, cumin, paprika, and bay leaves. Continue to cook for another 2 minutes. Add the beans with the stock, tomatoes, and thyme leaves. Bring to a boil, reduce the heat, cover, and simmer for 20 minutes.

3 Remove the bay leaves, then take out 2 cups (450 ml) of the soup and blend with an immersion blender or in a food processor. Return the puréed soup to the pan, stir, and heat through. Season to taste with salt and pepper. Serve garnished with thin slices of red onion, chopped cilantro, and a squeeze of lime juice.

WITH MIXED BEANS
Prepare the basic recipe, but use 1 x 154-oz. (400-g) can each of lima beans, pinto beans, and fava beans instead of the black beans. If you want to cook beans from scratch, select a prepared bean mix that uses beans with similar cooking times.

WITH CHIPOTLE
Prepare the basic recipe, using 1–3 tbsp. chopped chipotle in adobo sauce instead of fresh chilis. Chipotle is very spicy so keep tasting until you add enough for your taste. For a more Mexican flavor, add 1 cup (250 g) fresh or frozen corn with the tomatoes.

WITH WHITE BEAN & GARLIC
Prepare the basic recipe, using white beans in place of the black beans. Increase the quantity of garlic to 4 cloves and omit the carrot, chilis, cumin, and tomatoes. Stir in ½ cup (125 ml) soy cream just before serving garnished with plenty of chopped parsley in place of cilantro.

WITH BLACK BEAN & CELERY
Prepare the basic recipe, adding 4 chopped celery stalks with the carrots.

Potato, Kale & Chipotle Soup

(GF) (V)

Chipotle is a hot chili much loved in Mexico for its smoky undertones and depth of flavor. Adding it here makes a budget potato and kale soup into something much more dynamic, but add a little at a time and taste until you find the spiciness that's right for you.

Serves 4

1 tbsp. olive or sunflower oil
1 onion, sliced
2 garlic cloves, crushed
½ tsp. ground cilantro
¼ tsp. ground cumin
4 cups (1 liter) vegetable stock (see page 71)
14 oz. (400 g) potatoes, cut into ½-in. (1.5-cm) cubes
1 x 14 oz. (400 g) can chopped tomatoes
2 tbsp. cashew or other nut butter
½–2 tsp. chipotle sauce
3½ oz. (100 g) chopped kale
salt
toasted cashew nuts, to serve

1 Heat the oil in a large saucepan and add the onion. Cook, stirring frequently, for 5–7 minutes until soft and translucent. Add the garlic, cilantro and cumin, and cook for a further minute.

2 Pour the stock and potatoes into the pan with a little salt and bring to a boil over a high heat, then reduce the heat, cover and simmer for about 10 minutes, until the potatoes are just tender. Stir in the tomatoes.

3 Transfer about 2 cups (450 ml) of the soup to a blender, add the nut butter and blitz to a purée; alternatively, use a deep bowl with a hand-held blender to blitz. Return the purée to the pan and add the chipotle sauce, tasting as you go and adjusting the salt. Add the kale and cook for about 7 minutes until tender but still firm. Ladle into bowls and sprinkle with a few toasted cashew nuts to serve.

WITH SWEET POTATO
Replace the potatoes with sweet potatoes.

WITH CURRIED POTATO
Replace the cumin and cilantro with 2 tsp. medium curry powder. Serve with a swirl of non-dairy yogurt before topping with the nuts and a sprinkling of garam masala.

WITH BEANS
Reduce the vegetable stock to 2 cups (450 ml) and omit the blending process. Add 1 x 14-oz. (400-g) can black or kidney beans with the tomatoes.

WITH RED BELL PEPPER & CHIPOTLE
Roast 2 red peppers rubbed in olive oil in a 400°F (200°C) oven for 30–40 minutes until just beginning to char. When cool enough to handle, pull out the stem, halve and deseed. Chop and add with the tomatoes. Alternatively, use two large jarred peppers.

Silky Lentil Soup

GF V

This soul-warming soup is a meal in itself, perfect for anyone feeling under the weather. As an added bonus, children love it and you can sneak all kinds of vegetables into it without their knowledge!

Serves 4–6

1 tbsp. olive oil
1 onion, roughly chopped
1 green or red bell pepper, seeded and roughly chopped
1 carrot, peeled and roughly chopped
1 zucchini, roughly chopped
1 garlic clove, minced
1 tsp. ground cumin
1 tsp. ground cilantro

1 cup (200 g) split red lentils, washed and picked over
5 cups (1.2 liters) vegetable stock (see page 71)
1 x 14-oz. (400-g) can plum tomatoes
2 tsp. tomato paste
1 bay leaf
sea salt and black pepper
fresh parsley or cilantro, to garnish

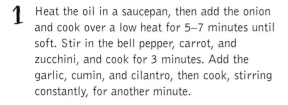

1. Heat the oil in a saucepan, then add the onion and cook over a low heat for 5–7 minutes until soft. Stir in the bell pepper, carrot, and zucchini, and cook for 3 minutes. Add the garlic, cumin, and cilantro, then cook, stirring constantly, for another minute.

2. Add the remaining soup ingredients, lentils, stock, tomatoes and juice, tomato paste, and bay leaf. Bring to a boil, then reduce the heat, cover, and simmer for 30 minutes, until the lentils and vegetables are very soft.

3. Remove the bay leaf and blend the soup with an immersion blender or in a food processor. The soup will be fairly thick, so dilute with a little more stock if you prefer it thinner. Season to taste, then reheat, and serve garnished with parsley or cilantro.

WITH GREEN LENTILS
Prepare the basic recipe, using 1 cup (200 g) green lentils in place of red lentils, 2 sliced celery stalks in place of the zucchini, and green not red bell pepper. Garnish with parsley.

WITH YELLOW PEAS
Prepare the basic recipe, using 1 cup (200 g) yellow split peas, soaked overnight in cold water, in place of red lentils. Increase the cooking time to 60 minutes.

WITH BABY SPINACH
Prepare the basic recipe. Stir ½ lb. (450 g) baby spinach into the soup when reheating, and cook just until wilted. There is no need to garnish this variation.

MULLIGATAWNY SOUP
Prepare the basic recipe, adding 1 peeled, cored, and chopped green apple with the vegetables. Use 1–2 tbsp. medium curry powder, to taste, in place of the ground cumin, and add 1 tsp. dried mint. Stir 1 tbsp. lime juice into the blended soup.

Lentil Comfort Soup

(GF) (V)

A soup to turn to when comfort food is the order of the day, this soup is a hug in a bowl. Serve with warm bread in front of the fire.

Serves 4

1 tbsp. olive or sunflower oil
1 onion, roughly chopped
1 garlic clove, crushed
1 tsp. ground cilantro
1 bay leaf

4 cups (1 liter) vegetable stock
  (see page 71)
1 small fennel bulb, roughly chopped
1 red pepper, roughly chopped
1 carrot, sliced

2 celery sticks, sliced
1 cup (200 g) red split lentils, washed
1 x 14-oz. (400-g) can plum tomatoes
1 tsp. tomato purée
salt and freshly ground black pepper
fresh cilantro or parsley, to garnish

1 Heat the oil in a large saucepan and add the onion. Cook, stirring frequently, for 5–7 minutes until soft and translucent. Add the garlic, cilantro and bay leaf and cook for a further minute.

2 Pour the stock into the pan, then add the remaining soup ingredients, seasoning to taste with salt and pepper. Bring to a boil over a high heat, then reduce the heat, cover and simmer for about 20 minutes, until the vegetables and lentils are soft.

3 Remove the bay leaf, then purée the soup with a hand-held blender, or process in batches in a blender. Add a little more stock or water if you prefer a thinner soup. Serve garnished with fresh cilantro or parsley.

CHUNKY LENTIL SOUP
Ensure that all the vegetables are cut into bite-sized pieces. Make the soup as directed, but do not blend it.

INDIAN LENTIL SOUP
Make the soup, omitting all the vegetables except the onion and garlic. With the garlic, bay leaf and cilantro, add 1 tsp. each grated fresh root ginger and turmeric and ½ tsp. each ground cumin and black mustard seeds. Add only one-third of the tin of tomatoes. When the soup is cooked, do not purée but stir in 3½ fl oz. (100 ml) coconut milk and 2 oz. (50 g) chopped spinach and cook for a few minutes to wilt.

MIDDLE EASTERN LENTIL SOUP
Make the soup, omitting all the vegetables except the onion and garlic. With the garlic, add 1 tsp. each turmeric and ground cumin. Purée and thin the soup, if desired, then stir in 4 tbsp. chopped fresh parsley and 2 tbsp. fresh mint along with the juice of ½ lemon.

GREEK LENTIL SOUP
Make the soup, but use 12 oz. (350 g) brown lentils (presoaked for 2 hours) instead of red lentils and omit the fennel, red pepper and tinned tomatoes. After cooking for 20 minutes, stir in an additional 3½ fl oz. (100 ml) olive oil and 1 tbsp. red wine vinegar. Cook for another 15–20 minutes until the lentils are tender and the soup has thickened. Serve with the herbs and an additional splash of red wine vinegar.

CHAPTER 4

Grazing Dishes

This collection of small dishes is designed to be versatile. Mix and match the plates to form a casual meal, select one for a quick supper, pack another for lunch, or use them as excellent sides. Many recipes here are made in fairly small quantities, making them perfect for sharing. The following notes on ingredients will help to ensure your grazing dishes are as delicious and nutritious as can be.

OILS

For most cooking purposes a reasonable quality olive oil is the oil of preference, although sunflower or rapeseed oil are excellent too, especially where a subtle-tasting oil is called for. Only splash out on expensive extra-virgin olive oil where it is exposed, such as where it is used for drizzling, or to make hummus (such as Butter Bean Hummus with Za'atar Topping on page 106)—then it is worth buying the best.

VEGETABLES

Choose the best-looking, freshest produce, which generally means buying seasonal foods. Frozen vegetables are suggested in a number of recipes in this chapter and there is nothing wrong with using them as a substitute for fresh. Vegetables used in these recipes are of average size, unless stated otherwise. It is also assumed that they are cleaned and peeled, when necessary.

GRAINS

Grains are carbohydrates that help to fuel the body. Whole grains release energy slowly, keeping you sustained and energized all day. Whole grains can also be an important source of fiber, and protein—which is particularly relevant to vegetarians and vegans—as well as immune system-boosting antioxidants. Other nutritional components of whole grains are calcium, iron, magnesium, phosphorus, potassium, sodium, zinc, copper, manganese, selenium, and vitamins, which are present in varying amounts in different grains. If you follow a gluten-free diet it's important to remember that grains such as barley, faro, bulgur wheat, freekeh, kamut, rye, wheat berries, oats, and spelt contain gluten. Gluten-free grains include corn, amaranth, quinoa, teff, rice, millet, buckwheat, and sorghum.

LEGUMES

Legumes, such as lentils, peas, and beans are a good source of low-fat protein and fiber. The protein is particularly important for people who do not obtain any protein from meat, fish, or dairy sources. Lentils contain about twice as much iron as beans and are also higher in most B vitamins and folate. However, beans contain iron, protein, fiber, and nutrients including potassium, zinc, and many B vitamins, as well as some calcium. Remember to rinse tinned beans well before using them as they can be salty.

NUTS

A useful source of protein, different nuts also provide you with different nutrients. Walnuts, peanuts, almonds, cashew nuts, pecans, macadamias, and Brazil nuts are rich in zinc, vitamin E, and omega-3 fatty acids. Almonds contain a reasonable amount of calcium and about four times as much fiber as cashew nuts. Cashew nuts, however, contain about twice as much iron and zinc as almost any other nut—boost your intake of these nutrients with the Cashew Spread on page 109.

EGGS

Large eggs are used in these recipes unless stated otherwise. It is best to buy free-range eggs, preferably organic. For frying or poaching, indulge in one that tastes good. Make sure your eggs are fresh: they have a thicker white near the yolk that will better hold a round shape as it cooks. Generally speaking, eggs cook better from a cool room temperature rather than refrigerated. Runny eggs are not recommended for people who are immune-suppressed, children, or the elderly.

CHEESE

Traditionally, most cheeses contained animal rennet (an enzyme that helps milk to separate into curds and whey). Today a wide number are made with vegetarians in mind, so always check the label. Cheeses such as Parmesan are strictly controlled and can only be made in a limited geographical location using traditional techniques, so are not suitable for vegetarians. However, substitutes are available, usually called "Italian hard cheese" or "Parmesan-style cheese." The quality of vegan cheeses varies, so try them out to find the ones that you prefer.

TOFU

Soft and smoked tofu can be consumed straight from the packet. Firm tofu, used in dishes such as the Gingered Tofu Lettuce Wraps on page 105, requires preparation to remove excess liquid. Remove the packaging and sandwich the tofu between two plates. Put a weight on top (a couple of cans of beans or a book or two will do), then leave for at least 30 minutes, or preferably a couple of hours, to press out the excess liquid. It is then ready for slicing and cooking or marinating.

Charred Lemon Broccoli

Charred broccoli is extremely versatile. It makes a great base for a salad, can be eaten hot with pasta or served as a side. Substitute toasted flaked almonds or nutritional yeast for the cheese if you want to make this dish vegan.

Serves 4

2 small heads broccoli
    (about 1 lb 2 oz./
    500 g), cut into florets
2 tbsp. olive oil
grated zest and juice of
    ½ lemon

salt and freshly ground
    black pepper
Parmesan-style cheese
    shavings, to garnish

1 Preheat the oven to 400°F (200°C). Spread the broccoli florets on a baking tray and drizzle with the olive oil. Gently toss the florets in the oil to combine. Place in the oven and roast for 20 minutes.

2 Remove the tray from the oven, sprinkle the lemon zest over the broccoli, trickle over the lemon juice and season with salt and pepper, to taste. Return to the oven for about 15 minutes until the broccoli is soft and slightly charred on the edges. Serve sprinkled with the Parmesan shavings.

WITH BRUSSELS SPROUTS
Substitute 1 lb 2 oz. (500 g) Brussels sprouts for the broccoli and add 1 crushed garlic clove and a pinch of chili flakes with the lemon. Proceed as directed, cooking the sprouts for 25–30 minutes.

WITH SWEET & SOUR SAUCE
Omit the lemon and Parmesan-style cheese. Instead, season midway through cooking with a sauce made from 2 tbsp. rice vinegar, 1¾ oz. (40 g) coarsely chopped unsalted peanuts, ½ tsp. superfine sugar, and a pinch of chili flakes. Season to taste with salt and pepper.

STEAMED LEMON BROCCOLI
Place a steamer basket in a large saucepan over boiling water. Add the broccoli, cover and steam over a high heat until bright green and just tender, about 4 minutes. Remove the steamer and drain the cooking water from the pan. Add the olive oil, lemon zest and juice, followed by the broccoli. Toss together, season, and serve with the Parmesan shavings.

Tapenade with Crudités

 GF V

This classic dish is usually flavored with anchovies, so if you are tempted to buy your tapenade, check the ingredients carefully. The vegetable sticks can be prepared a few hours in advance and kept in an airtight container in the refrigerator until needed.

Serves 4

for the tapenade
20 black olives, pitted
2 tbsp. capers
zest and juice of 1 lemon
5 garlic cloves, minced
⅔ cup (150 ml) olive oil
sea salt and black pepper
lemon slices, to garnish
   (optional)

for the vegetable sticks
1 red bell pepper
8 celery stalks
8 baby carrots
½ cucumber
8 radishes

1   To make the tapenade, put the olives, capers, lemon juice and zest, garlic, and oil in a food processor, and blend until smooth. Season to taste with salt and pepper, being careful with the salt because the olives and capers are both already high in salt. Transfer to a serving bowl and garnish with lemon slices.

2   Cut the pepper into strips. Scrub the carrots with a brush under cold running water to clean. Cut in half lengthways. Wash the celery and cut into strips. Cut the cucumber into sticks. Wash and trim the radishes. Arrange decoratively on a plate and serve with the tapenade.

WITH MUSHROOMS
Prepare the basic recipe, using 3 cups (225 g) sliced mushrooms, cooked in ¼ cup (50 ml) olive oil. Do not add any more oil to the tapenade.

WITH SUN-DRIED TOMATOES
Prepare the basic recipe, using rehydrated sun-dried tomatoes or drained sun-dried tomatoes in oil in place of the olives. Reduce the oil to ⅓ cup (40 ml) and flavor with 2 tablespoons chopped fresh basil.

WITH GREEN OLIVES
Prepare the basic recipe, using green olives in place of the black olives.

WITH PIQUILLO PEPPERS
Prepare the basic tapenade, then use it to stuff 1 x 7-oz. (200-g) can piquillo peppers, drained. Omit the vegetable sticks.

Garlicky Miso Cavolo Nero

Serves 4

1 tbsp. miso paste
1 tbsp. water
1 tbsp. dark brown sugar
1½ tbsp. sunflower oil

1 tsp. sesame oil
2 tbsp. grated fresh root ginger
4 garlic cloves, sliced

3 cups (300 g) cavolo nero, hard stems
  discarded and leaves torn into pieces
1 tbsp. sesame seeds

1 In a small bowl, whisk together the miso, water, and sugar until combined, then set aside.

2 Heat the sunflower and sesame oils in a wok or large frying pan. Add the ginger and garlic and stir-fry until the garlic is very lightly browned, 1–2 minutes.

3 Add the cavolo nero to the pan and stir-fry until the greens are wilted and almost tender. Then add the miso mixture and continue to stir-fry for another minute until evenly combined and the edges of the greens are just beginning to char. Serve sprinkled with the sesame seeds.

WITH RED PEPPER
Follow the base recipe, adding 1 romano red pepper, thinly sliced to the cavolo nero.

WITH TOFU
Follow the base recipe as directed. With the garlic and ginger, add 8 oz. (225 g) smoked tofu, cut into pieces. Serve on a bed of rice noodles or rice.

WITH TAHINI & CHILI SAUCE
Follow the base recipe as directed, omitting the ginger and the miso-sugar mixture. Stir-fry only 2 garlic cloves and add 1 deseeded and thinly sliced red chili at the same time. Cook the greens until tender-crisp, then drizzle with a sauce made by mixing together 3 tbsp. tahini paste with 2 tbsp. each soy sauce or tamari and water and 1 tbsp. sweet chili sauce. Sprinkle over the sesame seeds to finish.

WITH TOMATOES
Follow the base recipe as directed, omitting the ginger, miso-sugar mixture, and sesame seeds. Toss 8 halved cherry tomatoes, 6 chopped black olives, and the zest and juice of 1 lemon into the just-cooked greens and stir-fry to heat through.

Kale Crisps with Sesame

Use tamari instead of soy sauce

Serves 2

2½ cups (250 g) kale or cavolo nero, hard
  stems discarded and leaves torn into
  medium-sized pieces

2 tsp. sunflower oil
few drops of sesame oil
½ tsp. soy sauce or tamari

1 tbsp. sesame seeds
flaky salt and freshly ground black pepper

1 Preheat the oven to 150°C (300°F). Line a large rimmed baking tray with baking paper.

2 Put the kale into a large bowl and massage with the oils and soy sauce until thoroughly coated. Sprinkle over the sesame seeds, season with salt and pepper and toss to combine.

3 Spread the kale over the prepared baking tray in a single layer, being careful not to overcrowd the kale. Bake for 10 minutes, then turn the tray around in the oven and bake for another 10–15 minutes, until the kale begins to firm up and shrink. Cool the kale on the tray for 3 minutes before eating within a few hours.

WITH SMOKED PAPRIKA
Make the kale crisps as directed, omitting the sesame oil, sesame seeds and soy sauce. Increase the quantity of sunflower oil to 1 tbsp. Add ¼ tsp. each smoked paprika and cumin with the seasoning. If you like your crisps extra spicy, add the same amount of chili flakes.

WITH RAS-EL-HANOUT
Make the kale crisps as directed, omitting the sesame oil, sesame seeds and soy sauce. Increase the sunflower oil to 1 tbsp. Add 1 tsp. of ras-el-hanout with the seasoning.

WITH SALT & VINEGAR
Make the kale crisps as directed, omitting the sesame oil, sesame seeds and soy sauce. Replace the sunflower with 1 tbsp. olive oil. Add 1 tbsp. cider vinegar with the oil.

WITH LEMON
Make the kale crisps as directed, omitting the sesame oil, sesame seeds and soy sauce. Increase the quantity of sunflower oil to 1 tbsp. Add ½ tsp. grated lemon zest with the seasoning.

Tofu Lettuce Wraps

Use tamari
instead of soy
sauce

These are perfect for a light meal and are really low in fat. There is a noodle version in the variations if you want to make this a more substantial dish.

Serves 2 as a main, or 4 as a starter

8 oz. (225 g) firm tofu, prepared as directed on page 101 and cut into ½-in. (1.5-cm) pieces
1 tbsp. sunflower oil

for the marinade
3 tbsp. soy sauce or tamari
2 tbsp. lime juice
¼ tsp. sesame oil
1½ tbsp. maple or agave syrup

1–2 tsp. hot sauce
1 tbsp. grated fresh root ginger
1 garlic clove, crushed

for the wraps
1 carrot, cut into matchsticks
½ red bell pepper, cut into matchsticks
2 radishes, thinly sliced
4 medium-sized romaine lettuce leaves
1 tbsp. sesame seeds

1 In a bowl, combine the marinade ingredients and toss in the tofu pieces. Set aside for 30 minutes, if possible.

2 Heat the oil in a frying pan over a moderate heat. Using a slotted spoon, transfer the tofu to the pan and fry for 5–6 minutes, turning occasionally, until golden brown and lightly crispy. Add any remaining marinade and cook until it has coated the tofu and become sticky.

3 In a bowl, toss together the carrots, red pepper and radish and place in the lettuce leaf cups. Top with the tofu and sprinkle with sesame seeds. Eat immediately. Or if serving cold, allow the tofu to cool before placing into the lettuce cups.

WITH TEMPEH
Substitute 8 oz. (225 g) precooked tempeh for the tofu. Steam the tempeh over boiling water for 10 minutes, then cool and dice. Marinate for 30 minutes, then fry with the excess marinade, cooking on all sides, until crisp, 10 minutes to crisp. Proceed as directed.

WITH SOBA NOODLES
Cook 4½ oz. (125 g) gluten-free soba noodles until just tender. Drain and coat with the marinade, then leave to cool. Spread 1 tbsp. hummus into the base of each lettuce wrap and top with the noodles and vegetables.

WITH GARBANZO BEANS
Use 1 x 14-oz. (400-g) can of garbanzo beans, drained and rinsed, instead of the tofu. Put the garbanzo beans and marinade in a saucepan and cook for a few minutes until the sauce becomes sticky and coats the garbanzo beans. Proceed as directed.

WITH SLAW & ALMONDS
Omit the tofu. Fill the lettuce wraps with Quick Side Slaw (see page 59) and top with a handful of roasted almonds.

Butter Bean Hummus with Za'atar Topping

(V)

This is so simple to make and less expensive than store-bought hummus, so it's worth making a batch at the weekend to use in your lunchbox during the week. The key to really smooth hummus is the addition of an ice cube, which helps smash the beans; if your blender isn't up to processing ice, leave it out.

Serves 2

1 x 14-oz. (400-g) can butter beans, drained and rinsed
2 garlic cloves
2 tbsp. extra-virgin olive oil, plus extra for drizzling
2 fl oz. (60 ml) lemon juice
1 tsp. ground cumin

1 tsp. sweet paprika
1 ice cube (optional)
salt

to serve
1 tsp. za'atar
pita breads or sweet potato flatbreads (see page 126)

1 Place the butter beans, garlic, three-quarters of the lemon juice, oil, cumin, and paprika in a blender or food processor. Add the ice, if using, then process until smooth. Season with salt and adjust the lemon and spices to taste. Thin with a little water to create a creamy texture.

2 Transfer to a serving bowl and drizzle over the olive oil, then scatter the za'atar over the top. Serve with warm pita breads or sweet potato flatbreads.

WITH BEETS
Make the hummus as directed, adding 1½ cups (200 g) cooked beets cut into chunks with the other ingredients.

WITH SUN-DRIED TOMATO
Make the hummus as directed, adding 1 x 6 oz. (170 g) jar drained sun-dried tomatoes in oil with the other ingredients.

WITH GARBANZO BEANS & TAHINI
Make the hummus as directed, using 1 x 14-oz. (400-g) can garbanzo beans, drained and rinsed, instead of butter beans. Increase the olive oil to 4 tbsp, and add 2 tsp. tahini and sufficient water to create a creamy texture.

WITH EDAMAME
Make the hummus as directed, using 14 oz. (400 g) frozen edamame beans, cooked, drained and cooled, instead of butter beans. Add 3 tsp. tahini and sufficient water to create a creamy texture. Replace the za'atar with fresh chopped cilantro.

Bissara

Omit the
flatbreads

This North African bean dish is very popular in Egypt where it is served with flat bread and fresh vegetable sticks. Fava beans are also known as broad beans.

Serves 6

2 cups (300 g) large dried
    fava beans, soaked
    overnight and drained
3 cloves garlic
½ cup (120 ml) olive oil
8 cups (1.8 liters) water
1 small green chili, seeded

    and chopped
4 tbsp. lemon juice
2 tsp. ground cumin
sea salt and black pepper
paprika
chopped fresh parsley, to
    garnish

1 Place the fava beans, garlic, half of the olive oil, and water in a saucepan. Bring to a boil, cover, then cook over medium heat until the beans are tender, about 1 to 1½ hours, depending on size and freshness of the beans. Drain and cool, reserving 1½ cups (375 ml) of the cooking liquor.

2 Place the beans and the green chili in a food processor with 1 cup (250 ml) of the reserved liquor. Blend until smooth, adding more of the liquid if necessary to achieve a firm but soft purée. Return the purée to a clean saucepan and stir in the lemon juice, cumin, and salt and pepper to taste. Cook gently for 5 minutes, stirring.

3 Transfer the bissara to a serving bowl. Drizzle with the remaining olive oil, sprinkle with paprika to taste, and garnish with parsley. Serve at room temperature with flat bread and vegetable sticks, if desired.

WITH GRILLED ZUCCHINI
Prepare the basic recipe and spread it onto a platter. Slice 2 zucchini lengthways and lay on a cookie sheet. Sprinkle with lemon juice and a little salt and pepper. Put under a hot broiler until just beginning to char around the edges. Place the zucchini slices over the bissara.

WITH PINTO BEANS
Prepare the basic recipe, using pinto beans in place of fava beans.

WHITE NAVY BEANS & GARLIC
Prepare the basic recipe, using navy beans in place of fava beans and adding 1 or 2 more garlic cloves.

WITH FRESH FAVA BEANS
Prepare the basic recipe, using 2½ lb (1.1. kg) fresh fava beans in place of the dried fava beans. To cook, remove the beans from their pods and cook in boiling water for 10 minutes, until tender; drain and refresh with cold water. Remove the skins from the beans to reveal the bright green beans inside. Continue as for basic recipe.

Hummus With Dukkah

Making your own hummus is a great money saver, and you get to select organic ingredients and adjust the acidity, spices, and texture to suit your tastebuds. You may not need all the dukkah, but keep it in a sealed container and use it on salads or vegetable dishes. Serve this hummus as a dip with toasted pita bread.

Serves 4–6

for the hummus
1 small onion, chopped
2 tsp. olive oil
4 garlic cloves, minced
1 x 14-oz. (400-g) can garbanzo beans (or equivalent in home-cooked beans)
½ cup (125 g) tahini
4 tbsp. lemon juice
4 tbsp. fresh chopped parsley

2 tbsp. chopped jalapeño peppers (optional)
1 tsp. cumin
¼ tsp. cayenne pepper
1 tsp. salt

for the dukkah
¼ cup (40 g) sesame seeds
¼ cup (40 g) slivered almonds
2 tbsp. cilantro seeds
1 tsp. cumin seeds
sea salt and black pepper

1 To make the hummus, heat the olive oil in a saucepan, and cook the onions for 5–7 minutes, until soft. Put the onions and all the other ingredients in a food processor, and blend until the hummus reaches your desired texture, adding a little water, if the mixture appears too stiff.

2 To make the dukkah, combine the seeds and almonds in a hot, dry skillet. Toast until golden, then cool. Coarsely grind mixture by pulsing a couple of times in a food processor, or by lightly crushing with a pestle and mortar. Season to taste with the salt and pepper. Sprinkle dukkah over the top of the hummus to serve.

WITH BLACK BEANS
Prepare the basic recipe, using black beans in place of garbanzo beans and cilantro in place of the parsley.

WITH PIMENTO & HARISSA
Prepare the basic recipe, adding 1 chopped roasted pimento (from a jar or freshly cooked). Serve with a small dish of harissa (hot chili sauce from North Africa) in place of the dukkah.

WITH PASTA
Prepare the basic recipe. Stir 1 cup (225 g) hummus into 1 x 14-oz (400-g) can crushed tomatoes and heat through without boiling. Serve over penne, garnished, if desired, with dukkah.

WITH WITH SHREDDED VEGETABLES IN PITA
Prepare the basic recipe and use the hummus to stuff 4 halved pita breads along with shredded iceberg lettuce, carrot, very finely cut green bell pepper, and alfalfa sprouts. Omit the dukkah.

Cashew Spread

(GF) (V)

This is the vegan version of a cheese spread. Serve it as a starter with vegetable crudités or crackers, but it is also a great sandwich filler and it works well on baked potatoes. Using raw cashews creates a delicately flavored spread, while toasted cashews produce a fuller flavor.

Serves 4–6

1¼ cups (175 g) raw or roasted unsalted cashews
juice of ½ lemon
4 tbsp. water
1 large garlic clove
2 tbsp. nutritional yeast
1 tsp. balsamic vinegar
½ tsp. sugar
½ tsp. sea salt, or to taste
½ tsp. white pepper, or to taste
2 tbsp. toasted sesame seeds
1 tbsp. chopped scallion
1 tbsp. chopped fresh parsley
2 tsp. chopped fresh thyme
fresh herbs and a slice of lemon, to garnish

1 Soak the cashews for at least an hour in water; drain. Combine the cashews, lemon juice, water, garlic, nutritional yeast, balsamic vinegar, and sugar in a food processor. Process until smooth, scraping down the sides once in a while. Season to taste with salt and white pepper.

2 Transfer the mixture to a bowl. Stir in the sesame seeds, scallion, and herbs. Serve at room temperature garnished with fresh herbs and lemon.

WITH COCONUT
Prepare the basic recipe, using full-fat coconut milk in place of water. Add the herbs, if desired.

WITH ALMOND
Prepare the basic recipe, using almonds or smoked almonds in place of the cashews and 3 tablespoons olive oil in place of the water. Add the herbs and sesame seeds, if desired.

WITH PEPPERS
Prepare the basic recipe, but omit the herbs and sesame seeds. Add 1 x 2-oz. (50-g) jar pimentos and 1 tablespoon smoked paprika to the food processor with the cashews. For additional bite, add 1–2 tablespoons finely chopped chipotle in adobo sauce.

WITH CARROT & RAISINS
Prepare the basic recipe, using ¾ cup (75 g) grated carrot and ½ cup (75 g) raisins in place of the scallion, parsley, and thyme.

Mushroom Herb Pâté

GF   V

Serve with
gluten-free
toast

Whether you serve this tasty pâté as an elegant starter or as a sandwich filling, you'll enjoy the pungent earthiness of the mushrooms. Portobello mushrooms are used here for their strong flavor, but there are many mushrooms to choose from. Just pick your favorite.

Serves 4

2 tbsp. olive oil
1 medium onion, chopped
2 garlic cloves, minced
1 lb. (450 g) portobello
   mushrooms, sliced
1 sprig fresh rosemary
¾ cup (125 g) sunflower
   seeds

zest of 1 lemon
2 tbsp. nutritional yeast
pinch ground nutmeg
1 tbsp. chopped fresh
   parsley
1 tbsp. chopped fresh
   thyme
sea salt and black pepper

1 Heat the oil in a large saucepan, then add the onion and cook over medium-high heat for 5–7 minutes until soft. Add the minced garlic, mushrooms, and rosemary, and cook until the mushrooms are tender. Continue to cook until most of the liquid from the mushrooms has evaporated; cool. Remove the rosemary.

2 Put the mushroom mixture in a food processor along with the remaining ingredients. Process until smooth, scraping down the sides once in a while. Shape the pâté into oval quenelles. Heat a dessert spoon in hot water, leave it wet, scoop up some pâté, and roll it between the bowl and the spoon to form a quenelle. Slide it off the spoon and onto a plate. Alternatively, press into ramekins and garnish with fresh herbs. Serve at room temperature with crackers or toast.

WITH CHILI & CILANTRO
Prepare the basic recipe, but add 1–2 chopped red chili peppers with the mushrooms and use 4 tbsp. chopped fresh cilantro in place of the rosemary, parsley, and thyme. Serve with chunks of avocado dipped in lime juice.

WITH HERB & WALNUT
Prepare the basic recipe, but replace the sunflower seeds with ¾ cup (75 g) chopped walnuts, which have been soaked in hot water for 2 hours.

WITH HERBS & FENNEL
Prepare the basic recipe. Toast 2 teaspoons fennel seeds in a dry skillet for a minute or two until they start to pop. Add to the pâté after blending.

WITH HERBS & EGGPLANT
Prepare the basic recipe, using 8 oz. (225 g) mushrooms and 1 small eggplant. Cut the eggplant into ½-in. (1-cm) thick slices. Sprinkle with salt and let sit for 1 hour, then wipe off the excess water with paper towel. Roughly chop and cook with the mushrooms.

Molletes

Mexican comfort food at its very best, and in Mexico molettes are often accompanied by a Bloody Mary. This recipe uses tinned beans for convenience, however home-cooked beans are a doddle and it's worth cooking them in bulk and freezing them in batches.

Serves 2–4

4 small white rolls (petit pain are ideal)
1 x 14-oz (400-g) can refried beans or home-cooked beans (see below)

7 oz. (200 g) Cheddar cheese, grated
2 x quantity of pico de gallo (see page 115)

1 Preheat the oven to 400°F (200°C). Line a baking tray with baking paper.

2 Halve the rolls lengthways and remove most of the bread from the middle of the rolls to accommodate the filling (crumble the bread and freeze it for use in another dish).

3 Warm the refried beans in a pan until they soften, then divide between the cavities in the rolls. Sprinkle over the cheese, then place the rolls on the baking tray and bake until the cheese is melted and bubbly and the bread is crispy, 15–20 minutes.

4 Serve while still hot, accompanied by the pico de gallo.

WITH AVOCADO
Make the molletes as directed, but sprinkle over just half of the cheese. Top with the slices of flesh from 1 avocado. Sprinkle over the remaining cheese and bake as directed.

WITH MANGO SALSA
Make the molletes as directed, replacing the pico de gallo with mango salsa (see page 115).

WITH HOME-COOKED BEANS
Replace the tinned beans with home-cooked. Combine 6¼ oz. (180 g) black beans (soaked in water for several hours and drained), 1 bay leaf, 1 onion cut into quarters, and 2 whole garlic cloves in a saucepan. Bring to a boil, cover, and simmer until the beans are tender, 45–60 minutes. Drain and remove the bay leaf, onion, and garlic. For refried beans, reserve the cooking liquid. Use a potato masher to mash the beans until some are smooth and others retain their texture. Add sufficient cooking liquid to form a thick soup. Season with 1 tsp. ground cumin and salt, pepper, and chipotle sauce, to taste, and cook for 10 minutes.

Quinoa & Black Bean Tacos

(GF) (V) Use a non-dairy cheese substitute

This is a great filling for tacos, and the quinoa provides both texture and protein. It can be used in many Mexican-style recipes, either as it is or with the addition of some fresh or canned tomatoes.

Serves 4

2 oz. (50 g) quinoa
1 tbsp. olive oil
1 small red onion, chopped
1 red or green bell pepper, chopped
1 garlic clove, crushed
1 tsp. chili powder
¼ tsp. paprika

1 tsp. ground cumin
3½ oz. (100 g) mushrooms, chopped
3½ oz. (100 g) frozen or tinned corn
1 x 14-oz. (400-g) can black beans, drained and rinsed
salt

to serve
8 corn taco shells, warmed
2 oz. (50 g) grated Cheddar cheese or non-dairy substitute
2 tbsp. chopped fresh cilantro
1 avocado, sliced and rubbed with lemon juice

1 Cook the quinoa in boiling water for about 20 minutes until tender, then drain and set aside.

2 Meanwhile, heat the oil in a frying pan and add the onion. Cook for about 3 minutes, then add the peppers and cook for another 3 minutes. Stir in the garlic, chili powder, paprika, and cumin and cook for 1 minute. Add the mushrooms and continue to cook until all the vegetables are tender. Stir in the corn, black beans, and the cooked quinoa and heat through. Season to taste with salt.

3 Stuff the tacos with the filling and top with the grated cheese, chopped cilantro, and the sliced avocado.

WITH REFRIED BEANS
Fill the tacos with refried beans, using a 14-oz. (400-g) can refried beans or home-cooked beans (see page 111). Top with 3 halved cherry tomatoes and the toppings from the base recipe.

TEN-MINUTE TACOS
Replace the filling: in a bowl, combine 1 x 14-oz. (400-g) can black beans, drained and rinsed; 1 x 5½ oz. (165 g) can corn, drained; 3 chopped tomatoes; 2 sliced scallions and 2 sliced radishes. Season with ½ tsp. ground cumin, a squeeze of lime juice, salt, and black pepper. Fill the tacos and use the toppings from the base recipe. Drizzle with hot sauce.

TEX MEX BAKE
Make the filling as described, adding a 14-oz. (400-g) can chopped tomatoes with the beans. Put into a baking dish. Boil 1 lb 2 oz. (500 g) sweet potato for 15 minutes, or until tender, then drain and mash with 2 fl oz. (50 ml) sour cream, grated nutmeg, and black pepper, to taste. Spread over the bean mixture and dot with butter. Bake in a 350°F (180°C) oven for 45 minutes until golden brown.

BEANY ENCHILADAS
Lay 4 warmed flour tortillas on a board, fill with a few tbsp. of the quinoa mixture, fold over the ends and roll up to seal. Place in the ovenproof dish. Run a portion of tomato sauce (see page 117) down the center of the dish and top with 2 oz. (50 g) Cheddar cheese or non-dairy substitute. Place under a hot grill and cook until bubbling. Serve with avocado slices.

Fig & Goat Cheese Crostini

Makes about 12

1 baguette, cut into ½-in. (1-cm) slices
2 tbsp. olive oil
4 oz. (125 g) soft goat cheese

1 tbsp. plus 1 tsp. honey
3½ oz. (100 g) moist dried figs, cut into thin
  slices lengthways

2 oz. (50 g) broken walnuts, toasted
small fresh basil leaves
salt and freshly ground black pepper

1. Preheat the grill to medium. Brush the bread slices with olive oil and season with salt and pepper. Place under the grill until lightly toasted.

2. In a small bowl, mix together the goat cheese and 1 tablespoon of honey until smooth. Spread over the toasted bread and top with slices of dried fig. Brush with the additional honey, sprinkle over the walnuts and basil leaves to serve.

WITH CARAMELIZED ONION
Heat 1 tbsp. olive oil in a frying pan and fry 2 sliced onions for 5–7 minutes until soft. Stir in 1 tbsp. each soft brown sugar and balsamic vinegar, and season with salt and pepper. Reduce the heat to low and cook for 30–35 minutes, stirring often, until caramelized. Prepare the crostini as described, omitting the honey, figs, and basil.

WITH HERBS
Omit the honey and figs and flavor the goat cheese with ½ tsp. grated lemon zest and 3 tbsp. mixed fresh herbs. Season generously with salt and pepper and serve topped with sliced sun-dried tomatoes and small fresh herb leaves.

WITH HUMMUS & FETA
In place of the suggested toppings, spread 1 tbsp. hummus over the toasted bread. Chop 10 green and black olives and mix with 2 oz. (50 g) crumbled feta cheese. Sprinkle over the hummus.

Cheesy Paprika Potato Wedges

Serves 4

4 medium potatoes, unpeeled
2 tbsp. olive oil
½ tsp. dried thyme
½ tsp. paprika

¼ tsp. garlic powder
4 tbsp. Parmesan-style cheese
salt and freshly ground black pepper

5 fl oz. (150 ml) soured cream mixed with
  1 tbsp. chopped fresh chives, to serve
  (optional)

1. Preheat the oven to 400°F (200°C). Slice the potatoes into even wedges.

2. Pour the olive oil into a rimmed baking tray. Add the thyme, paprika, garlic powder, and a little salt and pepper and mix with the olive oil. Put the potatoes on the tray and use your hands to coat them with the olive oil-spice mix.

3. Spread them out into a single layer and bake for 15 minutes. Use a fish slice to turn the wedges over, then sprinkle with the Parmesan cheese. Bake for another 15–20 minutes until golden brown.

4. Remove from the oven and allow to rest for 2–3 minutes to enable them to be removed from the trays more easily. Serve immediately with the soured cream and chives, if using.

WITH JERK SEASONING
Replace the thyme, paprika, garlic powder, salt, and pepper with 1 tbsp. jerk seasoning.

WITH SRIRACHA MINT MAYO
Omit the soured cream and serve with the Sriracha Mint Mayo (see page 118).

WITH LEMON & GARLIC
Replace the garlic powder with 8 unpeeled garlic cloves and the juice of 1 lemon. Bake as directed, omitting the Parmesan-style cheese. When cooked, squeeze the garlic out of the papery skin into a small bowl, mash slightly with a fork and toss into the wedges. Serve with the soured cream and chives.

PATATAS BRAVAS
Cook the wedges as directed, omitting the Parmesan-style cheese. Make the tomato sauce on page 117, substituting 1 tsp. paprika for the red chili. Toss the sauce through the potatoes once golden brown, and continue to roast until the sauce dries out a little, about 10 minutes.

Use gluten-free bread

Avocado Toast with Pico de Gallo

Maybe the greatest quick-fix meal ever. With the ingredients so exposed, the key is to use really good avocados and tasty fresh bread; ripe avocados should yield a bit to a gentle squeeze when purchased. Ideally, make more pico de gallo than you need and keep in the fridge to use with salads or as a dip.

Serves 1

1 small ripe avocado
2 tsp. lemon or lime juice
pinch of chili flakes
2 thick slices sourdough, seeded or wholemeal bread
1 tbsp. extra-virgin olive oil
salt and ground black pepper

for the pico de gallo
2 plum tomatoes, finely chopped
¼ onion, finely chopped
½ jalapeño or mild green chili, deseeded and finely chopped
¼ garlic clove, crushed
grated zest and juice of ¼ lemon or lime
1 tbsp. chopped fresh cilantro

1 Combine all the ingredients for the pico de gallo in a small bowl, season to taste with salt and set aside. This is best made 15 minutes in advance for the flavors to meld, though this is not imperative if you can't wait.

2 Cut the avocado in half lengthways, then into quarters, making it easier to twist and remove the stone and skin. Scoop the avocado flesh into a bowl, discarding any stringy, bruised or black bits before mashing with a fork to your desired texture. Squeeze in the lemon or lime juice, then season to taste with sea salt, black pepper, and chili flakes.

3 Toast the bread on both sides, drizzle over the oil, then pile on the avocado and top with the pico de gallo.

WITH MINT
Replace the cilantro in the pico de gallo with chopped fresh mint leaves.

WITH MANGO SALSA
In the pico de gallo, replace the tomatoes with the flesh of ½ ripe mango and add 1 tsp. grated orange zest.

WITH DUKKAH
Dukkah can be purchased or make your own. Warm a small frying pan over moderate heat and add 2 oz. (50 g) finely chopped hazelnuts or pistachios. Cook, stirring often, for 3–4 minutes until toasted, then tip into a bowl. To the same pan, add 4 tbsp. sesame seeds and 2 tbsp. cumin seeds (or 2 tsp. ground cumin) and 1 tbsp. cilantro seeds (or 1 tsp. ground cilantro) and cook for 1–2 minutes until just toasted; add to the bowl. Stir in 2 tsp. dried oregano and salt and pepper to taste. Cool and sprinkle 1 tsp. or so over each slice of avocado toast in place of the pico de gallo. Store excess dukkah in a lidded jar for up to 1 month.

Mozzarella & Spinach Pita Pizza

You can vary the toppings on this pizza to use up what is to hand. If you want a shortcut, use a good-quality shop-bought tomato sauce for the base—heat the sauce for a few minutes to thicken it.

Serves 2

1 oz. (25 g) baby spinach
2 wholemeal pita breads
½ red pepper, sliced
2 oz. (50 g) mozzarella, torn

for the tomato sauce
1 tbsp. olive oil
½ x 14-oz. (400-g) can chopped tomatoes
1 garlic clove

½ red chili, deseeded
pinch of superfine sugar
salt and ground black pepper

1 Preheat the oven to 400°F (200°C), or heat the grill to its highest setting.

2 For the tomato sauce, heat the oil in a small saucepan and add the garlic. Fry lightly until golden brown, then remove the garlic and discard. Add the tomatoes, chili and a pinch of sugar. Bring the sauce to the boil, then reduce the heat and simmer for about 5 minutes, stirring frequently, until thickened. Remove the chili, season to taste and set aside.

3 Meanwhile, put the spinach in a sieve, hold over the sink and pour a kettle of boiling water over the spinach to blanch it. Allow to cool until it can be handled.

4 Arrange the pita breads on a baking tray. Spread them with a layer of tomato sauce, arrange the spinach and red pepper slices over the top and sprinkle with the mozzarella cheese. Bake in the oven for 5–10 minutes, until the mozzarella is bubbling and the bases are crisp; alternatively, cook under the grill for 3–4 minutes, checking frequently as these can burn easily.

WITH FLATBREAD
Make the pizzas as directed, using 2 regular wholemeal flatbreads or 4 mini flatbreads instead of pitas. Alternatively, make your own sweet potato flatbreads (see page 126).

WITH WALNUTS & BLUE CHEESE
Make the pizzas as directed, substituting 2 oz. (50 g) blue cheese for the mozzarella and adding 4 broken walnut halves with the cheese.

WITH RICOTTA & ARTICHOKE
Make the pizzas as directed, omitting the pepper and mozzarella. Add ½ x 14 oz. (400 g) can artichokes (or equivalent in jarred or deli artichokes), drained and quartered, to the pizzas on top of the spinach. Dot the ricotta over the top.

WITH PINE NUTS & RAISINS
Make the pizzas as directed. Add 2 tbsp. each of pine nuts and raisins with the spinach along with a few capers.

Halloumi Chips with Sriracha Mint Mayo

Panko breadcrumbs are Asian-style breadcrumbs which are used to coat fried foods. They are dried at a low heat, resulting in breadcrumbs that stay crispier longer. Make them at home by drying finely grated day-old breadcrumbs in a 300°F (150°C) oven for 10 minutes until crisp but not colored. Store in an airtight container once cool.

Serves 3

1 x 9-oz. (250-g) pack of
    halloumi
1 tbsp. plain flour
1 tsp. smoked paprika
1 egg, beaten
2 oz. (50 g) panko
    breadcrumbs
sunflower or rapeseed oil,
    for frying

for the Sriracha mint
    mayo
4 fl oz. (120 ml)
    mayonnaise
½ garlic clove, crushed
1½ tbsp. Sriracha or
    similar hot chili sauce
1 tbsp. lemon juice
1 tbsp. chopped fresh
    mint leaves
salt, to taste

1 Combine all the ingredients for the Sriracha mayo and set aside.

2 Slice the halloumi into six pieces, then halve lengthways, making twelve chips. Line up three bowls, one containing the flour mixed with smoked paprika; the next containing the beaten egg; and the third bowl with the breadcrumbs. Coat each halloumi chip first in the flour mixture, then dip in the egg, and finally coat with breadcrumbs.

3 Fill a shallow heavy-bottomed pan or deep frying pan with oil to a depth of about ½ in. (1 cm) and heat to 350°F (180°C) on a cooking thermometer (or until a piece of bread browns in the oil in 20 seconds). Working in batches, carefully lower the halloumi chips into the oil and fry for about 2 minutes on each side until crisp and golden, then drain on kitchen towel. Serve hot, using the Sriracha mayo as a dip.

WITH ZA'ATAR
When making the chips, add 1½ tbsp. za'atar to the bowl containing flour, and reduce the smoked paprika to ¼ tsp. Continue as directed. This is also good with the polenta chips (below).

WITH POLENTA CHIPS
Make up 3 oz. (80 g) polenta following the packet directions and stir in 3 tbsp. grated hard, strong cheese. Line a baking dish with baking paper, pour in the polenta to a depth of about ½ in. (1.5 cm), smooth to flatten, cool, then chill until solid. Cut into chips. Continue as directed, using dried polenta instead of breadcrumbs.

WITH YOGURT-MINT DIP
In a serving bowl, combine 4 fl oz. (125 ml) Greek yogurt, 4 tbsp. fresh chopped mint, 1 crushed garlic clove, ½ tbsp. lemon juice, ½ tsp. ground cumin, and ½ tsp. cayenne pepper with salt and pepper to taste. Serve instead of the Sriracha mayo.

Baked Zucchini Falafels

Use gluten-free oats and gram flour

These falafels are baked to reduce the oil used in cooking, but traditionally they would have been fried. If you wish to follow tradition, fry them in plenty of olive oil for 3–5 minutes per side, making sure they cook evenly. Either way, serve stuffed in pita bread with hummus, lettuce, cucumber, and tomato or on top of a grainy salad.

Makes 12

1 zucchini, coarsely grated
1 x 14-oz. (400-g) can garbanzo bean, drained and rinsed
2 oz. (50 g) porridge oats
2 tbsp. chopped spring onion
1 garlic clove, crushed
1 tbsp. harissa paste
1 tsp. tahini
½ tsp. paprika
½ tsp. ground cumin
1 tsp. lime juice
gram (garbanzo bean) flour or plain flour, to coat
salt

1 Preheat the oven to 350°F (180°C). Line a baking tray with baking paper.

2 Place the grated zucchini on a clean tea towel, gather up the edges and squeeze gently to remove the water. Place in the bowl of a food processor with the garbanzo bean and pulse on low to pulverise; alternatively, you could use a potato masher. Add the remaining ingredients, except the flour, and pulse to combine. Adjust the seasoning as needed.

3 Divide the mixture into twelve pieces and, with damp hands, roll each one into a ball, adding a little flour if the mixture is too sticky to hold together. Roll each ball lightly in the flour and arrange on the baking tray. Bake for 15 minutes, then carefully turn them over and bake for another 10–15 minutes until golden all over. The longer they cook, the more they will dry out, so do not overbake.

WITH QUINOA
Replace the oats with 2 oz (50 g) cooked quinoa.

WITH BEETS & CILANTRO
Replace the zucchini with 2 small peeled, grated beets and add 1 tsp. ground cilantro with the other spices. This also works with carrot.

WITH ALMOND
Replace the oats with 1½ oz. (40 g) ground almonds.

INDIAN FALAFELS
Replace the spices with 1–2 tsp. curry powder, to taste, and add 1 tbsp. chopped fresh cilantro to the mixture.

Smoky Cheese Delights with Raw Tomato Dip

These cheese balls are much simpler to prepare than they look, although you do need to leave time to chill the mixture. They can also be cooked from frozen—just add a few minutes to the cooking time.

Makes 16

12 oz. (350 g) whole milk ricotta
4 oz. (125 g) smoked Cheddar cheese, finely grated
4 oz. (125 g) mozzarella, grated
2 oz. (50 g) plain flour
2 eggs, lightly beaten

3½ oz. (100 g) panko or dry breadcrumbs
sunflower or rapeseed oil, for frying

for the raw tomato dip
14 oz. (400 g) fresh tomatoes
2 tbsp. chopped fresh mint

2 tbsp. chopped fresh parsley
grated zest and juice of ½ lemon
olive oil, for drizzling
salt and freshly ground black pepper

1 Combine the cheeses in a bowl. Scoop 1 tablespoon of the mixture into your damp hand and roll gently into a ball. Place on a baking tray lined with baking paper and repeat until all the mixture is used up. Place the tray in the freezer for at least 30 minutes to firm up.

2 Put the flour, eggs and breadcrumbs in three separate bowls and roll each ball in the flour, then in the eggs, and lastly in the breadcrumbs, returning to the baking tray. Freeze again for 30 minutes. The cheese balls can be frozen and bagged up for storage at this stage.

3 Meanwhile, make the dipping sauce. Grate the tomatoes into a bowl. Discard the skins. Combine the grated tomato with all the other ingredients; ideally, prepare this 30 minutes in advance to allow the flavors to blend.

4 Fill a shallow heavy-bottomed pan or deep frying pan with oil to a depth of about ½ in. (1 cm) and heat to 350°F (180°C) on a cooking thermometer (or until a piece of bread browns in the oil in 20 seconds). Working in batches, carefully lower the cheese balls into the oil and fry for 2–3 minutes, turning to cook on all sides until crisp and golden. Drain on kitchen towel and serve warm with the dipping sauce.

WITH GOAT CHEESE
For the cheese, use 12 oz. (350 g) crumbly goat cheese (the log type works well), 4 oz. (125 g) grated hard goat cheese and 4 oz. (125 g) grated mozzarella. Make the fritters as directed.

WITH SWISS CHEESE
For the cheese, use 12 oz. (350 g) ricotta, 4 oz. (125 g) grated Gruyère cheese, and 4 oz. (125 g) Emmental cheese. Make the fritters as directed.

WITH BALSAMIC GARLIC DIP
Put 4 fl oz. (120 ml) olive oil in a small pan and add 3 crushed garlic cloves. Gently warm through, stirring continuously—do not cook the garlic, simply heat through then cool and discard it. Transfer to a bowl and stir in 1 tsp. dried oregano and 4 tbsp. balsamic vinegar. Season with salt and pepper, to taste. Serve with the cheese balls instead of the tomato dip.

WITH BLACK PEPPER DIPPING SAUCE
Beat 1 egg yolk until smooth, then stir in 1 tbsp. soy sauce, 1 tsp. freshly ground black pepper, 2 tbsp. lemon juice, ½ tbsp. superfine sugar and 1 tsp. salt. Thin down with 2 tbsp. hot water or vegetable stock. Place into a hot pan for 30–60 seconds, stirring. The mixture will thicken slightly, but do not overcook or it will scramble. Taste and adjust the sweet, sour, salt balance; cool to room temperature. Serve with the cheese balls instead of the tomato dip.

(V)

Summer Rolls with Peanut Dipping Sauce

Don't be put off by the long list of ingredients and the detailed instructions—these are much easier to make than first appears, and once you've made a couple you've mastered them for life.

Makes 4

for the peanut dipping sauce
5 fl oz. (150 ml) hoisin sauce
6 tbsp. peanut butter
3½ fl oz. (100 ml) water
3 tbsp. lime juice
1½ tbsp. soy sauce

for the summer rolls
4 spring roll wrappers
2 oz. (50 g) straight to wok rice noodles
½ red pepper, cut into matchsticks
3-in. (7.5-cm) piece cucumber, cut into matchsticks

½ carrot, cut into matchsticks
2–3 medium radishes, thinly sliced
2 scallions, cut into strips
16 fresh mint leaves
few drops of sesame oil
¼ tsp. chili flakes

1 Whisk together all the sauce ingredients in a bowl until smooth. Set aside. One at a time, soak the spring roll wrappers in warm water for about 10 seconds to moisten. Lay the wrappers on the work surface for around a minute to allow the water to soak through, making the wrappers flexible.

2 Lay one quarter of the rice noodles about ¾ in. (1.5 cm) in from the bottom edge of the wrapper, then line up the vegetables and top with four mint leaves. Drizzle the noodles with a few drops of sesame oil and a sprinkling of chili flakes. Bring the bottom edge of the wrapper tightly over the filling, the fold the sides in over it. Roll up the wrapper from the bottom, tucking in the filling as you roll. Place on the plate, seam side down. Repeat with the remaining wrappers and serve with the dipping sauce.

CRISPY SUMMER ROLLS
Prepare the summer rolls. Heat 8 fl oz. (250 ml) sunflower oil in a wok or large frying pan over a medium heat. Fry the spring rolls until crisp and golden brown on both sides, about 5 minutes. Drain on kitchen towel and serve with the dipping sauce.

WITH JAPANESE DIP
Omit the peanut dipping sauce. Whisk together 4 tbsp. tamari, ¼ tsp. sesame oil and about ¼–½ tsp. prepared wasabi, to taste. Serve with the summer rolls.

WITH SWEET CHILI DIPPING SAUCE
Omit the peanut dipping sauce. Place 1 finely chopped red chili (deseeded for a milder taste) in a small saucepan with 3½ fl oz. (100 ml) water. Add 1 finely chopped garlic clove, 2 oz. (50 g) superfine sugar and 3 tbsp. rice or white wine vinegar. Bring to a boil, stirring, until the sugar has dissolved, then simmer for 3–5 minutes until reduced by half. Remove from the heat and pour into a small dish. Leave to cool and serve with the summer rolls.

WITH TOFU
Prepare 12 oz. (350 g) tofu (see page 101), cutting it into fingers. Spread the tofu onto a baking tray and bake at 400°F (200°C) for about 25 minutes until golden brown. Cool, then sprinkle with the sesame oil and chili flakes and add to the spring rolls instead of the rice noodles. Serve with the dipping sauce.

Sweet Potato Steaks with Balsamic Glaze

GF · V
Use maple syrup instead of honey

Oh so simple, but a dish that works well as a side or can be the focus of a main course when served on top of a bed of steamed green vegetables. Do take the time to line the baking tray or you will regret it when it comes to the washing up.

Serves 2

2 sweet potatoes, unpeeled
2 tbsp. olive oil
2 tbsp. balsamic vinegar
2 tbsp. maple syrup or honey
small sprig of fresh rosemary, finely chopped, or ¼ tsp. dried rosemary

1 garlic clove, crushed
salt and freshly ground black pepper
raw tomato dip (see page 121), to serve

1 Preheat the oven to 400°F (200°C). Line a baking tray with baking paper. Cut the sweet potatoes lengthways into "steaks" about ½-in. (1-cm) thick.

2 Combine all the remaining ingredients together in a large bowl and season to taste. Add the sweet potatoes steaks and toss to coat. Turn out onto the lined baking tray and roast in the oven for 30 minutes, or until browned and tender, turning halfway through. Serve with a raw tomato dip.

WITH PAPRIKA & CINNAMON GLAZE
Reduce the maple syrup or honey to 1 tsp. and add 1 tsp. each paprika, ground cinnamon, and a pinch of chili flakes to the glaze.

WITH SPICE RUB
Replace the balsamic glaze with a spice rub: toast 1 tbsp. each of cilantro and fennel seeds and ½ tsp. cumin seeds in a dry non-stick frying pan for about 1 minute, until fragrant. Add the seeds to a pestle and mortar with a garlic clove and grind together. Pour in 2 tbsp. olive oil and mix together. Brush over the sweet potato slices and cook as directed.

WITH CAULIFLOWER
In place of the sweet potatoes, cut a cauliflower head into slices about ½-in. (1.5-cm) thick. Proceed as directed, cooking the steaks for about 20 minutes.

Spinach Vadai & Coconut Chutney

(V)

Serves 4

1 cup (200 g) yellow split peas (chana dal)
2 cups (125 g) shredded fresh spinach, washed
1 small onion, finely chopped
1–1½ green chilis, finely chopped
1 tsp. minced gingerroot
5 curry leaves, finely chopped
½ tsp. garam masala or turmeric
2 tbsp. chopped fresh cilantro

sea salt
sunflower oil, to fry

for the coconut chutney
1 cup (125 g) freshly grated coconut
2 tbsp. chopped onion
1 fresh green chili
2 tbsp. chopped fresh cilantro
1 tbsp. lemon or lime juice
1 tbsp. black mustard seeds

1 Soak the split peas for at least 2 hours, and then drain. Meanwhile, cook the washed spinach until wilted in a saucepan with no water other than that clinging to the leaves; drain and cool.

2 To make the chutney, combine all the ingredients except the mustard seeds in a blender until coarsely ground, adding a little water if necessary. Heat the mustard seeds in a hot dry pan until they pop. Add to the chutney and adjust the seasoning to taste. Set aside until ready to serve.

3 Put the drained peas in a food processor and blend to a coarse paste without adding any water. Tip into a bowl and stir in the cooked spinach and the remaining ingredients. Using wet hands, form the mixture into small round patties about 1½ in. (4 cm) in diameter.

4 Heat a little sunflower oil in a skillet and fry the vadai in batches, turning to ensure that they are golden brown all over. Drain on paper towels and keep warm until serving.

WITH YOGURT SAUCE
Prepare basic vadai, omitting the spinach. In place of the chutney, make a sauce with 2 cups (500 ml) soy yogurt, 2 tablespoons water, and ¼ teaspoon each of salt and sugar or to taste. Pour over vadai and garnish with red chili powder, ground cumin, and fresh cilantro leaves.

WITH FRESH TOMATO CHUTNEY
Prepare basic vadai. Make a tomato chutney by combining 3 skinned and chopped tomatoes with 1 finely chopped red onion, ½ cup (25 g) freshly chopped mint, 1 tablespoon chili-flavored oil, and 1 teaspoon toasted cumin seeds.

WITH FRESH MANGO CHUTNEY
Prepare basic vadai. Serve with mango chutney (page 128).

WITH RED CHILI
Prepare the basic recipe, but make a hotter version by using red chilis in place of the green chilis.

Muhammara Dip with Sweet Potato Flatbreads

(V)

Two versatile recipes in one. Use muhammara as a filling for potatoes, thinned down as a pasta sauce or with vegetables in a wrap. The sweet potato flatbread is a two-ingredient miracle food that is great with curries or stews.

Serves 2–4

for the muhammara dip
2 red bell peppers
1½ tbsp. extra-virgin olive oil
1½ oz. (40 g) walnuts, toasted
1 small garlic clove, crushed
1½ oz. (40 g) fresh breadcrumbs

½ tbsp. lemon juice
1 tbsp. pomegranate molasses
½ tsp. Aleppo chili flakes, or ¼ tsp. each of
   sweet paprika and cayenne pepper with a
   pinch of cumin
½ tsp. soft brown sugar

salt
½ tsp. sumac (optional)

for the flatbreads
1 large sweet potato, cut into chunks
approximately 4 oz. (125 g) plain flour

1 Preheat the oven to 425°F (220°C). Put the peppers on a baking tray and roast for 30 minutes, turning them once or twice, until just charred. Allow to cool. Skin and remove the core and seeds when cool enough to handle, and slice into chunks.

2 Transfer the peppers to the bowl of a food processor and add all the remaining ingredients for the dip. Pulse until you have a fairly smooth paste. Taste and adjust the salt and sugar, then transfer to a serving bowl.

3 To make the flatbreads, boil or steam the sweet potato for 20 minutes, until tender, then drain, mash and leave to cool. Combine the mashed sweet potatoes with approximately the same quantity of flour and knead to a soft dough. Divide the dough into six pieces and roll each piece into a round on a well-floured surface.

4 Heat a frying pan over a moderate heat. Place a flatbread in the pan, press down with a spatula and cook until bubbles form on the bread. Flip and cook the other side, then remove from the pan and keep warm. Repeat with the remaining flatbreads and serve with the dip.

WITH TOMATO DIP
Make the muhammara as directed and stir in 2 skinned and chopped tomatoes. Serve with flatbreads or pitas.

WITH VEGETABLE KEBABS
Thread a selection of small mushrooms, zucchini chunks, green pepper chunks and cherry tomatoes on four small skewers. Whisk together 1 tbsp. each olive oil and lemon juice, season with salt and pepper, and use to baste the kebabs. Put the kebabs in a 400°F (200°C) oven and roast for 10–12 minutes, turning once until just cooked. Alternatively, barbecue over a medium–high heat for 5–6 minutes per side. Serve with the muhammara dip.

WITH JARRED PEPPERS
For a quicker version, use jarred roasted red peppers in place of oven roasted peppers. About ½ x 1 lb 1 oz. (480 g) jar should be sufficient. Drain on kitchen towel before adding to the food processor.

WITH GRAINS
Cook 7 oz. (200 g) grains such as spelt or buckwheat following the packet directions. Toss with the muhammara dip and 1–2 tbsp. olive oil. Toss in 10 halved cherry tomatoes and a handful of chopped fresh parsley and mint leaves.

Samosas & Fresh Mango Chutney

These delicious, spicy Indian starters are easy to make with phyllo pastry. Once you have mastered the first one, constructing the samosas is really easy.

Serves 4

4 tbsp. sunflower oil
1 tsp. mustard seeds
2 small onions, finely chopped
2 tsp. curry powder
¼ tsp. salt
2 potatoes, peeled and finely chopped

1 carrot, peeled and finely chopped
1 cup (125 g) diced green beans
1 cup (125 g) frozen peas
½ cup (150 ml) water
1 x 8-oz. (225-g) package phyllo pastry
sunflower oil, for deep-frying

for the chutney
1 ripe mango
1 large shallot, peeled and roughly chopped
2 green chilis, roughly chopped
2 garlic cloves
sea salt

1   Warm the oil in a skillet, add the mustard seeds, and cook over a moderate heat until they begin to pop. Stir in the onions and fry for 5 minutes until they are soft. Add the curry powder and salt, fry for 1 minute, then add the potatoes, carrot, beans, peas, and water. Cook for 15 minutes on a low heat, stirring occasionally, until the vegetables are tender and the liquid almost evaporated. Remove from the heat and let cool.

2   Cut the phyllo pastry sheets in half to make long strips. Work with one strip at a time, covering the remaining strips with wax paper or a damp cloth to prevent drying out. Place a spoonful of the filling at one end of the strip. Fold over the corner diagonally to form a triangle. Continue the folding to the end of the strip. Seal the ends with a little water. Repeat with the remaining strips.

3   Two-thirds fill a deep-fryer or wok with sunflower oil and heat to 350°F (180°C). Fry the samosas two at a time for 2–3 minutes until golden. Drain on paper towel, then serve hot or at room temperature.

4   To make the chutney, peel the mango and slice the flesh from the pit, roughly chop, and set aside. In a food processor, process the shallot, chilis, and garlic until smooth. Add the mango and pulse to roughly chop. Season with salt. Transfer to a serving bowl.

WITH MINTED YOGURT
Prepare the basic samosas. In place of the chutney, serve with 1 cup (250 ml) Greek-style yogurt mixed with 4 tbsp. chopped fresh mint and 2 teaspoons lime juice. Serve garnished with paprika and fresh mint leaves.

WITH POTATO, SPINACH & CASHEW
Prepare the basic samosas, omitting carrots, beans, and peas. After the potatoes are tender, add ⅔ cup (125 g) broken cashews and cook for 2 minutes, then add 2 cups (125 g) chopped fresh spinach and cook until wilted. Stir in 4 tablespoons chopped fresh cilantro. Let cool, then proceed with recipe.

WITH SWEET POTATO & GINGER
Prepare the basic samosas, using chopped sweet potato in place of the potato and omitting the carrots and beans. Add 2 teaspoons minced gingerroot and 1 finely chopped green chili with the curry powder.

OVEN-BAKED SAMOSAS
Prepare the basic recipe, but instead of deep-frying, brush samosas with sunflower oil and put on a parchment-lined cookie sheet. Bake at 400°F (200°C) for 10–12 minutes.

CHAPTER 5

Quick & Tasty

When you need something filling fast, look to this chapter. With recipes that can be on the table in no time at all, you'll be able to serve-up a nutritious and delicious home-cooked meal without a lot of effort and clean-up. Here you'll find recipes for healthy lunches, filling salads, one-pot curries, speedy pasta dishes, and super-fast stir-fries. Home cooking need never be a chore again.

ONE-POT MEALS

One-pot meals are perfect for busy people. They are not only time-saving, but offer the pleasure of cooking at home with much less fuss. The very nature of one-pot cooking means that the equipment needed is kept to a minimum and the pots and pans required will be large. Everything you will need, you probably already have in your kitchen drawers and cupboards. Basic utensils such as knives and a vegetable peeler and basic equipment such as a chopping board are the staples of every keen (or even reluctant) cook.

For the actual cooking, the pots and pans will need to accommodate a lot of ingredients. A large ovenproof frying pan with a lid will be necessary. If it is nonstick, that's even better. For the recipes cooked in a baking dish or roasting tin, this will also need to be roomy enough, but, as the food will shrink in size as it cooks, you can crowd the dish or tin a little. Large cast-iron casseroles or Dutch ovens with lids are perfect for browning vegetables on the hob, as they can then be transferred straight into the oven to finish cooking. Slow cookers are a great investment for busy families. The pot should be used at least half-full, but not more than three-quarters full, so choose a size suitable for the number you will be cooking for.

SPEEDY STIR-FRIES

Stir-frying is an easy way to make a meal. Like the best quick and easy cooking, all of the ingredients are cooked in the same pan. The method uses a small amount of very hot oil, and the heat cooks everything quickly, saving time, and retaining nutrients. All the preparation can be done ahead (including cooking the rice or noodles), which means you can get a meal to the table in just five to seven minutes —perfect when you are short on time but want to serve a healthy and delicious dish. What's more, this method of cooking is fun and easy to learn.

The beauty of stir-frying is that you can substitute foods and still make an authentic meal. For example, if you don't enjoy eating hot, bird's eye chiles, use long ones with a milder flavor; use ginger if you can't find galangal; or green beans rather than snow peas. Once you heat your wok to begin cooking, everything happens very quickly. Therefore, it is critical that all your ingredients are prepared, your utensils are ready and next to your wok, and your serving plates are waiting. If you are serving your stir-fry with a starch, such as rice or noodles, have this cooking before you begin so that it is ready once your stir-fry is cooked.

PACKED LUNCHES

Packing a lunch is usually cheaper then buying something every day, plus you can tailor it to your budget and health concerns, and personal tastes. Spend some time at the weekend making a few batches of lunch ideas and packing in individual containers ready to pick up and go. Write a list and stick it on the fridge so you don't forget to pack everything you need. And leave a note with your keys to remember your lunch! Nothing more annoying than leaving it behind in the chaos of the morning rush. Keep a few supplies at work like a set of cutlery, some napkins, chopsticks, or salt and pepper so you can dress up your lunch. Why not make up a batch of one of the tasty recipes here and take it into work to share with colleagues? They might return the favor and then you all get to try all kinds of new dishes.

GARNISHES & CONDIMENTS

Garnishes add flavor, texture, and visual appeal, making them an easy way to elevate a humble dish to an elegant offering fit for guests. Many recipes in this chapter suggest appropriate garnishes, but do experiment to find your own favorite presentations. Finely chopped or shredded fresh herbs such as chives, basil, Italian parsley, mint, sage, and cilantro all look pretty as well as adding a flavor punch. Zested citrus peel or finely sliced scallions can be an effortless way to add zing to a dish, just as croutons or lightly toasted seeds (sesame, pumpkin, or sunflower) can contribute texture and nutrients to a meal. Condiments like salsas, relishes, chutneys, and hot sauce can offer an element of spice to milder dishes, while plain yogurt, sour cream, tzatziki, or raita will balance out curries and other spicy dishes.

Mediterranean Roasted Vegetable Wrap

(V)

These deeply satisfying warm wraps are equally good when served cold. Try them as a lunchbox meal. Simply allow the vegetables to fully cool before constructing the wrap.

Serves 4

1 tbsp. olive oil
1 garlic clove, minced
sea salt and black pepper, to taste
1 red bell pepper, seeded and cut into strips
1 green bell pepper, seeded and cut into strips
1 small yellow squash, seeded and cut into strips

1 small zucchini, cut into strips
1 cup (185 g) cherry tomatoes
1–2 tsp. balsamic vinegar
1 cup (225 g) hummus
4 tortillas, warmed
4 oz. (125 g) baby spinach leaves, washed and dried

1 Preheat oven to 425°F (220°C). In a bowl, combine the oil, garlic, salt, and pepper. Lay all the vegetables in an oiled baking pan, pour in the oil mixture, and toss, taking care to coat each strip. Bake, turning once, until the vegetables are slightly charred and tender, about 40 minutes. Sprinkle with a little balsamic vinegar to taste. Cool slightly; the vegetables should be warm, not hot.

2 Spread the hummus on the warmed tortillas, lay the raw spinach on the hummus, and top with the roasted vegetables. Roll up the tortillas and tuck in the ends. Serve immediately.

WITH EGGPLANT
Prepare the basic recipe, replacing the zucchini and squash with 1 eggplant, which has been cut into strips, salted, allowed to stand, and patted dry.

WITH EXTRA PROTEIN
Prepare the basic recipe, adding ½ soy-based "chicken" cutlet, or sliced, smoked, or flavored tempeh, to each wrap. Cook the cutlet or tempeh according to the manufacturer's instructions.

WITH "MOZZARELLA"
Prepare the basic recipe, adding 4 slices mozzarella-style dairy-free "cheese" to each wrap.

WITH SATAY SAUCE
Prepare the basic recipe, using 1 tbsp. soy sauce in place of the balsamic vinegar and spreading the tortillas with satay sauce (page 184) in place of the hummus.

Sweet Potato & Avocado Wraps

This recipe calls for speedy steamed sweet potatoes. If you prefer your sweet potatoes roasted, you could toss the chunks in a little oil and roast for 30–40 minutes at 400°F (200°C).

Makes 2

1 sweet potato, cut into
    ½-in. (1.5-cm) chunks
1 tbsp. mayonnaise
½ tbsp. pesto
2 large flour tortillas
1 romano or red pepper,
    thinly sliced

1 avocado, sliced
1 tsp. lemon juice
    (optional)
2 small handfuls of
    arugula or other
    peppery leaves
freshly ground black
    pepper

1   Place the sweet potato chunks in a steamer over a pan of boiling water. Cover and steam for 7–10 minutes, until tender. Set aside to cool slightly (or leave to cool completely if you're not planning to eat the wraps immediately).

2   Meanwhile, combine the mayonnaise and pesto in a bowl and spread down the center of the flour tortillas. Top with the sweet potato, peppers and a little fresh ground black pepper.

3   Toss the avocado with the lemon juice (you can omit this step if you are eating the wraps immediately) and lay on top of the sweet potato. Top with a handful of arugula. Tuck in the top and bottom ends of the tortilla and roll up.

WITH COUSCOUS SALAD
While the sweet potato is cooking, tip 2 oz. (50 g) couscous into a large bowl and pour over 3½ fl oz. (100 ml) water and 1 tsp. vegetable stock powder. Cover, then leave for 10 minutes until tender and all the stock has been absorbed. Leave to cool and fluff up with a fork. Toss with the sweet potato, red pepper, avocado, and 1 tbsp. each pesto and lemon juice, then season with salt and pepper. Omit the mayonnaise, arugula, and tortillas.

WITH TOMATO, BEAN & AVOCADO
Omit the sweet potato and use 3 tbsp. canned cannellini beans (drained and rinsed) on each wrap instead. Slice a ripe tomato and lay on top of the beans. Continue as directed, adding a few fresh basil leaves.

SWEET POTATO & FETA TART
Prepare a puff pastry tart following the instructions on page 139. Spread 2 tbsp. pesto over the base and top with the sweet potato, peppers and 10 halved cherry tomatoes. Season with salt and pepper. Sprinkle with 2 oz. (50 g) crumbled feta cheese. Bake as directed on page 139 then serve with the arugula and avocado on the side, drizzled with mayonnaise.

Sun-Dried Tomato Soufflé Omelette

(GF)

Sun-dried tomatoes come in three varieties. The least expensive are the dried tomatoes, which need to be hydrated—the quickest way is to put them into a bowl, cover with water, then microwave, covered, for 2 minutes.

Serves 1

2 eggs, lightly beaten
2 sun-dried tomatoes, drained or rehydrated and roughly chopped
1 tsp. butter
1 scallions, sliced

1 tbsp. chopped fresh basil
salt and freshly ground black or white pepper

to serve
mixed salad leaves
balsamic vinegar

1 Separate the eggs, putting the yolks into a small bowl and the whites into a large clean bowl. Beat the egg yolks with a fork, seasoning well with salt and pepper.

2 Put a small frying pan over a low heat to warm and turn on the grill to medium. Whisk the egg whites until they form soft peaks. Then, using a silicone spatula, fold the egg yolks into the egg whites.

3 Add the butter to the pan and increase to a moderately high heat. Once the butter is foaming, slip the egg mixture into the pan and swirl the pan to even it out. Cook for 1 minute, then loosen the edges with the spatula. Sprinkle over the tomatoes, scallions, and basil and continue to cook until the underside is golden brown, 3–4 minutes. Place under the grill and cook until the top is just set.

4 Ease one half of the omelette over the other and transfer to a plate. Serve immediately with the salad and drizzled with balsamic vinegar.

WITH ASPARAGUS
Cook 2 oz. (50 g) asparagus tips in boiling water for 3–4 minutes until just tender. Add to the omelette with the sun-dried tomatoes.

WITH ARTICHOKE & PARMESAN
Drain 2 oz. (50 g) jarred or deli artichokes and cut into pieces. Add to the omelette instead of the tomatoes. Sprinkle with 2 tbsp. grated Parmesan-style cheese and proceed as directed.

WITH MUSHROOM & THYME
Add 3 sliced chestnut mushrooms, the scallions, and a pinch of dried thyme to the foaming butter and cook gently for 3 minutes until softened. Remove them from the pan and set aside. Add another small knob of butter and, when foaming, continue to make the soufflé omelette as described, using the cooked mushrooms as the filling in place of the tomatoes and basil.

WITH STRAWBERRY
Macerate 3 oz. (75 g) sliced strawberries in 1 tbsp. vanilla or superfine sugar for 15 minutes. Prepare the soufflé omelette as described, omitting the filling. Pile the strawberries into the cooked omelette, fold in half and serve sprinkled with a little more sugar.

Irish Soda Bread

Makes 1 loaf

3¾ cups (475 g) all-purpose flour   1 tsp. salt
1 tsp. baking soda   1⅔ (395 ml) cups buttermilk

1 Preheat the oven to 425°F (220°C) and line a large
cookie sheet with parchment paper. In a large bowl,
mix the flour, baking soda, and salt together. Make
a well in the center and add the buttermilk. Mix
quickly to form a sticky dough. Turn it out onto a
lightly floured work surface and form quickly into
a ball.

2 Place it on the cookie sheet, flatten the ball slightly
with your hand, and cut a deep cross in the top.
Dust with a little flour and bake for 30 minutes,
or until the bottom of the loaf sounds hollow when
tapped. Cool on a wire rack.

WITH DILL & POPPY SEED
Prepare the basic recipe, adding
1 tsp. dried dill and 1 tbsp. poppy
seeds to the flour mix.

WITH CHEESE & MUSTARD
Prepare the basic recipe, adding
¼ cup (30 g) shredded Cheddar
cheese and 2 tsp. dry mustard to
the flour mix.

WITH CHILI & CHEESE
Prepare the basic recipe, adding
4 finely chopped green onions,
1 deseeded finely chopped red chili,
and ¼ cup (30 g) finely shredded
Cheddar cheese to the flour mix.

SUNDRIED TOMATO SODA BREAD ROLLS
Prepare the basic recipe, adding
¼ cup (30 g) finely chopped
sundried tomatoes and 1 tsp. thyme
to the flour mix. Handling as little
as possible, cut the dough into
5 equal portions and form into balls.
Flatten, place on lined cookie sheet,
mark a cross in the top, and bake in
a preheated oven at 400°F (200°C)
for 20–25 minutes.

Quick & Easy Ciabatta

Makes 1 loaf

4 cups (510 g) white bread flour   1¾ cups (440 ml) + 2 tbsp. warm   1 tbsp. extra virgin olive oil
½ tsp. sugar   water, divided
1½ tsp. active dry yeast   1 tsp. salt

1 Line a large cookie sheet with parchment paper.
In a large bowl, mix the flour with the sugar and
yeast, add the warm water and salt, and stir with
your hands. Raise the dough up high and slap it
down again to aerate the mixture to develop the
dough's characteristic airy texture. Pour over the
olive oil, cover with plastic wrap, and leave in a
warm place for about an hour, until doubled in size.

2 Preheat the oven to 400°F (200°C). Carefully
pour the dough onto a well-floured work surface
and, without knocking the air out, fold the dough
over lengthways like an envelope to create the flat
ciabatta loaf.

3 Transfer the dough onto the cookie sheet and bake
for 30–40 minutes, or until the bread is golden and
sounds hollow when tapped on the bottom.

WITH GARLIC
Prepare the basic recipe, adding
2 minced garlic cloves to the flour
in the bowl.

WITH SALT & PEPPER
Prepare the basic recipe, adding
2 tbsp. freshly ground black pepper
to the flour. While still hot, brush
with melted butter and sprinkle with
flaked sea salt.

WITH CHILI
Prepare the basic recipe, adding
2 tsp. crushed red pepper flakes to
the bowl with the flour.

CIABATTA ROLLS
Prepare the basic recipe. After
folding the dough like an envelope,
very carefully cut the dough into
8 or 9 rectangles with a sharp knife.
Try not to knock out the air. Place
on the cookie sheet and proceed
as directed.

Upscale Beans on Toast

Omit the cheese

There is nothing wrong with a can of beans, except that it is full of sugar. These beans are equally satisfying but with a fresher taste and can be served to friends without apology!

Serves 2

1 tbsp. olive oil
1 onion, finely chopped
1 garlic clove, crushed
1 tbsp. red wine vinegar
½ x 14-oz. (400-g) can chopped tomatoes
pinch of superfine sugar
¼–½ tsp. chili flakes (optional)
1 x 14-oz. (400-g) can cannellini beans,

drained and rinsed
2 tbsp. chopped fresh parsley
4 thick slices sourdough or wholemeal bread
butter, for spreading
2 tbsp. grated Cheddar cheese (optional)
salt and freshly ground black pepper

1 Heat the oil in a saucepan, add the onion and cook over a moderate heat for 5–7 minutes until soft and translucent. Add the garlic and cook for a further minute. Stir in the vinegar and cook for 2 minutes until it evaporates. Add the tomatoes and sugar, along with the chili flakes if you like a bit of heat in your beans, then simmer for 10 minutes until thickened. Add the beans, season to taste with salt and pepper, then cook until piping hot. Check the seasoning and stir in the parsley.

2 While the beans are heating through, toast then butter the bread. Pile the beans on top and sprinkle with grated Cheddar cheese, if desired.

IN A BENTO BOX
Place a portion of cold beans in one compartment of a bento box, stuff another with arugula sprinkled with a few drops of balsamic vinegar and sesame seeds. Fill the third compartment with Cheddar cheese cubes and the final one with pineapple chunks. Take the buttered bread too, but leave it untoasted.

WITH PASTA
Cook 5 oz. (150 g) chunky pasta, such as penne, in boiling water according to the packet directions until al dente. Drain, reserving a ladleful of the cooking water. Toss the hot beans through the cooked pasta using a little of the cooking water to loosen, as required. Serve sprinkled with grated Parmesan-style or Cheddar cheese. Omit the toast.

WITH BAKED POTATOES
Prick 2 Maris Piper or similar baking potatoes several times with a fork. Rub the potatoes with a little olive oil, then scatter with salt flakes, which should stick to the oil. Place directly on the shelf in a 400°F (200°C) oven and bake for 60–90 minutes. Check that the flesh is soft with a knife. Cut a large cross in the top of the potato and squeeze the sides to open; stuff with the hot beans and sprinkle with Cheddar cheese. Omit the toast.

Three-Tomato Goat's Cheese Tart

Using ready-rolled puff pastry makes this a quick favorite. It takes minutes to construct yet is impressive enough to serve at any occasion.

Serves 4

13-oz. (375-g) pack ready-rolled puff pastry
3 tbsp. pesto
1½ oz. (40 g) sun-dried tomatoes, roughly chopped
2 large tomatoes, sliced

4 oz. (125 g) cherry tomatoes, ideally a mix of red and yellow, halved
8 pitted black olives, halved
4 oz. (125 g) goat cheese, chopped into small pieces

leaves from a sprig of fresh rosemary
salt and freshly ground black pepper

1 Preheat the oven to 400°F (200°C). Grease a 8-in. (20-cm) baking dish.

2 Unroll the puff pastry sheet and use to line the prepared baking dish. Trim then neaten the edges.

3 Spread the pesto over the pastry base, and top with the sun-dried tomatoes, followed by the large tomato slices and the cherry tomatoes. Season with salt and freshly ground black pepper.

4 Distribute the olives evenly over the tomatoes and sprinkle over the cheese and rosemary. Bake for 15–20 minutes, or until the pastry is golden brown. Serve warm or cold.

WITH OLIVE TAPENADE
Make the tart as directed, replacing the pesto with 3 tbsp. black olive tapenade.

WITH ARTICHOKE
Make the tart as directed, replacing the black olives with the drained artichokes from a 9-oz. (250-g) can; the artichokes will need chopping into quarters before placing on top of the tomatoes.

WITH BEETS
Prepare the tart as directed. Instead of the pesto-tomato topping, slice 7 oz. (200 g) cooked beets and distribute over the pastry base. Sprinkle over the grated zest of ½ orange and a few chili flakes. Top with the goat's cheese.

INDIVIDUAL TARTS
Unroll the puff pastry onto a work surface, trim the edges to neaten and cut in half widthways and in half again to form four equal-sized pieces of pastry. Transfer to the lined tray. Score a ¾-in. (2-cm) border around the edge of each. Proceed as directed, distributing the ingredients evenly between the tarts.

Buddha Bowl

Use tamari
instead of soy
sauce &
gluten-free
noodles

A Buddha bowl is a fresh, clean meal in a bowl, containing greens,
vegetables, grains, protein, and some good fats. They couldn't be easier
and make perfect lunchbox meals as well as a quick, feel-good supper.

Makes 2

3½ oz. (100 g) quinoa, cooked
½ x 14-oz. (400-g) can black-eyed beans,
   drained and rinsed
1 tbsp. extra-virgin olive oil

1 tbsp. lime juice
1 tsp. sweet chili sauce
2-in. (5-cm) piece cucumber, sliced
1 large carrot, grated

1 avocado, sliced
4 tbsp. hummus
seeds of ½ pomegranate
salt and freshly ground black pepper

1   In a bowl, toss together the quinoa, beans, olive
   oil, lime juice, and sweet chili sauce and season
   with salt and pepper. Divide between two
   serving bowls.

2   Divide the cucumber, carrot, and avocado
   between the bowls. Place 2 tbsp. of hummus in
   the center of each bowl and sprinkle over the
   pomegranate seeds.

WITH ROASTED VEGETABLES
Make the roasted vegetables following the instructions on page
181. Use in the Buddha bowl in place of the raw vegetables.

WITH TOFU & NOODLES
Omit the quinoa and its dressing, along with the beans. Cook
6 oz. (175 g) udon noodles according to the packet directions and
toss in 2 tbsp. tamari, ½ tsp. sesame oil, sprinkle with sesame
seeds, and season with salt and pepper. Make the sticky tofu cubes
on page 105. Add to the raw vegetables in the Buddha bowl.

WITH GARBANZO BEANS
Replace the black-eyed beans with the same quantity of drained
and rinsed garbanzo beans.

ASIAN BUDDHA BOWL
Make a dressing from 2 tbsp. each peanut butter and water,
1 tbsp. soy sauce or tamari, 1 tsp. each grated fresh root ginger
and hot chili sauce, ½ tsp. superfine sugar, and a crushed garlic
clove. Use this in place of the oil and lime juice dressing.
Substitute cooked rice for the quinoa, and orange slices for the
pomegranate. Sprinkle with sesame seeds.

Warm Burrito Bowls with Chipotle Sauce

(V)

These spicy burrito bowls have almost everything you would find in a regular burrito, but deconstructed as a warm salad.

Serves 2

6 oz. (175 g) cooked
  brown rice
1 x 14-oz. (400-g) can
  black beans, rinsed
  and drained
3½ oz. (100 g) lettuce
  leaves, roughly
  chopped
1 avocado, stoned, flesh
  removed and diced
2 tomatoes, chopped
cilantro leaves, to serve

for the chipotle sauce
1 tbsp. chipotle paste
1 tbsp. olive oil
1 clove garlic, crushed
1 tsp. maple or agave
  syrup
1 tsp. salt
juice of ½ lime

1 For the chipotle sauce, place a small pan over a medium heat and stir together the chipotle paste, olive oil, garlic, honey, and salt. Cook for 2 minutes, then remove from the heat.

2 Divide the rice between two bowls, and top with the drained beans, lettuce, avocado, and tomatoes. Sprinkle with cilantro leaves, pour over the sauce, toss together and serve immediately.

WITH CILANTRO DRESSING
Prepare the basic recipe, and omit the sauce. Blend 1 bunch chopped fresh cilantro, 8 fl oz. (240 ml) olive oil, 5 tbsp. white wine vinegar, 2 crushed cloves garlic, 1 tsp. ground cumin, and 1 tsp. minced deseeded serrano chili, until smooth.

WITH CORN & FAJITA SEASONING
Prepare the basic recipe. Add 1 tbsp. fajita seasoning and 8 oz. (225 g) canned corn to the bowls with the rest of the salad ingredients.

WITH CREAMY AVOCADO DRESSING
Prepare the basic recipe, and omit the sauce. Process the flesh of 3 avocados, juice of 1 lemon, 4 tbsp. olive oil, 3 chopped cloves garlic, 2 tsp. salt, 3 fl oz. (75 ml) water, 4 tbsp. chopped parsley and 2 tbsp. agave or maple syrup until smooth.

Crunchy Asian Salad

A crunchy, satisfying salad that is easy to throw together for lunch, and full of healthy ingredients.

Serves 4

6 oz. (175 g) red kidney beans, rinsed and drained
4 scallionss, thinly sliced
6 oz. (175 g) red cabbage, finely sliced
1 medium carrot, peeled and grated
4 mushrooms, sliced
1 celery stalk, finely chopped
3 oz. (75 g) crispy lettuce leaves

for the dressing
4 tbsp. grated onion
2 fl oz. (60 ml) peanut or sesame oil
2 tbsp. rice vinegar
1 tbsp. finely chopped fresh ginger
1 tbsp. finely chopped celery
1 tbsp. tomato ketchup
2 tsp. soy sauce
1 tsp. sugar
1 tsp. lemon juice
½ tsp. grated garlic
¼ tsp. salt
¼ tsp. freshly ground black pepper

1 In a large bowl, toss together the beans, scallionss, red cabbage, grated carrot, mushrooms, celery, and lettuce leaves.

2 For the dressing, put all the ingredients in a blender and blend until smooth. Pour over the salad and toss to combine.

WITH QUICK SOY DRESSING
Prepare the basic recipe, omitting the ginger dressing. In a small jug, mix together 2 tbsp. soy sauce, 2 tbsp. mirin, and 2 tsp. sesame oil.

WITH APPLE, BLUE CHEESE & PECANS
Prepare the basic recipe, adding 1 crispy apple, peeled, cored and chopped, 2 tbsp. crumbled blue cheese, and 2 tbsp. chopped pecans to the other ingredients in the bowl.

WITH TOMATOES & PEANUTS
Prepare the basic recipe, adding 1 chopped tomato and 2 tbsp. salted peanuts to the other ingredients in the bowl.

WITH VIETNAMESE DRESSING
Prepare the basic recipe. Omit the dressing. Whisk together 3 fl oz. (80 ml) each of lime juice and fish sauce, 1 chopped red chili, and 2 tbsp. brown sugar in a small jug until the sugar has dissolved.

Baby Greens Shakshuka

GF
Use gluten-
free pasta

This recipe is based on a Middle Eastern breakfast dish, in which the eggs are traditionally cooked in a tomato sauce. There are lots of vegetables in this dish too, enough for a hearty meal for two or a lighter meal for three. Serve with flatbread.

Serves 2–3

4 oz. (125 g) asparagus tips
3½ oz. (100 g) French beans
3½ oz. (100 g) peas
7 oz. (200 g) baby spinach
2 tbsp. olive oil
4 oz. (125 g) baby leeks, sliced

2 baby zucchini
2 garlic cloves, crushed
1 tsp. cumin seeds
1 tsp. paprika
8–9 cherry tomatoes
2 tsp. lemon juice

2–3 eggs (one per person)
1 tbsp. chopped fresh dill
4 tbsp. Greek yogurt
sumac, for sprinkling
salt and ground black pepper
flatbreads, to serve

1 Bring a saucepan of water to the boil, add the asparagus and cook for 30 seconds, then add the beans and peas and cook for another 30 seconds, then dunk in the spinach to wilt. Immediately tip all the blanched vegetables into a colander to drain.

2 Heat the olive oil in a large frying pan and gently cook the leeks, zucchini, and garlic until soft, then add the cumin seeds and paprika. Stir in the blanched vegetables and tomatoes, lemon juice, and salt and pepper to taste. Cook for 2 minutes to blend.

3 Using a spoon, make 2 or 3 indentations in the vegetable mixture, ensuring they are well spaced out. Gently crack an egg into each hole. Cover the pan and cook gently until the eggs are as you like them, with soft or hard yolks. Scatter the dish with the dill and spoon a little yogurt over each egg, then sprinkle with sumac. Serve hot.

WITH VEGETABLE SAUCE
Make the vegetable sauce on page 151. Use this as the basis of your shakshuka instead of the baby vegetables and seasonings suggested. Make indentations in the sauce for the eggs, then cook and finish as for the base recipe.

WITH BURRATA
Omit the eggs, yogurt, dill, and sumac. Plate up the cooked greens and top with half a ball of burrata, at room temperature, per person.

WITH PASTA
Omit the eggs, dill, and sumac. Stir the yogurt into the cooked greens. Serve on a bed of fusilli or farfalle pasta, cooked according to the packet directions.

WITH RICE
Cook the greens and divide between 2 or 3 bowls. Hardboil 2 or 3 eggs, as required and cut into quarters. Add a portion of cooked brown rice per bowl, top with the yogurt, hardboiled eggs, and sumac and garnish with dill.

WITH CURRY SAUCE
Cook the greens as directed. Hardboil 2 or 3 eggs, as required and cut into quarters. Toss a 12 fl oz. (350 ml) jar of your favorite curry sauce into the greens and simmer for 10 minutes. Top with the hardboiled eggs and yogurt. Omit the dill and sumac.

Zucchini "Spaghetti" with Raw Tomato Sauce

GF · V

Use gluten-free pasta

The raw tomato sauce is an Italian classic that tastes like Mediterranean sunshine. It is a fresh, vibrant recipe that results in a dish remarkably low in calories but still satisfying.

Serves 2

2 ripe beefsteak tomatoes, cut in half across the center
2 tbsp. chopped fresh basil
grated zest and juice of ½ lemon
2 tbsp. chopped fresh parsley
2–3 zucchini

1 tbsp. olive oil
4 tbsp. water
salt and ground black pepper

to serve
2 tbsp. pine kernels, toasted
torn basil leaves

1 Using a box grater and keeping your fingers flat against the tomato and parallel to the grater, grate the tomatoes into a bowl. Discard the skins. Combine the grated tomato with the basil, parsley, lemon zest and juice and season to taste. Set aside for 30 minutes to allow the flavors to blend.

2 Meanwhile, trim and julienne the zucchini or process them through a spiralizer, placing the "spaghetti" in a colander with a sprinkling of salt. Toss, then leave over a bowl to drain for 10 minutes. Dab dry with kitchen towel or a clean tea towel.

3 Heat the olive oil in a frying pan over a medium heat. Add the zucchini and cook for 1 minute, turning gently. Add the water and cook for 5–7 minutes, until softened. Divide between two bowls and serve with the sauce and garnished with the pine kernels and basil.

WITH OLIVE-CAPER SAUCE
Prepare the raw tomato sauce, adding 10 roughly chopped pitted black olives and 1 tsp. capers.

WITH SPAGHETTI SQUASH
In place of the zucchini, take 1 medium spaghetti squash and prick it in a few places with a skewer but leave whole. Bake for about 1 hour in a 350°F (180°C) oven until tender. Cut in half lengthways, taking care that the steam escapes away from you. Remove and discard the seeds, then fluff the flesh with a fork to form spaghetti-like strands. Add ½–1 tsp. chili flakes (to taste) to the tomato sauce and finish as directed.

WITH SPAGHETTI
Replace the zucchini with 5 oz. (150 g) spaghetti, cooked according to the packet instructions. Drain, then immediately tip into the tomato sauce, tossing to mix.

Squash & Peanut Stir Fry

Use tamari instead of soy sauce

Serves 4

⅓ cup (85 g) peanut butter
⅔ cup (160 ml) water
1 tbsp. dark soy sauce or tamari
1 tbsp. sweet chili sauce
1 tbsp. sesame oil

1 tsp. chili sauce
1 medium butternut squash
2 tbsp. peanut or vegetable oil
1 oz. (25 g) fresh ginger, finely chopped
2 cloves garlic, finely chopped

1 medium red onion, sliced
2–3 tbsp. water, if needed
½ cup (65 g) roasted peanuts, chopped
1 small bunch fresh cilantro, roughly chopped

1. Put the peanut butter, water, dark soy sauce, sweet chili sauce, sesame oil, and chili sauce into a small bowl and whisk to combine. Set aside. Cut the butternut squash in half lengthways, peel, seed, and slice each half into ½-in. (1.25-cm) slices.

2. Heat a wok until a drop of water evaporates in a second or two. Add the peanut or vegetable oil, ginger, garlic, and red onion and stir-fry until fragrant and golden. Add the butternut squash and stir-fry for 5 to 6 minutes, until the squash is starting to soften and color.

3. Add the peanut butter mixture and stir-fry for 4 to 5 minutes, until the squash is tender. Reduce the heat, adding a little water if needed. Toss the peanuts and half the cilantro through the stir-fry.

WITH ZUCCHINI
Prepare the basic recipe, but substitute 2 sliced large zucchini for the butternut squash.

WITH CASHEWS
Prepare the basic recipe, but substitute ¼ cup (50 ml) light soy sauce and 2 tsp. cornstarch for the peanut butter and ½ cup (65 g) roasted cashews, chopped, for the roasted peanuts.

WITH BOK CHOY
Add 4 chopped baby bok choy to the wok just before the end of cooking, and allow them to wilt, but remain crisp, before adding the peanuts and cilantro.

WITH BASIL & GARLIC
Prepare the basic recipe, but omit the peanut butter, roasted peanuts, and cilantro. Add ¼ cup (50 ml) light soy sauce and 2 tsp. cornstarch to the sauce mixture, increase the garlic to 4 cloves, and replace the cilantro with 1 small bunch basil.

Broccoli & Cashew Nut Stir-Fry

GF V

Use tamari instead of soy sauce

Serves 4

3 oz. (75 g) cashew nuts
1 tbsp. sunflower oil
½ tsp. sesame oil, plus extra to finish
1 garlic clove, crushed

1 tbsp. chopped fresh root ginger
14 oz. (400 g) broccoli, cut into small florets
1 tbsp. water
1 romano pepper, thinly sliced

½–1 large red chili, deseeded and finely chopped
2 tbsp. soy sauce or tamari

1. In a hot wok, dry toast the cashew nuts over a medium heat, turning constantly until fragrant and just beginning to brown. Remove from the pan and set aside.

2. Heat the oils in the same pan and cook the garlic and ginger for 1 minute. Add the broccoli and stir-fry for 1–2 minutes until it turns bright green. Add the water and cover immediately so the broccoli cooks in the resulting steam, about 2 minutes.

3. Add the romano pepper and the chili and stir-fry for 1 minute, or until tender-crisp. Toss in the toasted cashew nuts and the soy sauce. Serve immediately, sprinkled with a few drops of sesame oil.

WITH SWEET & SOUR SAUCE
Before cooking the vegetables, make a sauce by mixing together 3 tbsp. rice vinegar or white wine vinegar, and 2 tbsp. each cornflour, agave or maple syrup and soy sauce or tamari, and set aside. Add this sauce instead of the soy sauce and cook, stirring, until the mixture has thickened slightly.

WITH NOODLES
Toss a 5 oz. (150 g) packet of straight to wok rice noodles into the finished stir-fry and heat through.

WITH PRE-PREPARED VEGETABLES
Substitute a 12 oz. (350 g) packet of prepared stir-fry vegetables for the broccoli and romano pepper. Add to the fried garlic and ginger and stir-fry for 2–3 minutes until tender-crisp (there is no need for the water and steaming step). Add the chili and cook for 1 minute before adding the soy sauce or tamari.

Tempeh & Green Vegetable Stir Fry

Tempeh is a traditional Indonesian food. This fermented soy bean product can be found in most grocery stores, but if unavailable, it can be easily substituted for an equal quantity of extra-firm tofu. Serve this dish with rice.

Serves 4

2 tbsp. peanut or
    vegetable oil
1 stalk lemongrass, outer
    leaves and root
    discarded, white part
    finely chopped
2 cloves garlic, finely
    chopped
1 x 12-oz. (350-g)
    package tempeh, sliced
    into bite-size pieces
1 head broccoli, cut into
    bite-size florets

1 lb. (450 g) green beans,
    topped and tailed
1 medium zucchini,
    halved lengthways and
    thinly sliced
2 tbsp. sweet chili sauce
2 tbsp. light soy sauce or
    tamari
1 small bunch fresh
    cilantro, roughly
    chopped

1   Heat a wok until a drop of water evaporates in a second or two. Add the oil, lemongrass, and garlic and stir-fry until fragrant and golden. Add the tempeh and toss for 1 to 2 minutes, until the tempeh is lightly golden.

2   Add the broccoli and green beans and stir-fry for 2 to 3 minutes more before adding the zucchini. Toss for 1 to 2 minutes, and then add the sweet chili and soy sauces, tossing to coat all the ingredients with the sauce. Once the vegetables are crisp-tender, toss through half the cilantro. Sprinkle with the remaining cilantro.

WITH HOT CHILI SAUCE
Prepare the basic recipe, but substitute hot chili sauce for the sweet chili sauce.

WITH RED BELL PEPPER
Prepare the basic recipe, but substitute 2 large red bell peppers, sliced into strips, for the green beans.

WITH SESAME
Prepare the basic recipe, but add 1 tbsp. sesame oil and 2 tbsp. sesame seeds to the wok with the sweet chili and soy sauces. Garnish with extra sesame seeds.

WITH TOFU
Substitute 12 oz. (350 g) of extra-firm tofu, cut into bite-size pieces, for the tempeh. Complete the recipe as directed.

Eggplant & Tofu Stir Fry

Use tamari
instead of soy
sauce

The tomatoes added toward the end of this stir-fry help to create a sauce as they soften; adding a little water can help this process if the mixture still seems a little dry.

Serves 4

1 x 12-oz. (350-g) package extra-firm tofu

3 tbsp. peanut or vegetable oil

1 oz. (25 g) fresh ginger, finely chopped

2 cloves garlic, finely chopped

1 yellow onion, halved lengthways and chopped

1 large eggplant, halved lengthways and sliced

2 tbsp. light soy sauce or tamari

3 large tomatoes, cored and cut into bite-size pieces

1 small bunch fresh Thai basil, chopped

1 Rinse, drain, and pat the tofu dry with paper towels, then slice it into bite-size pieces.

2 Heat a wok until a drop of water evaporates in a second or two. Add the oil, fresh ginger, garlic, and onion and stir-fry until fragrant and golden. Add the eggplant and toss for 1 to 2 minutes, until it starts to color and soften, then add the tofu.

3 Stir-fry the tofu and eggplant for 2 to 3 minutes before adding the soy sauce and tomatoes. Toss for 1 to 2 minutes more, until the tomatoes are heated through and beginning to soften. Toss through half the Thai basil. Sprinkle with the remaining Thai basil.

WITH BUTTERNUT SQUASH
Substitute ½ a butternut squash, peeled, seeded and thinly sliced, for the eggplant.

WITH BROCCOLI
Substitute 1 large head of broccoli cut into bite-size florets for the tofu.

WITH BOK CHOY
Omit the eggplant. Add the tofu to the stir-fry after the ginger, garlic, and onion. Add 6 baby bok choy, quartered, with the tomatoes.

WITH ZUCCHINI
Substitute 2 medium zucchini, sliced, for the tomatoes. Add a little vegetable broth or water if the stir-fry seems a little dry.

Pasta with Ricotta

One of the simplest pasta sauces, very easy to make and fresh and delicious. Make sure the ricotta is as fresh as possible for the best possible results. Using ewe's milk ricotta will give the sauce a stronger flavor.

Serves 6

1 lb. (450 g) pasta of
   your choice
sea salt
8 oz. (225 g) ricotta
4 tbsp. freshly grated
   Parmesan-style cheese,
   plus extra to serve

freshly ground black
   pepper
2 tbsp. extra-virgin olive
   oil

1 Bring a large pot of salted water to a rolling boil. Meanwhile, mix the ricotta with a little salt and the Parmesan and pepper. Slacken the sauce slightly with a little boiling water from the pot to make sure you can distribute it smoothly through the pasta.

2 Add the pasta to the boiling water and stir, return to a boil, and cook until al dente, then drain and mix with the ricotta. Drizzle with the olive oil just before serving.

WITH LEMON
Make the basic recipe, adding the grated zest of 1 lemon to the ricotta.

WITH BASIL
Make the basic recipe, adding a handful of torn basil leaves to the ricotta.

WITH PARSLEY
Make the basic recipe, adding a handful of finely chopped flat-leaf parsley to the ricotta.

WITH CHERRY TOMATOES
Make the basic recipe, adding about 15 quartered cherry tomatoes to the pasta and mix both together with the ricotta. Add 2 tbsp. of finely chopped parsley to the mixed pasta.

WITH CAPERS & OLIVES
Make the basic recipe, adding a handful of washed and chopped capers and one of chopped stoned green olives to the ricotta and pasta. Mix together and proceed with basic recipe.

Pasta Primavera

The word primavera, which means "spring" in Italian, is often used to identify various pasta dishes dressed with a vegetable-based sauce. This is one versions of the basic recipe.

Serves 6

4 tbsp. olive oil
1 small red onion, peeled and chopped
1 carrot, scraped and chopped coarsely
2 small zucchini, topped and tailed and cubed
1 small green or red bell pepper, seeded and cubed
1 x 16-oz. (450-g) can chopped tomatoes

2 tbsp. water
large pinch dried oregano
8 oz. (225 g) cherry tomatoes, washed and halved
1 lb. (450 g) pasta of your choice
sea salt and freshly ground black pepper
freshly grated Parmesan-style cheese, to serve

1 Bring a large pot of salted water to a boil for the pasta. In a separate large pan on medium-high heat, heat the oil. Add the vegetables, stirring to coat with oil. Cook for about 10 minutes, stirring only occasionally, until the vegetables are just cooked. Turn off the heat, but keep the pan on the burner. Add the canned tomatoes to the vegetables, with the water to thin the sauce if necessary. Gently mix in the oregano and cherry tomatoes.

2 Meanwhile, add the pasta to the boiling water and cook until al dente. Drain the pasta and put into the pan with the vegetables. Adjust seasoning and mix together, adding a little more olive oil if necessary. Serve on a warmed serving dish or individual plates, sprinkled with a little freshly grated Parmesan.

WITH PEAS
Replace bell pepper with 2 cups (300 g) fresh or frozen peas.

WITH OVEN-ROASTED PEPPERS
Prepare basic recipe, omitting bell pepper from sauce and roasting it separately instead. Cool, peel, and seed pepper, then stir into the sauce at the very end for a really sweet flavor.

WITH EGGPLANT
Replace carrot, zucchini, and pepper with a large cubed eggplant, salted and allowed to purge before rinsing and drying. Offer grated pecorino instead of Parmesan to serve.

WITH GARLIC & BROCCOLI
Replace the onion with 3 cloves of crushed garlic, and carrot, zucchini, and pepper with about 14 small florets of fresh broccoli.

WITH CREAM
Stir about 4 tbsp. of heavy cream through the sauce at the end.

Greek Tortellini Salad

Tortellini are available with a huge variety of fillings. For this recipe, choose one that will go well with zucchini and sheep cheese, such as spinach and ricotta, sun-dried tomato, or wild mushroom.

Serves 6

2 medium zucchini
6 tbsp. olive oil
2 small red bell peppers, diced
1 tsp. finely grated lemon zest
juice of 1 lemon
1 tsp. fresh thyme leaves
1 tsp. chopped fresh rosemary leaves

1 tbsp. chopped fresh parsley
salt and freshly ground black pepper
14 oz. (400 g) pre-prepared tortellini
8 oz. (225 g) crumbled feta, to garnish
approx. 20 sliced black olives, to garnish

1 Wash the zucchini, quarter lengthways, and cut into bite-size pieces. Heat 2 tbsp. of the olive oil in a skillet and sauté the diced bell peppers and zucchini for 3–4 minutes. Remove and let cool.

2 Mix the remaining 4 tbsp. oil with the lemon zest and juice, herbs, salt, and pepper to make a dressing. Mix with the sautéed vegetables and let stand.

3 Meanwhile, cook the tortellini according to the package instructions. Drain and add to the vegetables. Mix and season to taste. Serve garnished with the feta and olives. Serve warm or room temperature.

WITH RAVIOLI
Prepare the basic recipe, using ravioli in place of the tortellini.

WITH PENNE
Prepare the basic recipe, using 14 oz. (400 g) penne in place of the tortellini.

WITH PARMESAN
Prepare the basic recipe, omitting the crumbled feta. Instead, serve the salad topped with shavings of Parmesan cheese.

WITH TAGLIATELLE
Prepare the basic recipe, using 14 oz. (400 g) tagliatelle in place of the tortellini.

Gnocchi in Creamy Cashew "Cheese" Sauce

Ⓥ

The focus of this recipe is the wonderful sauce, which is a nutritious and delicious vegan alternative to cheese sauce and can be used instead of cheese sauce in most dishes. It is speedy, but some people like to soak their cashew nuts for a couple of hours in advance; if you do this you may need a little less water in the recipe.

Serves 2

3½ oz. (100 g) frozen
    peas
9 oz. (250 g) packet
    gnocchi

for the cashew sauce
5 oz. (150 g) raw or
    roasted unsalted

cashew nuts or cashew
    nut pieces
4–6 tbsp. water
2 tbsp. lemon juice
2 tbsp. nutritional yeast
1 garlic clove, crushed
salt and freshly ground
    black pepper

1 Place all the sauce ingredients in a food processor or blender, pulse to combine, then process for 3–5 minutes until completely smooth. Add extra water until you achieve your desired consistency. Taste and adjust the seasoning.

2 Bring a saucepan of water to the boil and add the peas. Once the water has returned to the boil, add the gnocchi and cook for 3 minutes, until all the gnocchi have risen to the top of the pan. Drain, then return the gnocchi and peas to the pan and add the sauce, tossing gently to mix. Heat through for a minute, stirring, then taste and adjust the seasoning before serving.

WITH MACARONI
Make the cashew sauce as directed, adding ½ tsp. Dijon mustard and ¼ tsp. paprika to the mixture. Replace the gnocchi with 6 oz. (175 g) macaroni or cooked in boiling water until al dente, following the packet instructions. Add the peas about 3 minutes before the end of the pasta cooking time.

WITH ZUCCHINI "SPAGHETTI"
Replace the gnocchi and peas with zucchini "spaghetti" (see page 146). Mix the cooked "spaghetti" with the cashew sauce and heat to warm through. Serve with plenty of black pepper and grilled cherry tomatoes.

ROOT VEGETABLE GRATIN
Steam 14 oz. (400 g) chopped root vegetables until tender. Place in an ovenproof dish with the cooked gnocchi and peas and cover with the cashew sauce. Sprinkle over 4 tbsp. fresh breadcrumbs and place under a hot grill until bubbling and golden brown.

Quick-Fire Antipasti Pizza

You could make this pizza in the time it takes to order one in! You only need self-raising flour and yogurt for the ingenious pizza base—or you could even buy a ready-made pizza base as a shortcut, and a jar of pizza sauce too!

Makes 1 pizza

for the pizza sauce
2 tomatoes, skinned and quartered
2 tbsp. tomato purée
2 tbsp. water
1 tbsp. olive oil
1 tsp. dried oregano
½ tsp. superfine sugar
pinch of chili flakes

1 garlic clove, halved
salt and freshly ground black pepper, to taste

for the pizza base
7½ fl oz. (225 ml) Greek yogurt
5–6 oz. (150–175 g) self-rising flour
¼ tsp. salt

for the topping
7 oz. (200 g) pack mixed antipasti
3 tbsp. grated Parmesan-style cheese
½ x 4½ oz. (125 g) mozzarella ball, torn
small fresh basil leaves, to serve

1 Preheat the oven to 425°F (220°C). For the pizza sauce, put all the ingredients in a blender and process until smooth. If you haven't got a blender, finely chop the tomatoes and combine with the remaining ingredients.

2 For the base, place the yogurt, 5 oz. (150 g) of the flour and the salt in a bowl. Mix with a spoon until combined. Turn out on to a well-floured work surface and knead for about 5 minutes, adding a little extra flour if necessary to form a firm dough. The dough is ready when you have a stretchy ball. This can also be done in a food processor. Using a floured rolling pin, roll and pull out the dough into a rough circle about ¼-in. (5 mm) thick—don't worry about trying to achieve a perfect circle.

3 Spread the tomato sauce over the pizza base, leaving a ½-in. (1-cm) border around the edge. Top with the antipasti, Parmesan and torn mozzarella. Bake the pizza until the crust turns a golden brown, about 10 minutes, and garnish with the basil leaves to serve.

WITH FIG & BLUE
Prepare the base and sauce recipe as directed, but omit the antipasti topping and cheeses. Instead, cut 3 figs into wedges and scatter over the pizza base with 3 oz. (75 g) crumbled blue cheese. Serve garnished with wild arugula.

WITH ZUCCHINI & RICOTTA
Prepare the base and sauce recipe as directed, but omit the antipasti topping and cheeses. Instead, cut 1 zucchini on the diagonal using a vegetable peeler. Toss with 1 tsp. olive oil, a grating of lemon zest, a pinch of chili flakes, and salt and pepper. Scatter the zucchini over the pizza and top with 2 tbsp. Parmesan-style cheese and 2½ oz. (60 g) ricotta cheese. Serve scattered with torn fresh basil leaves.

WITHOUT PIZZA SAUCE
Prepare the base recipe as directed, but omit the pizza sauce. Combine 3¼ oz. (90 g) ricotta cheese with 3 oz. (75 g) frozen spinach (defrosted and well drained). Mix in 1 tbsp. olive oil, a pinch of chili flakes and garlic powder, and season with salt and pepper. Spread over the pizza base. Top with antipasti and sprinkle with Parmesan (omit the mozzarella).

WITH CARAMELIZED ONION
Prepare the base and sauce recipe as directed, but omit the antipasti topping and cheeses. Instead, make a portion of the caramelized onions (see page 204) and scatter on top of the pizza sauce. Top with 3½ oz. (100 g) feta cheese.

Kale Pesto with Linguine

Serves 4

12 oz. (350 g) linguine or spaghetti
1 garlic clove
3 oz. (75 g) kale, hard stems discarded and
    leaves torn

2 oz. (50 g) walnuts or pecans, toasted
2 oz. (50 g) Parmesan-style cheese, plus
    extra, grated, to serve
juice of ½ lemon

5 tbsp. extra-virgin olive oil
salt and freshly ground black pepper

1 Cook the linguine or spaghetti according to the packet directions. Meanwhile, start a food processor running and drop the whole garlic clove down the tube to finely chop. Stop the motor and add the kale, nuts, Parmesan, lemon juice, and 4 tbsp. of olive oil to the bowl of the processor. Pulse to combine, then process until smooth. Thin with a little more olive oil, if required, and season to taste with salt and pepper.

2 Drain the pasta, reserving a little of the cooking water. Stir 4 tbsp. pesto into the pasta, loosening with a little of the reserved cooking water. Serve with an additional grating of Parmesan, if desired.

3 Keep the excess pesto in a sealed container or jar, covering the surface with olive oil. Refrigerate for up to 1 week, or freeze for up to 1 month.

WITH BASIL
Follow the base recipe but use the following ingredients: 1 garlic clove, 2 oz. (50 g) each fresh basil, toasted pine nuts and Parmesan-style cheese, plus 2–2½ fl oz. (60–75 ml) olive oil.

WITH PUMPKIN SEEDS
Follow the base recipe but use the following ingredients: 1 garlic clove, 2 oz. (50 g) each fresh cilantro and toasted pumpkin seeds, 1 oz. (25 g) Parmesan-style cheese, ½ tsp. chili flakes, and 2½–3 fl oz. (75–90 ml) olive oil.

WITH ARUGULA & HAZELNUTS
Follow the base recipe but use the following ingredients: 1 garlic clove, 1 oz. (25 g) each arugula and fresh parsley, 2 oz. (50 g) each toasted hazelnuts and Parmesan-style cheese, the juice of ½ lemon, and 3½–4 fl oz. (100–125 ml) olive oil.

VEGAN PESTO
Follow the base recipe, or any of the variations, but omit the Parmesan-style cheese. In its place add 3 tbsp. nutritional yeast, then taste and add another tbsp. for a more cheese-like flavor, if desired.

Marinated Tofu

Use tamari instead of soy sauce

Serves 4

2 cloves garlic, finely chopped
¼ cup (50 ml) light soy sauce or tamari
1 tsp. coconut palm sugar or brown sugar

2 tsp. rice wine
1 lb. (450 g) extra-firm tofu
2 tbsp. peanut or vegetable oil

1 large red onion, peeled and chopped
8 oz. (225 g) tatsoi leaves

1 Combine the garlic, soy sauce, sugar, and rice wine in a bowl. Rinse, drain, and pat the tofu dry with paper towels before cutting it into bite-size pieces and adding it to the soy sauce mixture. Toss it through the marinade to coat, and set aside for 5 minutes.

2 Heat a wok until a drop of water evaporates in a second or two. Add the oil and onion and stir until fragrant and golden. Add the tofu and the marinade and stir-fry for 3 to 4 minutes. Add the tatsoi and toss until just wilted. Serve immediately.

WITH MUSHROOMS
Prepare the basic recipe, but substitute 1 lb. (450 g) sliced mushrooms for the tofu.

WITH SAMBAL OELEK
Add 1 to 2 tsp. sambal oelek to the marinade for the tofu. Garnish the stir-fry with sliced red chilis, if desired.

WITH ASIAN GREENS
Prepare the basic recipe, but reduce the tatsoi to 4 oz. (125 g), and add 2 quartered baby bok choy and ⅛ of a Chinese cabbage, shredded, to the wok with the tatsoi.

WITH SESAME
Prepare the basic recipe, but add 1 tbsp. sesame oil to the marinade and 1 tbsp. sesame seeds to the wok with the onion. Garnish the stir-fry with extra sesame seeds.

Omit the cheese

Tomato & Eggplant One-Pot Pasta

Unlike most pastas, orzo cooks well in a one-pot dish, and being so small it takes very little time to do so.

Serves 2

1 tbsp. olive oil
1 small onion, sliced
1 garlic clove, crushed
1 bay leaf
pinch of chili flakes
1 eggplant, cut into ½-in.
  (1.5-cm) chunks
5 oz. (150 g) orzo
1 x 14-oz. (400-g) can
  chopped tomatoes

15 fl oz. (450 ml)
  vegetable stock
2 tsp. dried mixed herbs
½ tsp. lemon zest
salt and freshly ground
  black pepper
2 tbsp. chopped fresh
  basil
Parmesan-style cheese
  (optional), to serve

1 Heat the oil in a small saucepan and cook the onion over a moderate heat for 5–7 minutes until soft and translucent. Add the garlic, bay leaf and chili flakes, then cook for another minute. Stir in the eggplant and cook for 3–5 minutes, stirring occasionally until the chunks have softened.

2 Add the orzo, tomatoes, stock, herbs, and lemon zest and stir well to combine, then season to taste with salt and pepper. Bring to a boil, then reduce the heat and simmer, stirring occasionally, for 10–12 minutes, or until the zucchini and orzo are cooked through.

3 Stir through the basil and serve with a grating of Parmesan cheese, if desired.

WITH ZUCCHINI
Substitute 2 sliced zucchini for the eggplant.

WITH MOZZARELLA
Add 3 oz. (75 g) mini mozzarella balls at the end of the cooking time and serve without the Parmesan-style cheese.

WITH PEA & MUSHROOM
Melt 1 tbsp. butter with the olive oil and add 4½ oz. (125 g) chopped mushrooms to the pan after the onions have softened. Cook for 3–4 minutes until the mushrooms have all wilted. Omit the eggplants, adding 3 oz. (75 g) frozen peas 5 minutes before the end of the cooking time.

WITH BEANS
Drain and rinse ⅔ can cannellini or borlotti beans. Add to the pasta 5 minutes before the end of the cooking time.

Portobello Halloumi Burger

GF

Use tamari instead of soy sauce and omit the buns

There are two ways of serving these: using the mushrooms in place of the bread roll, or enclosing the whole lot in a bread roll … the choice is yours.

Makes 2

for the sweet chili sauce
2 tbsp. honey
2 tbsp. dark soy sauce or tamari
1½ tbsp. soft brown sugar
¼ tsp. ground ginger
1 tbsp. Sriracha or similar hot sauce, or to taste

for the burgers
3½ tbsp. balsamic vinegar
2 tbsp. olive oil
4 large portobello mushroom caps, stems removed
2 slices halloumi, thickly sliced

2 slices tomato
2 thinly sliced red onion rings
a few torn basil leaves
2 burger buns (optional)
salt and freshly ground black pepper

1 Combine all the sauce ingredients in a small pan. Bring to a boil, then reduce the heat and simmer for 2–3 minutes until slightly thickened —it will thicken up further when cooling.

2 Preheat the broiler to medium-high. In a shallow bowl, combine the balsamic vinegar, olive oil, and a grinding of salt and pepper. Wipe the mushroom caps with damp kitchen towel, add to the vinegar mixture with their caps facing upwards, and leave for 5 minutes.

3 Broil the mushrooms, underside first, for about 5 minutes, or until they start to sweat, then flip and broil the cap side for 2–3 minutes until tender. Set aside and keep warm. Put the halloumi under the grill, cooking for 2 minutes on each side under a relatively high heat until golden brown, soft and pliable, then sprinkle with pepper and set aside.

4 Lay one mushroom on a plate to use as the bun base. Top with half the halloumi cheese and drizzle with sweet chili sauce. Place a slice of tomato and one of the onion rings on top and add a few torn basil leaves. Top with a second mushroom. Repeat to create two burgers. To eat, half-wrap the burger in baking parchment to facilitate a hand-hold. Alternatively, enclose it in a bun. Serve any remaining sauce on the side.

WITH HARISSA & LEMON-MINT MAYO
Heat 1 tbsp. sunflower oil in a non-stick frying pan over a moderate heat. Thinly spread harissa paste on the halloumi slices and fry for 2 minutes each side or until golden. Replace the sweet chili sauce with lemon-mint mayo: in a small bowl combine 4 tbsp. mayonnaise, 1 tbsp. chopped fresh mint, and 1 tsp. lemon juice. Serve naked or in a bun.

WITH RED PEPPER & HUMMUS
Replace the mushrooms with 2 pieces of grilled red pepper from a jar, and the sweet chili sauce with 1 tbsp. shop-bought hummus (the red pepper variety would be nice). Cook the halloumi as directed, or use the harissa version (as above). This burger must be served in a bun.

WITH CURRIED PANEER
In place of the halloumi and mushroom, heat 1 tbsp. sunflower oil in a non-stick frying pan over a moderate heat. Fry 2 slices of paneer until golden brown on each side. Reduce the heat and add a knob of butter and 1 tsp. curry powder. Baste the paneer with the butter for 1 minute. Replace the basil with cilantro and omit the sauce. Serve in a bun or a chappati.

WITH SWEET POTATO & SWEET CHILI SAUCE
Follow the base recipe, as directed, replacing the mushrooms with 4 sweet potato steaks. Serve naked or in a bun.

Quick Green Thai Curry

(GF) (V)

This recipe uses mostly frozen vegetables for speed; you can substitute fresh, but they will take longer to prepare and cook. Nutritionally, frozen vegetables are roughly the same as fresh, although freezing may change the vitamin content.

Serves 4

1 tbsp. sunflower or coconut oil
1 onion, chopped
1 tbsp. grated fresh root ginger or ginger paste
1 garlic clove, crushed, or 1 tsp. garlic paste
2 tbsp. green curry paste, or to taste

1 x 14-oz. (400-g) can coconut milk or light coconut milk
7 fl oz. (200 ml) vegetable stock
12 oz. (350 g) frozen vegetables
1 x 7 oz. (200 g) packet mangetout and baby corn

1–2 tsp. soft brown sugar
1–2 tbsp. lime juice
2 oz. (50 g) peanuts, roughly chopped
salt

1 Heat the oil in a deep frying pan and gently cook the onions for 5–7 minutes until soft and translucent. Add the ginger and garlic and cook for 1 minute. Add the curry paste and cook for a further minute.

2 Pour the stock and coconut milk into the pan and bring to a boil. Add the frozen vegetables, mangetout and baby corn. Reduce the heat and simmer over a moderate heat for 3–4 minutes until the vegetables are tender.

3 Stir in the sugar, lime juice, and salt to taste. Taste and adjust the sweet, sour, and salt balance. Top with the crunchy chopped peanuts and serve.

WITH PAK CHOI
Replace the mangetout and sweetcorn with 3¼ oz. (90 g) pak choi; add this when the vegetables have already been cooking for 5 minutes so it retains its crispness.

WITH FRESH VEGETABLES
Use 12 oz. (350 g) fresh mixed vegetables in place of the frozen vegetables and cook for 5 minutes before adding the mangetout and sweetcorn, then simmer for 5 minutes and finish as directed.

WITH EGGPLANT & POTATO
Before adding the curry paste, add 1 lb 2 oz. (500 g) sliced new potatoes and 11 oz. (300 g) chopped eggplant. Cook for 10 minutes, turning often, then add the curry paste and cook for 1 minute. Pour in the stock and coconut milk and continue as directed. Omit the frozen vegetables, mangetout and sweetcorn.

WITHN RED THAI CURRY PASTE
Use the milder red Thai curry paste instead of the green. Add a 14 oz. (400 g) can chickpeas, drained and rinsed, with the coconut milk.

CHAPTER 6

Hearty Comfort Food

Comfort foods tend to satisfy our longing to eat something familiar and filling. They are generally a little higher in calories than our more frugal meals, and carbohydrates tend to feature more prominently. The cooking methods remain simple though, so if you are in need of a little cosseting, look no further than this chapter—there are comforting recipes from all over the globe.

Here you will find a tempting mix of hearty meals, including Creamy Mushroom Lasagne (see page 177) and Sweet Potato Mac & Cheese (see page 178), as well as ideas for side dishes including Wholegrain Mustard Mash and Creamed Spinach (both page 164). Some of the recipes are perfect for healthy, filling weekend brunches, especially when you are pressed for time—look no further than Pumpkin & Tofu Kebabs and the Pappardelle with Mushroom Sauce (both page 186). You will also find some starter ideas, which will tempt your taste buds but not fill you up completely.

SOUPS
Soup is one of the most versatile dishes imaginable, and can be served in a mug or bowl for a cheering winter lunch or late-night snack. Here the humble soup is given a new twist and is served in a roll (see page 165) for added heartiness. The variety of flavors that can be added to a soup, from herbs to honey and ginger, are endless. Soup is also a great way of using up leftovers, so don't be afraid to experiment with what you have to hand.

BURGERS
Vegetarian burgers are healthy, colorful, and delicious, and there are so many possibilities to choose from. The humble patty can be made more exciting by adding a fruity salsa (see page 171) or some hot sauce. Simply add a salad from the Super Salads chapter on pages 40 to 69 for a hearty yet wholesome meal.

PASTA & RICE
Pasta is a great vehicle for sauces, while rice is highly nutritious and an excellent food to include in a hearty diet. Here you will find comforting dishes pasta such as Penne with Ricotta & Gorgonzola (see page 187) and Butternut Squash Ravioli (see page 188), as well as the utterly delicious Triple Tomato Risotto (see page 175).

STEWS & CASSEROLES
One-pot stews and casseroles are not only super simple to prepare, but are perfect for days when a filling meal is needed without fuss or ceremony. The spicy West African Peanut Stew (see page 169) and flavorful Vegetable Mole Oaxaca (see page 189) can both be made with minimal equipment. What's more they are simple, nutritious, and satisfying, and can be prepared ahead of time so they are ready when you need them.

PIES & BAKES
Nothing comforts and nurtures like a homemade pie or bake. There aren't many people who don't inwardly melt at the sight of a golden glazed pie crust or "ahhh" the smell emanating from a roast. The Potato & Mushroom Phyllo Pie (see page 180) is just the dish for a cold wintry day—what could be more tempting than the filling of creamy potato and mushroom nestled under a topping of crisp phyllo pastry? And the Winter Vegetable Bake (see page 182) makes good use of seasonal vegetables to create this delicious and filling biscuit-topped crowd-pleaser.

NOODLES
Noodles are perfect for a quick and comforting meal that can be on the table in minutes. Yakisoba is a classic Japanese street food dish that is loved by adults and children alike—just go easy on the chili sauce—and on page 185 you'll find a vegan version that is packed with vegetables and plant-based protein.

DAIRY-FREE BÉCHAMEL SAUCE
Béchamel sauce is used in many comforting dishes, and this vegan version of the classic white sauce is really versatile—use it as the basis of a creamy vegetable sauce, as a pie filling with ingredients such as spinach or mushrooms, or stir in 4 oz. (125 g) cheddar-style vegan "cheese" after the sauce has thickened for a cheesy version.

3 tbsp. soy margarine
3 tbsp. all-purpose flour
1½ cups (375 ml) soy milk
pinch ground nutmeg
sea salt and white pepper

Makes 1½ cups (375 ml)

Melt the soy margarine in a saucepan, then stir in the flour and cook over low heat for 2 minutes, stirring constantly. Slowly add the soy milk, then increase the heat slightly and bring to a boil, stirring until the sauce thickens. Add the nutmeg and season to taste.

Wholegrain Mustard Mash

Serves 4–5

2 lb. (900 g) medium Yukon Gold or similar floury potatoes
2 garlic cloves
1 cup (250 ml) soy milk

3 cups (250 ml) soy cream
1 bay leaf
sea salt
2 tbsp. olive oil

1½ tbsp. wholegrain mustard
black pepper

1 Peel the potatoes and cut each into 6 pieces. Peel and lightly crush the garlic. Put potatoes and garlic in a saucepan with the soy milk, cream, bay leaf, and a generous pinch of salt. Cook for about 15–20 minutes, until the potatoes are very tender. Strain, reserving the cooking liquid but discarding the bay leaf and garlic.

2 Mash the potatoes thoroughly (do not use a blender because the potatoes will become gluey), then fold in enough cooking liquid for the mashed potatoes to become soft and smooth. Stir in the olive oil and the mustard, then season to taste with salt and pepper.

WITH ROASTED GARLIC
Prepare the basic recipe, using the flesh from 6 roasted garlic cloves with the potatoes.

WITH PESTO
Prepare the basic recipe, using 2 tbsp. vegan pesto (see page 156) in place of the mustard.

WITH CELERIAC MASH
Prepare the basic recipe, using 1 lb. (450 g) potatoes and 1 lb. (450 g) celeriac, and 1 tsp. Dijon mustard in place of the wholegrain mustard.

WITHOUT MUSTARD
Prepare the basic recipe, omitting the mustard.

Creamed Spinach

Serves 4

1 tbsp. olive oil
1 small onion, finely chopped
1 garlic clove, minced
1 lb. (450 g) fresh baby spinach, washed

1 cup (125 g) non-dairy cream cheese
½ cup (50 g) non-dairy mayonnaise
¼ tbsp. nutritional yeast
¼ tsp. garlic granules

¼ tsp. ground nutmeg
sea salt and black pepper
3 tbsp. toasted slivered almonds, to garnish

1 Heat the olive oil in a saucepan, add the onion, and cook over a medium-high heat for 5–7 minutes until the onion is soft. Add the minced garlic and cook another minute. Add the spinach and cook with only the water clinging to the washed leaves until just tender; drain and transfer to a warmed serving dish.

2 Meanwhile, combine the non-dairy cream cheese, mayonnaise, nutritional yeast, garlic granules, and nutmeg in a saucepan. Heat gently without boiling, then season with salt and pepper to taste. Pour the sauce over the spinach, toss gently, and garnish with the toasted almonds.

WITH PASTA
Prepare the basic recipe and serve it over 12 oz. (350 g) cooked pasta such as gnocchi or fusilli.

WITH LEEKS
Prepare the basic recipe, adding 3 sliced leeks (white part only) to the pan with the onion. Use just 8 oz. (225 g) pound spinach.

CAULIFLOWER "CHEESE"
Prepare the basic recipe, replacing the spinach with 1 cauliflower, broken into florets and cooked in boiling water until tender. For a more cheesy flavor, add 1½ cups (175 g) shredded non-dairy "hard cheese" to the sauce.

WITH KALE
Prepare the basic recipe, using 1 lb. (450 g) kale in place of the spinach.

Soup in a Roll

These bread bowls are best used for thicker, chowder-type soups, as thin soups might seep through the bread.

Makes 4 bread bowls

2 tsp. active dry yeast	1 tbsp. cornmeal for
1¼ cups (300 ml) warm	sprinkling
water	1 egg white
3½ cups (450 g) white	1 tbsp. water
bread flour	oil for greasing
1 tsp. salt	

1 Lightly grease a large cookie sheet with a little oil and sprinkle with cornmeal. Dissolve the yeast in the warm water and set aside for 10–15 minutes, until creamy. In a large bowl, combine the flour and salt. Make a well in the center and pour in the yeast liquid. Mix until a dough comes together. Knead for about 10 minutes, until the dough is soft, smooth, and elastic. Place the dough in a large lightly oiled bowl, cover, and put in a warm place for an hour or so, until doubled in size.

2 Turn the dough out onto a lightly floured work surface and punch down. Divide into 4 equal portions. Shape each one into a 4-in. (10-cm) round loaf and place on the cookie sheet. Place inside a greased plastic bag and leave for about 35 minutes, until doubled in size.

3 Preheat the oven to 400°F (200°C). In a small bowl, beat the egg white and water together, and brush half of it over the dough. Bake for 15 minutes, brush with the rest of the egg white, and bake for another 10–15 minutes, until golden brown. Cool on a wire rack.

4 Cut a ½-in. (1.5-cm) thick slice from the top of each loaf and scoop out the centers, leaving ¾-in. (2-cm) thick shells. Fill bread bowls with hot soup (see right) and serve.

WITH CREAMY SQUASH SOUP
Prepare the basic recipe. Make soup by cooking 1 large deseeded and chopped butternut squash, 1 finely chopped onion, 1 peeled and chopped carrot, 1 tsp. ground cumin, and salt and freshly ground black pepper in 5 cups (1.25 liters) chicken or vegetable stock until tender. Blend until smooth. Reheat, fill bowls, and garnish with chopped cilantro.

WITH ARTICHOKE & SPINACH DIP
Prepare the basic recipe. In a medium bowl, combine 1 cup (200 g) mayonnaise, 6 oz. (175 g) grated Parmesan-style cheese, one 14-oz. (400-g) can drained artichoke hearts, 4 oz. (125 g) washed and chopped spinach, and 1 tbsp. hot sauce. Transfer to a shallow greased baking dish and bake at 325°F (170°C) for 35–40 minutes until browned. Transfer to the bread bowls and garnish with chopped parsley.

WITH THREE BEAN CHILI
Prepare the basic recipe, filling the rolls with Three Bean Chili (see page 200).

Cheese & Potato Patties

These little potato cakes will remind you of old-style home cooking. They're great for a midweek dinner with a bowl of baked beans or a salad for a lighter option.

Makes 8–10

3 large potatoes (about 1 lb 11 oz./750 g), cut into quarters
5 oz. (150 g) strong Cheddar cheese, grated
3 scallions, sliced
2 garlic cloves, crushed
½ tsp. paprika
2 tbsp. chopped fresh parsley
1 egg, lightly beaten
2–3 tbsp. olive oil or butter, plus extra if required
1–2 tbsp. milk, if required
salt and freshly ground black pepper
soured cream, to serve
chopped fresh chives, to serve

1 Bring a saucepan of water to a boil, add the potatoes, then reduce the heat, cover and simmer for about 20 minutes, or until tender. Drain, cool slightly, then mash until smooth. Add the cheese, scallions, garlic, paprika, and parsley to the potatoes with sufficient egg to bind the mixture. Season with salt and pepper to taste. If the patties are still a little dry and crumbly, add 1–2 tbsp. milk to reach the desired consistency.

2 Scoop about 2 tbsp. of the mixture at a time into damp hands and form into round patties about ½-in. (1.5 cm) thick.

3 Heat the oil or melt the butter in a frying pan over a medium heat. Add the patties in batches, taking care not to overcrowd the pan, and cook for 5–6 minutes until golden and crispy. Using a spatula, carefully flip them and cook the other side. Add a little more oil between batches, if required. Serve with a dollop of soured cream scattered with chives.

WITH SWEET POTATO
Replace the potatoes with 3 medium–large sweet potatoes, peeled and cut into chunks. Add 1 oz. (25 g) soft breadcrumbs to the mixture. Replace the paprika with ½ tsp. chili flakes. If liked, dredge the completed patties in additional breadcrumbs before frying.

WITH SPICES
Heat 1 tbsp. oil in a frying pan and add 1 tbsp. grated fresh root ginger, 1 tsp. each of cumin seeds, ground turmeric, garam masala and ½–1 tsp. chili powder, to taste. Cook the spices for 1 minute, then add to the mashed potato with the other ingredients along with 2 oz. (50 g) cooked frozen peas. Omit the cheese and paprika.

WITH EGG
Divide the mashed potato mixture into four and form into large potato cakes. Fry as directed and keep warm. Fry 4 eggs to your liking, adding a little more oil or butter to the pan as necessary. Top each patty with a fried egg.

Zucchini Fritters with Tzatziki

These fritters use both spelt and rice flours. If these are unavailable, use whole wheat, all-purpose, or even buckwheat flour—or a combination of flours.

Serves 4

for the tzatziki
1½ cups (350 ml) soy yogurt
1 tbsp. olive oil
½ cucumber, shredded
1 clove garlic, crushed or minced
1 tsp. chopped fresh dill or ½ tsp. dried dill
sea salt and black pepper

for the fritters
½ cup (125 g) rice flour
½ cup (125 g) spelt flour
1 tsp. baking powder

⅓ cup (25 g) quick-cooking oats
2 tbsp. nutritional yeast
2 tbsp. chopped fresh mint or 1 tsp. dried mint
1 tsp. ground cilantro
2 medium zucchini, coarsely shredded
3 scallions, finely chopped
1 red chilipepper, finely chopped
sea salt and black pepper
½ cup soy yogurt
canola oil, to fry

1 In a small bowl, combine all the ingredients for the tzatziki. Chill until ready to serve. In a bowl, combine the flours, baking powder, oats, yeast, mint, and cilantro. Place the zucchini in a clean towel and squeeze out any excess liquid, then add to the flour mixture, tossing to ensure that the pieces are coated in flour.

2 Add the scallions, red chili, and salt and pepper to taste. Gently stir in the yogurt, adding a little water if the mixture feels too dry. Set aside for 10 minutes for the baking powder to begin to activate.

3 Heat a skillet or griddle until very hot, then coat with a little oil. Using about ¼ cup of fritter batter, drop the batter onto the hot skillet and spread out with a spatula. Cook until bubbles rise to the surface of the fritter and the base is golden brown, then turn and cook the other side. Remove and keep warm while you make the next fritters. Serve with the tzatziki.

WITH CARROT
Prepare the basic recipe, using 2 cups (225 g) shredded carrots in place of zucchini (there is no need to squeeze the liquid out of the carrots).

WITH CORN
Prepare the basic recipe, using 2 cups (300 g) frozen or canned corn in place of the zucchini (there is no need to squeeze the liquid out of the corn). Use parsley in place of mint.

WITH PARSNIP
Prepare the basic recipe, replacing zucchini with 2 cups (225 g) shredded parsnips, which have been blanched in boiling water for 2 minutes, then drained and squeezed dry. Use sage in place of mint.

WITH TAHINI SAUCE
Prepare the basic fritters, but replace tzatziki with tahini sauce. Combine 1 minced garlic clove, ¼ cup (75 g) tahini, 4 tbsp. lemon juice, 4 tbsp. soy yogurt, and 1 tsp. freshly chopped parsley. Season to taste with a little sea salt, a pinch of cayenne pepper, and a few drops of agave syrup.

West African Peanut Stew

(GF) (V)

Is it a soup or is it a stew? Either way, this is a warming, wholesome dish. Serve with brown rice, accompanied by your favorite hot chili sauce, if you like your food spicy.

Serves 4

2 tbsp. peanut or sunflower oil
1 red onion, chopped
2 garlic cloves, crushed
2 tbsp. chopped fresh root ginger
2 tsp. chili flakes, or to taste
1¼ pints (750 ml) vegetable stock (see page 71)

1 x 14-oz. (400-g) can chopped tomatoes
7 oz. (200 g) unsweetened chunky peanut butter
3 tbsp. tomato purée
3 small sweet potatoes, cut into ¾-in. (2-cm) chunks

5 oz. (150 g) spring greens or kale, hard stems discarded and leaves roughly chopped
salt and freshly ground black pepper, to taste
1 oz. (25 g) crushed toasted peanuts, to serve

1 Heat the oil in a large frying pan and gently cook the onion for 5–7 minutes until soft and translucent. Add the garlic and ginger and cook for 1 minute. Stir in the chili flakes and cook for a further minute, then pour in the stock and tomatoes and bring to a boil over a high heat. Cover, reduce the heat and simmer for 10 minutes.

2 Meanwhile, in a small bowl, mix together the peanut butter and tomato purée. Add a ladleful of the hot cooking liquid, stir to combine, then pour into the pan, stirring well to combine.

3 Stir in the sweet potato and cook for 5 minutes, then add the spring greens or kale, season with salt and pepper, and cook for 10 minutes until the vegetables are tender. Add a little water if the sauce is too thick; it should be quite sloppy. Serve sprinkled with the peanuts.

WITH CASHEW NUTS
Replace the peanut butter with cashew butter and finish with crushed toasted cashew nuts in place of peanuts.

WITH PEAS & SPINACH
Replace the sweet potatoes and greens with 3½ oz. (100 g) frozen peas, 3½ oz. (100 g) sugar snap peas and 3 oz. (75 g) baby spinach leaves. Cook for about 5 minutes after adding these vegetables, or until just tender.

WITH EGGPLANT & OKRA
Roughly chop an eggplant, place in a colander, sprinkle with salt and leave for 30 minutes. Drain and pat dry with kitchen towel. Add to the stew instead of the sweet potato. Replace the greens with 5 oz. (150 g) small okra (trimmed around the stem without piercing the pod). Cook for 10 minutes, or until tender.

WITH COCONUT MILK
Add 1 x 14-oz. (400-g) can of coconut milk with the tomatoes and reduce the water to 14 fl oz. (400 ml).

Vegetable Pastitsio

This is a vegetarian version of a flavorful Greek layered casserole. Serve with a tossed salad and crusty bread.

Serves 4

2 cups (400 g) conchiglie
4 tbsp. extra-virgin olive
  oil
2 garlic cloves, minced
2 x 14-oz. (400-g) cans
  whole tomatoes in
  liquid
2 oz. (50 g) tomato paste
salt and freshly ground
  black pepper
4 fresh basil leaves,
  roughly torn

1 tbsp. finely chopped
  fresh oregano
1 tbsp. finely chopped
  fresh thyme
1 onion, finely sliced
1 small eggplant, cut into
  small cubes
2 small zucchini, cut into
  small cubes
2 eggs, lightly beaten
½ cup (120 ml) plain
  yogurt

1 Preheat oven to 190°C (350°F). In a large saucepan of salted boiling water, cook pasta until al dente, about 8 minutes. Drain and set aside.

2 Heat 2 tbsp. olive oil in large saucepan over medium heat. Fry garlic until golden, about 4 minutes. Add tomatoes and tomato paste, and stir well, breaking up tomatoes into smaller pieces. Season with salt and pepper and stir in basil, oregano, and thyme. Reduce heat to low and simmer for 10 minutes.

3 In a separate pan, heat remaining oil over medium-high heat and sauté onion, eggplant, and zucchini for 5 minutes, until tender. Season with salt and pepper. In a small bowl, combine the eggs and yogurt.

4 Spread half the tomato sauce in a medium casserole dish. Arrange the eggplant–zucchini mixture on top, then top with remaining tomato sauce. Layer pasta over tomato sauce, and spoon the yogurt–egg mixture over pasta. Bake for 45 minutes, until yogurt topping is browned and casserole is bubbly.

WITH MACARONI
Prepare the basic recipe, replacing the shell-shaped pasta with an equal quantity of macaroni.

WITH BÉCHAMEL
Prepare the basic recipe, replacing the yogurt–egg topping with béchamel sauce (see page 163). Spoon over pasta and bake as directed.

WITH CHILI
Prepare the basic recipe, adding 2 chopped fresh chilis (or to taste) to the tomato sauce with the garlic.

WITH SOYA MINCE
Prepare the basic recipe, adding 1 lb. (450 g) soya mince to the tomato sauce.

WITH VEGAN "CHICKEN"
Prepare the basic recipe, adding 1 lb. (450 g) vegan chicken-style pieces to the tomato sauce.

Lentil & Quinoa Burgers with Mango Salsa

(v)

These lentil and quinoa burgers have a good texture and go well in a bun or served on their own with the salsa and a green salad.

Serves 4

1 cup (200 g) green or brown lentils
½ cup (125 g) quinoa
1 tbsp. olive oil
1 small onion, finely chopped
1 small carrot, grated
2 tsp. ground cumin
¾ cup (40 g) soft breadcrumbs
2 tbsp. chopped fresh parsley
3 tbsp. tomato paste
1 tbsp. soy sauce
1 tbsp. nutritional yeast
2 tbsp. peanut butter
sea salt and black pepper
cornmeal or oats for coating

olive oil, for frying

for the mango salsa
1 mango, peeled and chopped
1 medium bell green pepper, seeded and chopped
1 small red onion, finely chopped
1 jalapeño pepper, finely chopped
2 tbsp. lime juice
1 tbsp. pineapple juice or orange juice
sea salt and black pepper
chopped fresh cilantro, to garnish

1 Put the lentils and quinoa in a saucepan of boiling water, reduce the heat, and simmer until soft. Drain and cool, then mash with a potato masher. To make the salsa, combine all the ingredients in a bowl and set aside.

2 Meanwhile, heat the oil in a skillet, add the onion, and cook over a medium-high heat until soft. Stir in the carrots and cumin, and cook for 2 minutes. Add the lentil-quinoa mixture, breadcrumbs, parsley, tomato paste, soy sauce, nutritional yeast, and peanut butter. Knead the mixture with your hands until it sticks together. Form the mixture into 8 burgers.

3 Coat each burger in cornmeal or oats. Heat 1 tbsp. olive oil in a skillet and fry over a medium-low heat until crisp and golden on each side, 4–5 minutes. Serve with the mango salsa.

WITH LIME & CHILI
Prepare the basic recipe adding 1–2 finely chopped red chilis and the grated zest and juice of 1 lime to the mixture. If the mixture is too soft, add extra breadcrumbs.

WITH ZUCCHINI
Prepare the basic recipe, using grated zucchini in place of the carrot.

WITH OATS
Prepare the basic recipe, omitting the quinoa. Add 1 cup (90 g) rolled oats with the breadcrumbs.

WITH RED LENTILS & WALNUTS
Prepare the basic recipe, using red lentils and omitting the quinoa. Add ¼ cup (50 g) rolled oats and 4 tbsp. finely chopped toasted walnuts with the breadcrumbs.

Beet & Bean Burger

Fill your bun as you choose—try iceberg lettuce, rocket, tomato, avocado, and a topping such as mayonnaise, perhaps. It's particularly good with horseradish sauce, too.

Makes 6

2–3 tbsp. olive oil
6 burger, ciabatta or sourdough buns

for the burgers
2–3 tbsp. sunflower oil
1 small onion, finely chopped
2 garlic cloves, crushed

1 large beet, grated
1 carrot, grated
1 x 14-oz. (400-g) tin black or borlotti
    beans, drained and rinsed
3½ oz. (100 g) cooked rice
2 oz. (50 g) walnuts, finely chopped
2 tbsp. plain or gram flour

2 tbsp. lemon juice
1½ tsp. ground cumin
1 tsp. smoked paprika
large handful of fresh parsley, chopped
1 egg, beaten
salt and freshly ground black pepper

1 For the burgers, heat the sunflower oil in a large frying pan and gently cook the onion for 5–7 minutes until soft and translucent. Add the garlic and cook for 1 minute. Stir in the beet and carrot, then cover and cook over a medium-low heat, stirring occasionally, for about 5 minutes, until the vegetables are just tender. Remove from the heat.

2 Stir the beans, rice, and walnuts into the vegetables and mix well to combine. Stir in the flour and mix really well. Add the lemon juice, cumin, and smoked paprika and season to taste with plenty of salt and pepper. Stir in the parsley. Using a potato masher or hand-held blender, mash the mixture so that about half of it is broken up—do not overwork it as a bit of texture is important. Add sufficient egg to bind and create a pliable mixture, but do not add too much or the mixture will become too soggy to shape; if you have overdone it, add a little more flour. With damp hands, form the mixture into six balls. Place on a chopping board and flatten into burgers.

3 Heat the olive oil in a large frying pan and cook the burgers over a medium-low heat until crisp on one side, about 4 minutes. Flip and repeat on the other side. Serve in the buns with your own choice of toppings.

WITH CORN, CHIPOLTE & CHILI
Use 4 oz. (125 g) frozen or tinned sweetcorn instead of the walnuts. Replace the smoked paprika with 1 tsp. chipotle sauce and use fresh cilantro in place of the parsley. Serve with slices of jalapeño chili from a jar, instead of the suggested toppings.

WITH SQUASH & WHITE BEANS
Replace the beet with ½ butternut squash cut into ½-in. (1-cm) chunks. Substitute a 14 oz. (400 g) can of cannellini beans for the black beans. Replace the parsley with fresh basil. Spread a little pesto over the burger and top with mayonnaise.

WITH SWEET POTATO & CAJUN SPICES
Replace the beet with sweet potato cut into ½-in. (1-cm) chunks. Replace the cumin and sweet paprika with 2–3 tsp. Cajun spice mix, to taste. Serve with mayonnaise flavored with a few drops of hot chili sauce.

WITHOUT NUTS
Replace the chopped walnuts with 4 tbsp. porridge oats.

Greek-style Stuffed Peppers

(V)

To boost the protein level, add a can of kidney beans or some diced firm tofu to the stuffing.

Serves 4

4 large green or red bell
  peppers
3 tbsp. olive oil
1 medium onion, chopped
2 garlic cloves, crushed
½ cup (100 g) brown rice
2½ cups (500 ml) tomato
  juice or vegetable juice
1 bay leaf
2 sprigs fresh parsley
2½ tsp. dried oregano

⅔ cup (100 g) chopped
  walnuts
1½ tbsp. nutritional yeast
2 tsp. lemon juice
pinch sugar
sea salt and black pepper
2 tbsp. breadcrumbs
½ tsp. lemon zest
1 tsp. toasted sesame
  seeds

1 Cut a slice off the top of each pepper and remove the center core and seeds. Brush the outside of the peppers with a little of the olive oil, then stand upright in an ovenproof dish. Heat the remaining olive oil in a saucepan, then add the onion and cook over a medium heat for 5–7 minutes until the onion is soft.

2 Add the garlic and cook for another minute. Add the rice, half of the tomato juice, bay leaf, parsley, and 2 tsp. of the oregano. Bring to a boil, cover, and simmer over low heat, adding a little extra water if the mixture dries out before the rice is cooked, about 40 minutes.

3 Discard the bay leaf and parsley sprigs. Add the walnuts, 1 tbsp. of the nutritional yeast, and lemon juice, then season with the sugar, salt, and pepper. Pile the mixture into the pepper shells.

4 Preheat oven to 350°F (175°C). Pour the remaining tomato juice and ½ tsp. oregano around the peppers. Combine the breadcrumbs, remaining ½ tbsp. nutritional yeast, lemon zest, and sesame seeds, and sprinkle over the peppers. Bake for 30–40 minutes until the peppers are tender. Serve hot.

WITH ZUCCHINI
Prepare the basic recipe, using 4 large zucchini, with seeds and some pulp scooped out, in place of the bell peppers.

WITH BARLEY
Prepare the basic recipe, using barley in place of rice.

WITH GRAPE LEAVES
Prepare the basic recipe, using 1 x 8-oz. (225-g) jar of grape leaves in place of the peppers and ½ cup (50 g) pine nuts in place of the walnuts. Rinse the leaves in warm water, shake dry, and lay out, vein-side up. Roll 1 tbsp. of the mixture in each leaf. Place the parcels in a baking dish, cover with tomato juice mixture, and weight the stuffed leaves with a plate to prevent unraveling. Omit the crumb topping. Serve cold.

WITH LENTILS & CURRANTS
Prepare the basic recipe, using ⅔ cup (150 g) cooked lentils (canned or home-cooked) in place of the walnuts, and 1 tbsp. each of fresh parsley and chives in place of the dried oregano. Add ½ cup (65 g) currants to the rice mixture before cooking.

Triple Tomato Risotto

This very special risotto combines the rich intensity of roasted cherry tomatoes and flecks of sun-dried tomato with the subtlety of tomato-flavored stock.

Serves 4

12 oz. (350 g) cherry tomatoes, halved
8 garlic cloves, unpeeled
1 tbsp. olive oil
4 cups (900 ml) vegetable stock (see page 71)
1 x 14-oz. (400-g) jar tomato sauce
1 tbsp. oil from sun-dried tomatoes
1 tbsp. soy margarine

4 shallots, finely chopped
2 cups (400 g) arborio (risotto) rice
½ cup (125 ml) white wine
¼ cup (40 g) sun-dried tomatoes, finely chopped
4 tbsp. chopped fresh basil
sea salt and black pepper

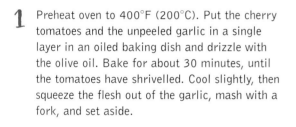

1   Preheat oven to 400°F (200°C). Put the cherry tomatoes and the unpeeled garlic in a single layer in an oiled baking dish and drizzle with the olive oil. Bake for about 30 minutes, until the tomatoes have shrivelled. Cool slightly, then squeeze the flesh out of the garlic, mash with a fork, and set aside.

2   In a small pan, heat the stock and tomato sauce. Heat the tomato oil and margarine in a saucepan on a medium-high heat, then add the shallots and cook for 5–7 minutes until soft.

3   Add the rice and stir to coat it with oil, then cook until the grains become translucent, about 1 minute. Add the wine and cook, stirring until absorbed, then add about 1 ladleful of the hot stock mixture and continue to cook, stirring frequently, until fully absorbed. Add another ladleful of stock and allow it to be absorbed before adding another. Continue this process until the rice is tender, but still firm, and just coated in a thick creamy sauce.

4   Gently stir in the roasted cherry tomatoes, mashed garlic, sun-dried tomatoes, and basil, and season with salt and pepper to taste. Serve immediately.

WITH ASPARAGUS
Prepare the basic recipe, using 1 bunch asparagus, chopped and blanched, in place of the cherry tomatoes and garlic.

WITH MUSHROOM
Prepare the basic recipe, using 1½ cups (100 g) cooked sliced button mushrooms, in place of the roasted cherry tomatoes.

OVEN-BAKED TRIPLE TOMATO RISOTTO
Prepare the basic recipe, using only 1½ cups (350 ml) tomato sauce and 3½ cups (850 ml) stock. After the wine has been absorbed, add all the remaining ingredients, cover, and bake at 350°F (180°C) for 20 minutes; stir, adding extra stock if required, and continue to bake for 10 minutes, or until the rice is tender-firm.

TRIPLE TOMATO RISOTTO CAKES
Prepare the basic recipe, then let it cool. Shape the risotto into small cakes and fry in olive oil until golden on both sides. This is an excellent way to use up leftover risotto.

Thyme & Taleggio Risotto with Mushrooms

Serves 4

1 tbsp. olive oil
½ oz. (15 g) butter
1 onion, finely chopped
8 oz. (225 g) mushrooms, sliced

small bunch fresh thyme sprigs
9 oz. (250 g) risotto rice
1 pint (600 ml) vegetable stock (see page 71)

4 fl oz. (120 ml) white wine or vegetable
 stock
100g (3½ oz) Taleggio cheese, cubed

1 In a large pan, heat the oil and the butter together over a medium heat. Add the onion and mushrooms and fry for 5 minutes, until softened. Remove the thyme leaves from their stalks and add most of them to the pan, along with the rice. Continue to cook for 2 minutes.

2 Start to add the stock, a ladle at a time, stirring until the stock has been absorbed each time. Continue adding the stock until it has all been absorbed, and the rice is cooked and creamy but still with a slight bite. Stir the Taleggio cheese into the risotto and serve immediately, sprinkled with thyme leaves.

WITH MUSHROOM & PARMESAN
Prepare the basic recipe. Increase the mushrooms to 12 oz. (350 g), omit the Taleggio, and substitute freshly grated Parmesan cheese.

WITH BUTTERNUT SQUASH & SPINACH
Prepare the basic recipe, omit the mushrooms and Taleggio, and substitute 8 oz. (225 g) diced butternut squash and grated Parmesan. Just before serving, add 2½ oz. (60 g) baby spinach leaves to the risotto.

WITH PARSLEY & BROAD BEAN
Prepare the basic recipe, omit the thyme, substitute parsley, and add 6 oz. (175 g) cooked broad beans with the cheese.

WITH ASPARAGUS & PARMESAN
Prepare the basic recipe, adding 1 bunch asparagus, chopped and blanched. Omit the Taleggio, and substitute freshly grated Parmesan cheese.

Hey Pesto Pasta

Serves 4

1 bunch (about 2½ oz./60 g) fresh basil
2 oz. (50 g) grated Parmesan cheese
1½ oz. (40 g) pine nuts

1 clove garlic, roughly chopped
¼ tsp. salt
¼ tsp. freshly ground black pepper

2 fl oz. (60 ml) extra virgin olive oil
12 oz. (350 g) pasta (ideally gemelli,
 spaghetti or orzo)

1 Place the basil, 1 oz. (25 g) grated Parmesan, pine nuts, garlic, salt, pepper, and olive oil in a blender or food processor, and blend until smooth. Set aside.

2 Cook the pasta according to the packet instructions, then drain, retaining some of the liquid. Off the heat, return the pasta to the pan and add the pesto, with a little of the pasta liquid. Serve immediately, sprinkled with the remaining grated Parmesan.

WITH WALNUTS & PECORINO ROMANO
Process 1 oz. (25 g) toasted walnuts with 1 chopped clove garlic, a good handful of fresh basil leaves, 5 tbsp. extra virgin olive oil, 1 oz. (25 g) grated Pecorino Romano, and ¼ tsp. each of salt and freshly ground black pepper.

WITH VEGAN "BACON"
Prepare the basic recipe. In a medium pan, over a medium–high heat, cook 6 chopped rashers of vegan "bacon" until crispy, and add to the pasta with the pesto.

WITH PEAS & SUNDRIED TOMATOES
Prepare the basic recipe, adding 1¼ oz. (30 g) thawed frozen green peas to the pesto with the rest of the ingredients in the food processor. Add 4 tbsp. chopped sundried tomatoes to the pasta with the pesto.

WITH SPINACH & AVOCADO
Prepare the basic recipe, adding 1¼ oz. (30 g) baby spinach leaves to the pasta with the pesto, and serve with a little chopped avocado on top.

Creamy Mushroom Lasagne

(V)

Supplement white mushrooms with crimini, chanterelle, portabello, oyster, porcini, or shiitake mushrooms to make this lasagne a taste sensation.

Serves 6–8

8 oz. (225 g) dried lasagne sheets
½ cup (50 g) dairy-free "Parmesan"
2 tbsp. olive oil
1 large red onion, sliced
3 garlic cloves, crushed
1 lb. (450 g) mixed fresh mushrooms, sliced

2 small leeks, white part only, chopped
2 tsp. dried thyme
¼ cup (50 ml) dry white wine
1 tbsp. tamari
sea salt and black pepper
1 quantity béchamel sauce (see page 163)
3 tbsp. nutritional yeast

1 Cook the lasagne sheets according to package instructions. If using a no-cook variety, blanch in boiling water for 2 minutes. Drain and lay out on a kitchen towel or parchment paper.

2 Meanwhile, heat the olive oil in a saucepan, then add the onion and cook over a medium-high heat for 5–7 minutes until soft. Add the garlic, mushrooms, leeks, and thyme, and cook over a low heat until tender. Increase the heat, add the wine, allow to bubble for 2 minutes, then remove from the heat. Stir in the tamari and salt and pepper to taste.

3 Make the béchamel sauce, then stir in the nutritional yeast. To assemble the lasagne, pour béchamel sauce over the bottom of a dish to form a thin layer, cover with a layer of pasta, coat with one-third of the béchamel sauce, followed by half the mushrooms, sprinkle with a third of the "Parmesan"; repeat, finishing with a generous coating of "Parmesan".

4 Preheat oven to 350°F (180°C). Cook for 30 minutes, then increase the heat to 400°F (200°C) and continue to cook until golden brown, preferably with almost burnt bits around the edges.

WITH "CHEESE"
Prepare the basic recipe, adding 2 cups (225 g) grated non-dairy "cheese" to the béchamel sauce (see page 163).

WITH FENNEL
Prepare the basic recipe, adding 2 sliced fennel bulbs, blanched for 5 minutes, with the mushrooms.

WITHOUT GLUTEN
Prepare the basic recipe, using spelt lasagne in place of the wheat-based lasagne sheets.

WITH BOLOGNESE SAUCE
Prepare the basic recipe, using a vegan bolognese sauce in place of the mushroom filling.

Sweet Potato Mac & Cheese

This has become a contemporary classic with its deliciously creamy sweet potato sauce. It needs nothing more than the simplest green salad on the side.

Serves 4

2 medium sweet potatoes, cut into chunks
1 pint (600 ml) whole milk
10 oz. (275 g) penne or macaroni
2 tbsp. unsalted butter

1 garlic clove, crushed
2 tbsp. plain flour
5 oz. (150 g) Cheddar cheese, grated
3 oz. (75 g) baby spinach

1 tsp. Dijon mustard or a grating of nutmeg
4 tbsp. Parmesan-style cheese
salt and ground black pepper

1 Preheat the oven to 375°F (190°C). Lightly grease a medium-sized ovenproof dish.

2 Bring a saucepan of water to a boil, add the sweet potato, then reduce the heat, cover and simmer for 10–15 minutes until tender. Drain the pan but retain the cooking water. Transfer the potato to a bowl and leave to cool slightly. Mash with 2 tbsp. of the milk. Add fresh water to the saucepan and bring to a boil, then cook the pasta according to the packet directions until al dente.

3 Meanwhile, in a small saucepan, melt the butter, then add the garlic and cook for 1 minute. Stir in the flour and cook for another minute. Using a balloon whisk, beat in the remaining milk, seasoning with salt and pepper to taste. Cook, stirring constantly, until the mixture thickens, about 5 minutes. Remove from the heat and beat in the puréed sweet potato, Cheddar cheese and Dijon mustard or nutmeg.

4 Transfer the drained pasta to the ovenproof dish and stir in the cheese sauce, then add the spinach, mixing well to encourage the spinach to wilt and to coat all the ingredients evenly in sauce. Add a little of the retained cooking water to loosen the sauce, if required. Sprinkle the Parmesan cheese on top and bake for 25–35 minutes, until the sauce is bubbling and the cheese is golden brown.

WITH A CRISPY TOPPING
Mix together 2 oz. (50 g) soft white or wholemeal breadcrumbs with the Parmesan-style cheese and 1 tsp. paprika. Sprinkle over the mac and cheese before baking as directed.

WITH PEAS & TOMATOES
Instead of the spinach, add 3 quartered tomatoes and 3½ oz. (100 g) frozen peas to the dish with the pasta and sweet potato purée. Bake as directed.

WITH ROASTED VEGETABLES
When constructing the mac and cheese, place half the pasta and sweet potato-cheese sauce in the base of the ovenproof dish and top with a layer of leftover roasted vegetables (around 10 oz./275 g would be ideal). Top with the remaining pasta and sauce and bake as directed.

WITH CAULIFLOWER
Replace the pasta with 1 head of cauliflower, cut into florets and steamed for 10 minutes or until tender. Carefully mix with the sweet potato-cheese sauce, 3 quartered tomatoes, a 14 oz. (400 g) can of butter beans (drained and rinsed), and the spinach. Bake as directed.

Potato & Mushroom Phyllo Pie

Ⓥ

When using phyllo pastry, work quickly to prevent it from drying out. Keep any unused sheets either covered in wax paper or a damp cloth.

Serves 4

1½ lbs. (675 g) floury
    potatoes, such as
    Idaho or Yukon Gold,
    thinly sliced
1 tbsp. olive oil
2 onions, finely sliced
8 oz. (225 g) cremini
    mushrooms, sliced
1 tsp. dried dill
1 tbsp. arrowroot
1 cup (250 ml) soy cream

¼ cup (50 ml) vegetable
    stock (see page 71)
1 tbsp. nutritional yeast
1 bunch scallions, sliced
pinch paprika
pinch ground nutmeg
sea salt and black pepper
6 sheets phyllo pastry
olive oil, to brush
sesame seeds, to sprinkle

1 Preheat oven to 375°F (190°C). Oil an 11 x 7 in. (28 x 18 cm) baking dish. In a large pan of boiling water, blanch the potato slices for 2 minutes, plunge into cold water, drain, and blot off any excess water with a cloth or paper towel. Heat the oil in a skillet, add the onions, and cook over a medium-high heat for 5–7 minutes or until soft. Add the mushrooms and cook until just wilted, then stir in the dill.

2 Mix the arrowroot with 2 tbsp. of the soy cream, then stir in the remaining soy cream, stock, and nutritional yeast. In the prepared dish, layer the potatoes, onion-mushroom mixture, and scallions, sprinkling a little of the cream mixture, paprika, nutmeg, salt, and pepper over each potato layer. Pour the remaining cream mixture over the top layer.

3 Working quickly, cut the phyllo slightly larger than the baking dish. Place the first sheet on top of the vegetables, tuck the overlap down inside the dish, then brush with olive oil. Repeat until all the sheets are used. Brush the top generously with oil and sprinkle with sesame seeds. Score the pastry into portions. Bake for 20–25 minutes, until golden; before serving test that the potatoes are cooked by inserting a knife through the scored pastry.

WITH PUFF PASTRY
Prepare the basic recipe, using non-dairy puff pastry in place of the phyllo.

WITH PEA & TOMATO
Prepare the basic recipe, but use 4 oz. (125 g) cooked frozen peas and 2 large peeled, seeded, and chopped tomatoes mixed together in place of the cooked mushrooms.

WITH SWEET POTATO & CORN
Prepare the basic recipe, replacing half of the potatoes with sweet potatoes and using 4 oz. (125 g) frozen corn in place of the cooked mushrooms.

WITH CARAMELIZED ONION
Prepare the basic recipe, omitting the onions, mushrooms and scallions. Instead, cook 1 lb. (450 g) sliced yellow onions in 4 tbsp. olive oil over a very low heat for about 30 minutes, stirring often. Stir in 1 tbsp. sugar, then continue to cook for 10–15 minutes until golden brown. Add the dill and proceed as with the basic recipe.

Speltotto with Roasted Veg

Risotto is a favorite comfort meal for many people, and this version, using spelt, has a deliciously nutty flavor.

Serves 4

for the roasted vegetables
1 eggplant, cut into large chunks
2 zucchini, cut into large chunks
1 red onion, cut into wedges
1 red bell pepper, cut into large chunks
1 green bell pepper, cut into large chunks
4 garlic cloves
3 tbsp. olive oil
7 oz. (200 g) cherry tomatoes
salt and ground black pepper

for the speltotto
2 tbsp. olive oil
3 shallots or a small red onion, finely chopped
7 oz. (200 g) pearled spelt
7 fl oz. (200 ml) white wine
17 fl oz. (500 ml) hot vegetable stock (see page 71)
7 oz. (200 g) frozen peas
2 oz. (50 g) unsalted butter
2 oz. (50 g) Parmesan-style cheese

1 Preheat the oven to 400°F (200°C). Tip the eggplant, zucchinis, onions, peppers, and garlic into a roasting tin. Toss through the oil and season with salt and pepper, then roast for 30 minutes, turning halfway through. Add the tomatoes and roast for another 10 minutes, squeeze the garlic out of its skin.

2 Meanwhile, make the speltotto. Heat the oil in a saucepan over a medium heat and fry the shallots for 4–5 minutes until soft. Add the spelt and cook for 2 minutes. Add the wine and bring to a boil, stirring; cook for 2 minutes. Reduce the heat and add sufficient stock to just cover, stirring frequently. Once the liquid is absorbed, add more stock 1 tbsp. at a time. Continue this process for 4 minutes.

3 Add the peas, return to a boil, and continue to cook, adding more stock as before for another 3–4 minutes, until most of the liquid has been used and the spelt is tender. Stir in the butter and Parmesan and season generously with salt and pepper. Serve with the roasted vegetables.

WITH RISOTTO RICE
Follow the base recipe, as directed, but in place of spelt use 9 oz. (250 g) arborio rice and increase the quantity of hot vegetable stock to 1½ pints (900 ml).

WITH BARLEY
Follow the base recipe, as directed, but in place of spelt use 6 oz. (175 g) pearl barley.

WITH PESTO & ASPARAGUS
While the speltotto is cooking, simmer 7 oz. (200 g) chopped asparagus for a few minutes until just tender, then drain. When adding the butter, stir in 4 tbsp. shop-bought or home-made pesto (see page 156) followed by the cooked asparagus. Omit the roasted vegetables.

WITH LEEK, TOMATOES & GOAT CHEESE
While the speltotto is cooking, heat 1 tbsp. oil in a frying pan and fry 2 sliced leeks and 6 oz. (175 g) cherry tomatoes for 3–4 minutes, stirring a few times until the leeks are softened. Set aside and keep warm. Stir into the speltotto after adding the butter. Top each portion with a slice of goat cheese. Omit the roasted vegetables.

Winter Vegetable Bake

(V)

Root vegetables make a star appearance in this one-pot wonder.

Serves 4–6

2 tbsp. olive oil
2 red onions, cut into wedges
½ butternut squash, diced
½ rutabaga, diced
3 medium carrots, thickly sliced
2 medium leeks, trimmed and sliced
2 medium parsnips, thickly sliced
3 raw beets, quartered
2 celery stalks, sliced

1 tsp. caraway seeds
2 garlic cloves, minced
3 tbsp. tomato paste
1¼ cups (300 ml) vegetable stock
1 x 14-oz. (400-g) can crushed tomatoes
1 tsp. mixed dried herbs
sea salt and pepper
1 tbsp. cornstarch
1 tbsp. water

for the biscuits
2 cups (250 g) all-purpose flour
1 tbsp. baking powder
½ tsp. salt
1 tsp. dried rosemary
4 tbsp. soy margarine
¾ cup (175 ml) soy milk
soy milk, to glaze

1 Heat the oil in a heavy-duty, ovenproof skillet, then add the onions, squash, rutabagas, carrots, leeks, parsnips, beet, celery, caraway seeds, and garlic. Cook over a medium-high heat for 5–7 minutes or until the onions are soft. Add the tomato paste, stock, crushed tomatoes and their juices, and herbs. Season to taste. Bring to a boil, cover, and simmer for 30 minutes.

2 Stir the cornstarch into the water, add a little of the pan juices, then pour the mixture into the pan, stirring, until the liquid thickens a little.

3 Meanwhile, to make the biscuits, put all the dry ingredients into a bowl. Blend in the margarine with your fingertips or a fork, until the mixture resembles fine breadcrumbs. Add the soy milk and stir until a soft, smooth dough is formed, adding more flour if the dough is sticky. Roll out the dough ¾ in. (2 cm) thick on a lightly floured surface and stamp out 8 to 9 rounds with a 2-in. (5-cm) cookie cutter.

4 Preheat oven to 400°F (200°C). Arrange biscuits around the edge of the vegetable mixture, brush the tops with soy milk, and bake for 20–25 minutes, or until risen and golden brown.

WITH SPICY BEANS
Prepare the basic recipe, but omit the beet and add 1 x 14-oz. (400-g) can navy or lima beans and 1–2 tsp. hot chili sauce.

WITH ROASTED WINTER VEGETABLES
Instead of the basic recipe, place all the vegetables in a roasting pan and toss with olive oil. Bake in a 425°F (220°C) oven until just beginning to char on the edges, about 50 minutes. Put in a skillet and add the tomato paste, stock, crushed tomatoes and juices, and herbs. Season to taste. Bring to a boil, and simmer, uncovered, for 15 minutes. Continue as with the basic recipe.

WITH APPLE & PEAR
Instead of the basic recipe, peel, core, and chop 3 pears and 3 Granny Smith apples, then toss with ¾ cup (170 g) sugar and 1 tsp. apple pie spices. Put in an ovenproof dish and sprinkle with 3 tbsp. water. Top with the basic biscuit mixture, adding 2 tbsp. sugar and omitting the rosemary, and bake as in the basic recipe.

Pappardelle with Mushroom Sauce

Serves 4

4 tbsp. extra-virgin olive oil
3 cloves garlic, peeled, and finely chopped
12 large fresh tomatoes, peeled, seeded, and
    coarsely chopped

2 cups (275 g) dried porcini mushrooms or
    similar full-flavored mushrooms, soaked in
    hand hot water for 20 minutes, then
    drained
14 oz. (400 g) pappardelle

2 tbsp. unsalted butter
salt and freshly ground black pepper
freshly grated Parmesan-style cheese, to serve
2 tbsp. fresh flat-leaf parsley, chopped

1 Heat the oil and gently fry the garlic for about 5 minutes, stirring frequently. Then add the tomatoes and stir thoroughly. Add the mushrooms and season. Stir gently and cook slowly for about 40 minutes, or until the sauce becomes creamy and the mushrooms very soft, adding a little water if necessary.

2 Bring a large saucepan of salted water to a boil. Put the pappardelle into the water and stir thoroughly. Replace the lid and return to a boil. Remove or adjust the lid once the water is boiling again. Cook according to the packet instructions until al dente. Drain the pasta and return it to the pot. Stir the butter through the sauce, season, and add to the pasta. Toss together, and serve immediately, sprinkled with the Parmesan cheese and parsley.

WITH FRESH MUSHROOMS
For a milder mushroom flavor, replace the dried porcini with fresh, sliced mushrooms of your choice.

WITH PASSATA
Use canned tomatoes or passata if suitable fresh tomatoes are out of season or not available.

WITH MASCARPONE
Make it creamy by adding 3 tbsp. mascarpone to the pasta and sauce when you mix it all together at the end.

WITH MILD GARLIC
For a milder garlic flavor, leave the garlic cloves whole, lightly crushed to just crack them, and then discard after heating with the oil at the beginning of the recipe.

Bangkok Satay Noodles

Serves 2

1 tbsp. olive oil
3½ oz. (100 g) fine green beans
1 small carrot, peeled and thinly sliced
3 scallions, sliced diagonally into 1 in.
    (2.5 cm) pieces

13 oz. (375 g) packet ready-to-eat egg
    noodles
2 tsp. sesame seeds
8 tbsp. chopped cilantro leaves
1 red chili, thinly sliced
4 tbsp. salted peanuts

for the sauce
5 tbsp. smooth peanut butter
1 tbsp. dark soy sauce
1 tsp. crushed dried chilies
juice of 1 lime
8 fl oz (250 ml) vegetable stock (see page 71)

1 To make the sauce, whisk together the peanut butter, soy sauce and crushed chilies in a medium jug. Stir in the lime juice and stock, adding a little extra stock if the sauce is too thick. Set aside.

2 In a wok, heat the olive oil, and when it is hot, but not smoking, add the vegetables and stir-fry for 3–4 minutes. Add the noodles to the wok, separating them out as you do.

3 Pour in the sauce and continue to stir-fry for a further 2 minutes. Serve either hot or cold, sprinkled with the sesame seeds, chopped cilantro, sliced red chili, and peanuts.

CHOW MEIN
Prepare the basic recipe, omitting the dressing and red chili. Add 1 deseeded and chopped red pepper, ½ small Chinese cabbage, shredded, 1 tbsp. curry powder, 4 tbsp. oyster sauce, and 2 tbsp. soy sauce to the other vegetables and the noodles.

WITH OMELETTE
Prepare the basic recipe. Make 2 omelettes, fill the omelettes with the Bangkok satay noodles and serve immediately.

WITH RED CURRY PASTE & TOFU
Prepare the basic recipe. Add 3 tbsp. red curry paste to the sauce, and substitute tinned coconut milk for vegetable stock. Add the olive oil to the wok, and fry 8 oz. (225 g) diced extra firm tofu. Proceed as before.

Yakisoba

Ⓥ

The Japanese equivalent of junk food, this noodle dish is often sold at festivals and as street food, sometimes in a bun, hotdog style. It is quick to make, but to cut down the preparation time further, look for bottled Yakisoba sauce in an Asian food market.

Serves 4

for the sauce
2 tbsp. teriyaki sauce
2 tbsp. mirin (rice wine) or apple juice
2 tsp. hot chili sauce
1 lemongrass stalk, soft inner core only, crushed and finely sliced
1 tsp. sugar
2 tsp. sesame oil

for the stir-fry
8 oz. (225 g) soba noodles
1½ tbsp. sunflower oil

1 small onion, sliced
2 garlic cloves, minced
2 carrots, thinly sliced
½ head cabbage, shredded
8 oz. (225 g) firm tofu, pressed, drained, and cut into ½-in. (1¼ cm) cubes
4 scallions, chopped
1 tbsp. toasted sesame seeds
chopped scallions or shredded seaweed, to garnish (optional)
pickled ginger, to garnish (optional)

1 Combine the sauce ingredients in a small bowl and set aside. Cook the soba noodles in boiling water for about 2 minutes or until they are just cooked. Do not overcook or the noodles become sticky. Drain, rinse in cold water, then drain again.

2 Heat the oil in a large skillet or wok over a medium-high heat. Add the onions, and stir-fry for 2 minutes, then add the garlic, carrots, and cabbage. Stir-fry for 3–5 minutes, until the vegetables are cooked but still firm.

3 Add the tofu, soba noodles, scallions, sesame seeds, and sauce, then cook, tossing to combine, until the noodles and tofu are hot. Serve garnished with chopped scallions or seaweed and strips of pickled ginger, if desired.

WITH CRISPY NOODLES
Prepare the basic recipe. Once the noodles have boiled, drain thoroughly and pat dry. Alternatively purchase pre-steamed noodles. Heat oil in a deep-fat fryer or deep frying pan to 340°F (170°C). Divide noodles into 4 portions, then fry a portion at a time for 6–7 minutes, until they are crunchy. Serve the vegetables and sauce over the noodles.

WITH YELLOW BEAN SAUCE
Prepare the basic recipe, omitting the sauce. Instead, combine ⅓ cup (30 ml) teriyaki sauce; 4 tbsp. yellow bean sauce; 2 tsp. minced gingerroot; 1 lemongrass stalk soft inner core only, crushed and finely chopped; and 2 tsp. sesame oil.

WITH "CHICKEN"
Prepare the basic recipe, using soy-based "chicken" in place of the tofu.

IN A BUN
Prepare the basic recipe and serve in a hotdog bun garnished with vegan mayonnaise and pickled ginger.

Pumpkin & Tofu Kebabs

(v)

Vegans often feel left out at barbecues. These delicious kebabs provide a tasty solution that will make any vegan feel special. They are easy to prepare, and can be made several hours in advance of the party, wrapped in aluminum foil, and refrigerated until required.

Serves 4

8 baby potatoes
1 x 12 oz. (350 g) young
   pumpkin
1 large zucchini
2 red, green, or yellow
   bell peppers, seeded
2 small red onions
8 cherry tomatoes
12 oz. (350 g) smoked
   firm tofu, cut into
   1-in. (2.5-cm) cubes
oil, to brush

for the glaze
½ cup (120 ml) olive oil
1½ tbsp. cider or white
   wine vinegar
2 tbsp. maple syrup
2 tbsp. orange juice
2 tbsp. chopped fresh
   parsley
1 tbsp. chopped fresh
   rosemary
2 tbsp. Dijon mustard

1 Cook the potatoes in a pan of boiling water until almost cooked; drain and pat dry. Meanwhile, whisk together the ingredients for the glaze. Cut the pumpkin, zucchini, and bell pepper into 1-in. (2.5 cm) pieces. Cut the onions into quarters.

2 Put the potatoes and vegetables in a shallow dish or container. Pour the marinade over the vegetables. Cover and refrigerate for at least 1 hour.

3 Heat the grill to medium-high and brush with a little oil. Alternately thread the vegetables and tofu onto 8 skewers, leaving a little space between each. Put the skewers on the grill and cook, turning frequently and basting with the marinade for about 10 minutes. Remove when the pumpkin and zucchini are tender-crisp.

WITH SHIITAKE MUSHROOMS
Prepare the basic recipe, using 16 shiitake mushrooms in place of the pumpkin and zucchini. Steam the mushrooms for 2 minutes prior to preparation to reduce the risk of them splitting and falling off the skewer.

WITH BUTTERNUT SQUASH
Prepare the basic recipe, using butternut squash in place of the pumpkin. Parboil the butternut squash with the potatoes.

WITH EGGPLANT
Prepare the basic recipe, using eggplant in place of the pumpkin. To prepare, cut a small eggplant into 1-in. (2.5-cm) cubes and sprinkle with salt. Let sit for 30 minutes, then wipe away the bitter juices with a paper towel.

WITH ADOBO GLAZE
Prepare the basic kebabs, but in place of the maple mustard glaze combine 1–2 tbsp. chopped canned chipotle chili, 1 tbsp. adobo sauce (from can), 4 tbsp. agave syrup, 4 tbsp. freshly squeezed mandarin orange juice, and 1 tbsp. cider vinegar.

Penne with Ricotta & Gorgonzola

A wonderful combination of two very different cheeses—one fresh and mild, the other salty, strong, and complex—melted together over pasta to make a simple supper dish full of flavor and comfort.

Serves 6

1½ cups (375 g) ricotta
½ cup (125 g) Gorgonzola
  dolce
1 lb. (425 g) penne
salt and freshly ground
  black pepper

1 Put the ricotta in the bottom of a large bowl and mash it with a fork. Add the Gorgonzola and some freshly ground black pepper and continue to blend them together.

2 Bring a large saucepan of salted water to a boil and use a little of the boiling water to slake the ricotta mixture until smooth. Put the penne into the water and stir thoroughly. Replace the lid and return to a boil. Remove or adjust the lid once the water is boiling again. Cook according to the packet instructions until al dente. Drain the pasta and transfer to the bowl containing the ricotta mixture.

3 Mix the penne and the ricotta mixture together thoroughly, adding a little more of the water in which the pasta was cooked if necessary to help distribute the cheese mixture through the pasta. Serve immediately.

WITH SPAGHETTINI
Use spaghettini instead of penne. Sprinkle the finished dish with chopped walnuts and finely chopped sage leaves.

WITH TALEGGIO & PINE KERNELS
For a milder flavor, use Taleggio instead of the Gorgonzola and finish the dish with a sprinkling of toasted pine kernels.

WITH GORGONZOLA PICCANTE
To make a much stronger tasting dish, substitute the Gorgonzola dolce for Gorgonzola piccante, the much more potent and piquant version. Add a couple of spoonfuls of cream to smooth the sauce.

WITH MASCARPONE & GORGONZOLA
For a creamier sauce, substitute the ricotta for mascarpone and add a few finely chopped chives to the finished dish.

WITH GOAT CHEESE, TALEGGIO & SUN-DRIED TOMATOES
Substitute the ricotta for creamy goat cheese and the Gorgonzola for Taleggio, then finish the dish with 3 or 4 finely chopped soft sun-dried tomatoes to give the dish a very different twist.

Butternut Squash Ravioli

This is lovely speciality from the south of Italy, with lots of flavor and wonderful colors.

Serves 8

3½ lb. (1.5 kg) butternut squash
2 oz. (50 g) hard amaretti biscuits, crushed
½ cup (50 g) freshly grated Parmesan cheese
6 eggs lightly beaten
large pinch freshly grated nutmeg
zest of half a lemon, finely grated
7 oz. (200 g) all-purpose flour
7 oz. (200 g) semola
1 beaten egg yolk

1 Peel and cut the squash into small pieces, bake on an oiled tray in a hot oven (375°F/190°C) until soft. Mash with a fork, and then mix in the crushed amaretti, Parmesan, one third of the beaten eggs, nutmeg, and lemon zest. Season to taste; the mixture should have a pleasant sweet/salty flavor. Allow to cool completely before using to fill the ravioli.

2 To make the pasta, work the flour, semola, and the remaining eggs into a soft dough and, use a pasta machine to roll out very thin sheets. Use a large cookie cutter to cut into as many discs as possible. Put a tsp. of the filling in the center of half of the discs. Brush the edges with beaten egg yolk and top each with an unfilled disc, pressing the edges together with your fingers. Use your fingers to gently ensure that any air is removed from the parcels.

3 Cook the ravioli in batches in boiling salted water for 4–5 minutes or until floating on the surface. Drain and coat lightly with pesto (see page 156) to serve.

WITH PUMPKIN
Use pumpkin instead of butternut squash to make the ravioli filling.

WITH PARMESAN CHEESE
Dress the ravioli with melted butter and freshly grated Parmesan-style cheese instead of the pesto.

WITH WALNUTS
Add a handful of finely chopped walnuts to the filling and dress the cooked ravioli with melted butter to change the texture and flavor.

WITH SAGE BUTTER
Dress the ravioli with sage butter instead of the pesto; melt 2 oz. (50 g) butter in a small heavy pan with a small handful of sage leaves over a pan of simmering water and leave to infuse for about 1 hour. Alternatively, for a nuttier flavor, melt the butter over direct heat with the sage until just browned, and then remove from the heat to infuse, and re-heat to foaming just before tipping over the cooked ravioli.

Vegetable Mole Oaxaca

Ⓥ

Every family in Mexico has their own way of preparing this fabulous dish, which originated in Oaxaca, so feel free to experiment with the recipe. Use your favorite chilis, vegetables, and beans, or add raisins or almonds.

Serves 4

4 tbsp. toasted pumpkin seeds
1 x 14-oz. (400-g) can tomatoes
4 tbsp. tahini
1 tbsp. sunflower oil
1 white onion, finely chopped
2 cloves garlic, minced
1 green bell pepper, seeded and chopped
1 large plantain, sliced
1 small butternut squash, chopped
2 medium potatoes
1 jalapeño (for mild) or habanero (for spicy) chili

2–4 dried chilis, torn
1 tbsp. paprika
2 tsp. ground cumin
¼ tsp. ground cloves
¼ tsp. ground cinnamon
½ cup (120 ml) vegetable stock (see page 71)
sea salt
1 x 14-oz. (400-g) can black beans
1 cup (175 g) frozen corn
1 tsp. sugar
1½ oz. (40 g) vegan dark chocolate
sliced avocados, lime juice, fresh cilantro, to garnish

1 Preheat oven to 350°F (180°C). Process the pumpkin seeds or almonds in a food processor until very fine. Add the tomatoes and tahini, and blend until smooth.

2 Heat oil in a flameproof casserole, add the onion, and cook over a medium-high heat for 5–7 minutes until soft. Add the garlic, bell pepper, plantain, squash, potatoes, and fresh chili. Cook for 3 minutes, then add the dried chili and remaining spices. Cook for 1 minute.

3 Add the tomato-tahini mixture and stock, and season to taste. Bring to a boil, cover, and cook in the oven for 30 minutes. Remove from the oven and add the beans, corn, and sugar, then stir in the chocolate. Adjust the seasoning.

4 Return to the oven for 10 minutes to heat through. Serve generously garnished with avocados dipped in lime juice and with plenty of fresh cilantro.

WITH SEITAN
Prepare the basic recipe. While the mole is cooking, fry 12 oz. (350 g) chopped seitan in 1 tbsp. oil for 5 minutes, stirring frequently, then add to the mole with the corn.

WITH TOFU
Prepare the basic recipe. Take a 1-lb. (450-g) block of tofu, which has been frozen and then thawed, and cut it into chunks. Fry the tofu in 1 tbsp. oil until crispy. Add to the mole with the corn.

WITH MANGO
Prepare the basic recipe, adding the chopped flesh of 1 mango with the corn.

IN TORTILLAS
Prepare the basic recipe. Place a generous portion of the stew in a wheat tortilla, roll up, and place in an oiled dish. Sprinkle with non-dairy cheese and bake for 20–25 minutes at 375°F (190°C) until crisp and golden. This is a good way to use leftover mole.

Egyptian Koshari

Many cultures have a rice and lentil, beans or pasta dish as one of their staples. This Egyptian version is topped with a tomato sauce tingling with a hit of chili.

Serves 6

for the base
3½ fl oz. (100 ml) olive oil
3 onions, finely sliced
2¼ oz. (60 g) vermicelli, broken into pieces
2 tsp. cumin seeds
1 tsp. cilantro seeds
1 tsp. mustard seeds
small cinnamon stick

7 oz. (200 g) long-grain rice
17 fl oz. (500 ml) water
2 tsp. vegetable stock powder
1 x 14-oz. (400-g) can Puy lentils, drained
    and rinsed
1 x 14-oz. (400-g) can garbanzo beans,
    drained and rinsed
salt and ground black pepper

for the spicy tomato sauce
1 onion, finely sliced
2 garlic cloves
14 fl oz. (400 ml) passata
1 tbsp. tomato purée
2 tsp. white wine vinegar
pinch of caster sugar
1 tsp. chili flakes

1 For the base, heat the oil in a large, deep frying pan or saucepan and gently cook the onions for 5–7 minutes until soft and translucent. Transfer a quarter of the cooked onions to a small saucepan for the sauce. Keep cooking the remaining onions in the frying pan until a deep golden brown and beginning to crisp.

2 Meanwhile, make the sauce. Crush 1 garlic clove, add to the onions in the saucepan and cook for 1 minute. Stir in the passata, tomato purée, vinegar, sugar, and chili flakes, and season with salt and pepper to taste. Simmer for 10–15 minutes, or until thickened.

3 Remove the onions from the frying pan with a slotted spoon and lay on kitchen towel to soak up any excess oil. Add the vermicelli to the oil in the pan and sauté until lightly browned, 2–3 minutes. Put the cumin, cilantro, and mustard seeds into the pan with the cinnamon stick and heat for 1 minute until fragrant. Add the rice and cook, stirring, for 1 minute, then add the water and stock powder. Bring to a boil, cover tightly, and simmer for 12–15 minutes until the rice is tender.

4 Remove from the heat and stir in the lentils, garbanzo beans, and half the onions. Cover and leave to sit for 10 minutes. Season with salt and pepper and serve hot with the sauce poured over and sprinkled with the remaining onions.

WITH RISOTTO RICE
Follow the base recipe, as directed, but in place of spelt use 9 oz. (250 g) arborio rice and increase the quantity of hot vegetable stock to 1½ pints (900 ml).

WITH PEARL BARLEY
Follow the base recipe, as directed, but in place of spelt use 6 oz. (175 g) pearl barley.

WITH PESTO & ASPARAGUS
While the speltotto is cooking, simmer 7 oz. (200 g) chopped asparagus for a few minutes until just tender, then drain. When adding the butter, stir in 4 tbsp. vegan pesto (see page 156) followed by the cooked asparagus. Omit the roasted vegetables.

WITH LEEK, TOMATO & GOAT CHEESE
While the speltotto is cooking, heat 1 tbsp. oil in a frying pan and fry 2 sliced leeks and 6 oz. (175 g) cherry tomatoes for 3–4 minutes, stirring a few times until the leeks are softened. Set aside and keep warm. Stir into the speltotto after adding the butter. Top each portion with a slice of goat cheese. Omit the roasted vegetables.

CHAPTER 7

Feed a Crowd

Cooking for a crowd needn't be daunting with these clever recipes that will satisfy meat-eaters, vegetarians and vegans alike. They keys to sucess are simplicity, the ability to scale recipes up or down as required, and serving-up meals packed with flavor. Below is a practical guide to some plant-based ingredients that may be less familiar to your guests.

BEANS

Beans have been a vital source of protein since ancient times. They are also high in fiber and complex carbohydrates. Being inexpensive and versatile, it is no wonder that they are central to the vegan diet. A wide variety of beans is available fresh, dried, or canned. As a rough guide, 1 lb. (450 g) of dried beans produces about three and a half 14-oz. (400-g) cans of beans. To cook dried beans, pick over the beans and remove any damaged ones. Soak the beans in cold water overnight, or for at least 4 hours, prior to cooking. Drain the soaked beans and put them in a saucepan and cover with water or stock (the liquid should be about 2 in./5 cm above the top of the beans). Do not salt until the beans are cooked, because the salt will toughen them during cooking. Bring to a fast boil for 5 minutes (10 for kidney beans to remove toxins), then simmer over a low heat until tender (see packaging for cooking times). As cooking times can vary, cooking several types of beans together is best avoided.

NON-DAIRY CHEESE

A number of manufacturers make soy-based cheese substitutes in a variety of flavors and textures, including hard cheeses such as cheddar and Parmesan, mozzarella, and soft cream cheeses. In general, they have the same cooking and melting qualities as those cheeses they are mimicking.

GRAINS

These include barley, buckwheat (kasha) corn, kamut, millet, oats, quinoa, rice, rye, spelt, and wheat berry. They form the backbone of the vegan diets and are either cooked whole or as a flour. To cook them whole, put in lightly salted boiling water, reduce the heat to a simmer, and cook until tender. Cooking time can take from 15 minutes for rice to 2 hours.

LENTILS

Lentils are legumes. They are low in fat and high in protein and fiber, and they are a vegan staple. Red, green, and brown lentils are the most commonly used, but Asian markets and health stores offer a wider range. Always pick over lentils to remove stray stones or broken lentils before cooking, then rinse in cold water. To cook lentils, use 3 cups (375 ml) water or stock to 1 cup (100 g) lentils. Add flavorings such as herbs, garlic, and onions to the liquid in the pan, but do not add salt until the lentils are soft. Bring the liquid to a boil, add the lentils, boil rapidly for 2–3 minutes, then simmer until tender. Cooking time varies from about 15 minutes for red lentils to about 20–25 minutes for other types. If using lentils in salads, drain as soon as they are tender; for purées, soups, and stews, a slightly softer texture is better.

Brown lentils Plumper than green lentils, can become mushy if overcooked, good for soups
French green lentils (puy lentils) Retain their shape after cooking, good in salads and stews
Green lentils A large flat lentil that holds its shape well, good in soups and salads
Red lentils Become mushy if overcooked, good in soups, stews, and purées

NUTRITIONAL YEAST

Don't be put off by its fish food-like appearance. Nutritional yeast has a strong, almost cheese-like flavor and is great as a Parmesan cheese substitute. It also adds a depth of flavor to any soup or stew that is in need of a little oomph. Do not confuse it with brewer's yeast, as they are not the same thing. Purchase in health food stores or gourmet food stores.

PHYLLO DOUGH

This dough is vegan and perfect for making quick and impressive pastries. It comes packaged, either fresh or frozen, in bundles of sheets. It is best to defrost phyllo slowly, use it at room temperature, and to work with it quickly, keeping the sheets covered with a clean damp cloth to prevent them from drying out.

TEXTURIZED VEGETABLE PROTEIN (TVP)

TVP is made from defatted soy flour, a by-product of the extraction of soybean oil, hence it is also known as soy protein. It is high in protein but low in fat. TVP comes in small dry chunks resembling dried vegetables, or in a ground form. Because of its varying texture and flavorless quality, TVP is manufactured to mimic meat in the form of ground beef and chicken fillets, for instance. It is often used in chili, tacos, veggie burgers, stews, curries, and soups, and can be useful for adding protein to vegetable-based dishes.

Overnight Oaty Pancakes

Makes 8–10

overnight
3 oz. (75 g) porridge oats
8 fl oz. (250 ml) buttermilk
1 oz. (25 g) raisins or sultanas
1½ tsp. superfine or light brown sugar

3 tbsp. plain flour
½ tsp. baking powder
½ tsp. bicarbonate of soda
generous pinch of ground cinnamon
¼ tsp. salt

in the morning
1 egg, beaten
1 oz. (25 g) butter, melted
1–2 tsp. sunflower oil
maple syrup, Greek yogurt, and fresh berries, to serve

1 Mix together the oats, buttermilk and raisins or sultanas in a bowl, then cover and refrigerate overnight. Sift the flour, sugar, baking powder, bicarbonate of soda, cinnamon, and salt into another bowl. Cover and leave overnight.

2 In the morning, slowly pour the oat mixture into the flour mixture, stirring, then add the egg and butter. Stir until just moistened but do not overmix. Allow the batter to rest for at least 10 minutes.

3 Heat a lightly oiled frying pan over a medium heat. Pour a ladleful of batter into the pan for each pancake. Cook the pancakes until bubbles appear, then flip and cook until lightly browned on the bottom. Serve with maple syrup, Greek yogurt and fresh berries.

WITH PROSECCO
Overnight, use 7 fl oz. (200 ml) buttermilk with the oats and increase the flour to 3¼ oz. (90 g). In the morning, add 6 fl oz. (175 ml) prosecco with the eggs and butter.

WITH CRANBERRY & LEMON
Substitute cranberries for the raisins and add ½ tsp. grated lemon zest to the batter. Omit the cinnamon.

WITH BANANA
In the morning, mash ½ banana and stir into the batter with the butter. Add about 2 tbsp. additional buttermilk or milk to thin to the required double cream consistency.

WITH CHOCOLATE
Add 1 tbsp. sifted cocoa powder to the flour mixture and leave overnight then proceed as directed. Substitute chocolate chips for the raisins, if liked.

Slow Cooker Blueberry Oatmeal

Serves 4

1 tbsp. coconut oil
5 oz. (150 g) jumbo rolled oats
2 bananas, sliced
6 oz. (175 g) blueberries

16 fl oz. (475 ml) water
16 fl oz. (475 ml) whole milk
2 tbsp. maple syrup
¼ tsp. salt

1 tsp. ground cinnamon
2 tsp. vanilla extract

1 Choose a baking dish that will fit inside your slow cooker, and grease the inside with a little coconut oil. Put all the ingredients in the baking dish and stir well. Place it inside the slow cooker and add enough water to come to 1 in. (2.5 cm) below the top of the baking dish, so that it is sitting in a water bath. Cover, and cook on low for 5–8 hours.

2 Stir well before serving, as it will initially look like it has separated. Divide the oatmeal between four serving bowls, and top with fresh fruit and cream, if desired.

WITH MANGO, PINEAPPLE & COCONUT
Prepare the basic recipe. Omit the blueberries, substituting ½ mango, chopped, 4 oz. (125 g) chopped fresh pineapple, and 1½ oz. (40 g) flaked or desiccated coconut.

WITH SULTANAS & ALMONDS
Prepare the basic recipe, adding 2½ oz. (60 g) sultanas to the oatmeal with the blueberries. Sprinkle the oatmeal with 1 tbsp. toasted flaked almonds just before serving.

WITH CRANBERRIES & WALNUTS
Prepare the basic recipe. Add 1½ oz. (40 g) dried cranberries to the oatmeal with the blueberries, and sprinkle with 1 tbsp. chopped walnuts before serving.

WITHOUT DAIRY
Prepare the basic recipe, substituting almond milk for the whole milk.

One-Pan Breakfast

(GF)

The ultimate way to make sure your friends keep coming back to stay! Pop the potatoes in the fridge overnight so that they grate more easily and hold their shape in the pan.

Serves 4

4 waxy potatoes
1 tbsp. butter
1 tbsp. olive oil
½ red bell pepper, chopped
½ green bell pepper, chopped
2 scallions, sliced

4 eggs
4 pinches of paprika
2 oz. (50 g) Cheddar cheese
8 cherry tomatoes
salt and freshly ground black pepper

1 Using the largest holes on a grater, grate the potatoes into the center of a clean tea-towel. Wrap up and squeeze over the sink to remove as much liquid from the potatoes as possible.

2 Heat the butter and olive oil in a large ovenproof frying pan over a moderate-high heat. When foaming, add the grated potatoes and cook for about 2 minutes, pressing down lightly with a fish slice. Add the peppers and scallions and season with salt and pepper. Stir to combine, then flatten everything again using the fish slice. Cook over a moderate heat, untouched, for 5 minutes, or until the potatoes are golden brown on the base.

3 Use a fish slice to flip the potatoes, working the pan a section at a time. Then, using the back of a spoon, make 4 shallow indentations into the hash. Crack an egg into each indentation and sprinkle with a pinch of paprika and a little salt. Sprinkle the grated cheese and cherry tomatoes around the eggs.

4 Transfer the pan to the oven and bake until the egg whites set, about 6–8 minutes. Serve immediately.

WITH SWEET POTATO
Replace half the potatoes with sweet potatoes.

WITH PAPRIKA & CHILI
With the red and green peppers, add 1 tsp. smoked paprika and 1–2 chopped red chilis to taste (deseeded for a milder flavor). Serve with slices of avocado on the side.

WITH APPLE
Add 1 peeled, grated Granny Smith apple to the potatoes after they have been squeezed dry. Proceed as directed, omitting the tomato. Serve with soured cream.

POTATO ROSTI
This calls for potato only, so omit the peppers and scallions. Cook the grated potatoes until golden and crisp on one side, then place a plate on top of the pan and invert it so the cake sits, cooked-side-up, on the plate. Add a little more butter and oil to the pan, slide the potato cake back into the pan and continue to cook until this side is golden brown. Serve with fried eggs and tomatoes. Omit the cheese.

Butternut Squash & Apricot Tagine

(V)

This quick version of the Moroccan classic is a good dish for entertaining and can be made up to 24 hours in advance.

Serves 4

for the tagine
2 tbsp. sunflower oil
1 red onion, finely chopped
2 garlic cloves, crushed
1 tsp. ground cumin
1 tsp. ground cilantro
1 tsp. ground turmeric
½ tsp. ground cinnamon
1 tbsp. harissa paste, or to taste
10 oz. (275 g) butternut squash, peeled, seeded and cut into chunks
10 oz. (275 g) new potatoes, cut into chunks
1 x 14-oz. (400-g) can chopped tomatoes

12 fl oz. (350 ml) vegetable stock (see page 71)
1 x 14-oz. (400-g) can garbanzo beans
2 oz. (50 g) dried apricots, roughly chopped
2 medium zucchini, sliced
2 tbsp. chopped fresh mint leaves, to garnish
salt and freshly ground black pepper, to taste

for the couscous
1 pint (600 ml) water
large pinch of salt
7 oz. (200 g) couscous

1 Heat the oil in a tagine or large frying pan over a medium heat, add the onions and fry gently for 5–7 minutes until soft. Add the garlic, cumin, cilantro, turmeric, cinnamon, and harissa paste and cook for 2 minutes.

2 Add the butternut squash and potato chunks and stir to coat in the oil. Stir in the tomatoes, stock and garbanzo beans. Cook for 10 minutes, then stir in the apricots and zucchini and cook for a further 10 minutes, adding a little water if the sauce becomes too thick.

3 Meanwhile, bring the water to a boil in a saucepan, add the salt and couscous and remove from the heat. Cover with a clean tea towel and stand for 5 minutes. When all the water is absorbed, fluff up with a fork and serve with the tagine, garnished with the mint.

WITH SWEET POTATO & PRUNE
Follow the base recipe, substituting 2 sweet potatoes for the butternut squash and 2 oz. (50 g) dried chopped prunes for the apricots.

WITH BITTER LEMON & OLIVES
Follow the base recipe, adding 1 preserved lemon, quartered and seeds removed, and 2 oz. (50 g) pitted green olives with the tomatoes.

WITH PUMPKIN & GREEN BEAN
Follow the base recipe, substituting a 4 lb 6 oz. (2 kg) piece of pumpkin, cut into bite-sized pieces, for the butternut squash, and 7 oz. (200 g) trimmed and halved green beans for the potatoes.

WITH FENNEL & OLIVE
Follow the base recipe, substituting 2 sliced fennel bulbs for the butternut squash, and adding 2 oz. (50 g) pitted green olives with the tomatoes.

Beer Bread Rolls

Use a good-quality, dark, and full-flavored beer, to produce a complex, nutty flavor.

Makes 12–16 rolls

1 tsp. sugar
¼ cup (50 ml) warm water
2 tsp. active dry yeast
3½ cups (450 g) white bread flour
2 cups (300 g) rolled oats, ground fine
¼ cup (25 g) wheat germ
½ tsp. salt
1½ cups (350 ml) brown ale
¼ cup (25 ml) maple syrup
2 tbsp. olive oil
1 egg + 1 egg white, room temperature, lightly beaten

1 Line 2 large cookie sheets with parchment paper. Dissolve the sugar in the warm water, sprinkle the yeast on top, and leave for 10–15 minutes until frothy. In a large bowl, combine the flour, ground oats, wheat germ, and salt. Make a well in the center and pour in the yeast liquid, brown ale, maple syrup, olive oil, and the whole egg. Mix until a soft dough comes together.

2 Turn out onto a lightly floured work surface and knead for 10 minutes, until the dough is smooth and elastic. Alternatively, knead in an electric mixer with a dough hook attachment for 5–8 minutes. Place the dough in a large lightly oiled bowl and turn to coat it all over. Cover and leave in a warm place for an hour or so, until doubled in size.

3 Turn out onto a lightly floured work surface and divide into 12–16 equal portions. Form each piece into a ball, tucking the dough underneath and pinching together. Place the rolls on the lined cookie sheets, seam underneath, and cover with lightly oiled plastic wrap. Leave to rise again for another hour, or until doubled in size.

4 Preheat the oven to 375°F (180°C). Remove cover, brush with the beaten egg white, and bake for 25–30 minutes, or until golden brown. Cool on a wire rack.

WITH MIXED SEEDS & PECANS
Prepare the basic recipe, adding 2 tbsp. each of sesame seeds, poppy seeds, nigella seeds, sunflower seeds, and chopped pecans to the flour with the yeast liquid.

WITH GARLIC & PARSLEY
Prepare the basic recipe, adding 2 minced cloves garlic and 2 tbsp. chopped parsley to the flour with the yeast liquid.

WITH SUNDRIED-TOMATO & OLIVE
Prepare the basic recipe, adding ¼ cup (25 g) finely chopped sundried tomatoes and 2 tbsp. pitted and finely chopped black olives to the flour with the yeast liquid.

BISCUIT BEER BREAD
In a large bowl, with a fork, mix together 4 cups (500 g) biscuit mix, 3 tbsp. sugar, and 12 fl oz. (360 ml) good-quality light beer or lager. Transfer to a 2 lb. (900 g) loaf pan and bake for 50 minutes at 375°F (190°C).

Cheesy Cauliflower Rice Cakes

Serves 4

1 small head cauliflower, cooked
7 oz. (200 g) cooked brown rice
1 tbsp. wholegrain mustard

3½ oz. (100 g) Cheddar cheese
2 eggs, beaten
2½ oz. (60 g) plain flour

2 tbsp. Parmesan-style cheese

1 Preheat the oven to 375°F (190°C). Line a baking tray with baking paper.

2 Break the cauliflower into small pieces and place them in a bowl. Add all the remaining ingredients, except the Parmesan, and use a fork to mash and mix the ingredients together—do not overwork as you want little chunks of cauliflower in the mixture.

3 Using damp hands, form the mixture into eight balls. Place on the lined baking tray and press down to form little cakes. Sprinkle the "cake" tops with the Parmesan and bake for about 20 minutes until golden brown. Serve warm or at room temperature.

COOKED IN THE PAN
Make the rice cakes as directed. Heat ½ tbsp. each butter and olive oil in a frying pan and cook the cakes for about 3 minutes each side until golden brown. It is best to cook the cakes in two batches to avoid overcrowding the pan; add a little more butter and oil to the pan to cook the second batch.

WITH QUINOA
Replace the rice with 7 oz. (200 g) cooked quinoa.

WITH JALAPEÑO
Add 3–4 tbsp. chopped jalapeño chilies to the cauliflower mixture and proceed as directed.

WITH SQUASH
Replace the cauliflower with the cooked and roughly mashed flesh of a small butternut or similar winter squash (about 10 oz./300 g) and ½ tsp. chili flakes.

Eggplant & Garbanzo Bean Stew

(V)

Serves 6

4 fl oz. (120 ml) olive oil
2 large eggplants (about 2 lb./900 g), cut into 2 in. (5 cm) cubes
1 large onion, coarsely chopped
4 cloves garlic, crushed

1 x 14-oz. (400-g) can chopped tomatoes
1 x 14-oz. (400-g) can garbanzo beans, drained and rinsed
1 tbsp. tomato purée
1 tsp. smoked paprika

¼ tsp. cayenne pepper
2 tbsp. chopped mint
salt and freshly ground black pepper

1 In a large deep frying pan, heat the oil, then add the eggplant. Cook over a medium heat, stirring occasionally, until tender and lightly browned. Add the onion and garlic, stir to combine, and cook for 3 minutes. Add the tomatoes, garbanzo beans, tomato purée, paprika, cayenne pepper, and salt and freshly ground black pepper to taste.

2 Bring the stew to a simmer, cover, and cook for about 30 minutes. If the stew becomes too thick, add extra water as necessary. When the stew is cooked and fragrant, stir through the mint and serve immediately.

WITH CELERY
Prepare the basic recipe, substituting 1 x 13½ oz. (385 g) can green lentils (drained) for the garbanzo beans, and adding 2 chopped celery stalks to the pan with the onion and garlic.

WITH CHILI
Prepare the basic recipe, adding 2 chopped green chilis to the pan with the onion and garlic. Omit the mint and substitute cilantro.

WITH BASIL
Prepare the basic recipe, omitting the mint and substituting 2 tbsp. freshly chopped basil to the stew.

WITH SWEET POTATO
Prepare the basic recipe. Omit the eggplant and substitute diced sweet potato. Add 2 tsp. chopped fresh ginger and 2 tbsp. red curry paste to the pan with the onion and garlic. Substitute tinned coconut milk for the water.

Hungarian Nut Loaf

(V)

Not the usual heavy nut roast but a lighter-textured loaf that uses lentils as well as nuts. The tomato-pimento sauce adds moisture and flavor.

Serves 6–8

1 cup (200 g) red lentils, rinsed
2½ cups (625 ml) vegetable stock (see page 71)
1 bay leaf
1½ tbsp. olive oil
1 large onion, finely chopped
1 leek, white part only, finely chopped
1 red bell pepper, seeded and chopped
4 oz. (125 g) cremini or button mushrooms, finely chopped
2 medium carrots, shredded
1 cup (125 g) whole Brazil nuts, toasted and roughly chopped

1 garlic clove, minced
1 tbsp. lemon juice
1 tbsp. tomato paste
1 tbsp. paprika
1 tsp. caraway seeds
3 tbsp. nutritional yeast
2 cups (90 g) wholemeal breadcrumbs
2 tbsp. chopped fresh parsley
sea salt and black pepper

for the sauce
1 tbsp. tomato paste
1 tsp. paprika
1 x 14-oz. (400-g) can crushed tomatoes
2 canned pimentos, drained and chopped
¼ cup (150 ml) red wine
1 tsp. dried sage

1 Preheat the oven to 375°F (190°C). Oil and line a 2-pint (1.2-liter) loaf pan with parchment paper. Put the lentils in a saucepan with the stock and bay leaf. Bring to a boil, cover, and simmer for 15 minutes. Discard the bay leaf.

2 Heat the oil in a saucepan, add the onion and cook over a medium-high heat for 5–7 minutes until soft. Set half the onion aside. Add the leek, red pepper, mushrooms, and carrot to the pan and cook for 5 minutes. Stir in all the remaining loaf ingredients. Press the mixture into the pan and bake for 60 minutes. Let cool for 10 minutes before removing from the pan.

3 To make the sauce, put the reserved onion and remaining sauce ingredients, except the parsley, into a pan. Bring to a boil, then reduce the heat, and simmer for 15 minutes. Serve with the loaf.

WITH HARISSA & CILANTRO
Prepare the basic loaf recipe, using 2–3 teaspoons harissa in place of the paprika and caraway seeds, and cilantro in place of the parsley. Also use cilantro in place of the sage in the sauce.

WITH SPICES
Prepare the basic recipe, using 1–2 tbsp. curry powder in place of the paprika and caraway seeds in the loaf. Add ½ teaspoon each of cumin and chili powder to the sauce, and use 1 tbsp. chopped fresh cilantro in place of the sage.

WITH OLIVES
Prepare the basic recipe, adding 12 sliced black olives and using herbes du Provence in place of the parsley and caraway seeds in the nut loaf. Use rosemary in place of the sage in the sauce.

WITH CHILI
Prepare the basic recipe, using 2–3 teaspoons hot chili sauce in place of the paprika and cumin seeds in place of the caraway seeds in the nut loaf. Divide 1 x 4-oz. (125-g) can chopped green chilis between the nut loaf mixture and the sauce. Omit the pimento in the sauce and season with hot chili sauce, to taste.

Three Bean Chili

(V)

Here's comfort food and one that is always a hit with meat-eaters too. Make this recipe in bulk for parties or potluck dinners, or freeze it in meal-size portions. It improves with keeping, so it is a great dish to prepare ahead of time.

Serves 6–8

2 tbsp. sunflower oil
1 large onion, chopped
3 carrots, chopped
2 green bell peppers, seeded and chopped
3 garlic cloves, minced
2–4 tbsp. chili powder, or to taste
1 tsp. smoked paprika
1 tsp. ground cumin
1 x 14-oz. (400-g) can kidney beans
1 x 14-oz. (400-g) can navy beans
1 x 14-oz. (400-g) can black beans
1 x 28-oz. (800-g) can crushed tomatoes
1 x 14-oz. (400-g) can green chilis, chopped and drained
½ cup (100 g) tomato paste
1 cup (125 g) quartered button mushrooms
2 cups (300 g) frozen or canned corn
1 tbsp. dried oregano
2 tsp. unsweetened cocoa powder
3 cups (750 ml) vegetable stock (see page 71) or beer
1 tsp. sugar
sea salt

1 Heat the oil in a saucepan, then add the onion and cook for 5–7 minutes until soft. Add the carrots, bell peppers, and minced garlic, and cook for 3 minutes. Add the chili powder, smoked paprika, and cumin, then cook for another minute.

2 Stir in all the remaining ingredients. Bring to a boil, then reduce the heat and simmer for at least 20 minutes. Alternatively, bake at 350°F (180°C) for 20 minutes. The chili matures with longer cooking.

WITH VEGAN CHEESE & SOUR CREAM
Prepare the basic recipe and serve it garnished with shredded vegan hard cheese substitute, such as cheddar or Monterey Jack, and some non-dairy sour cream or soy yogurt.

WITH TVP
Prepare the basic recipe. Ten minutes before the end of the cooking time, add ½ cup (125 g) TVP (texturized vegetable protein) and up to ½ cup (125 ml) water, as needed.

WITH ENCHILADAS
Prepare half of the basic recipe. Warm 2 x 10-oz. (275-g) cans enchilada sauce. Take 8 medium-size corn or flour tortillas and dip each one in the sauce, fill with the chili, roll up, and put in a baking dish, then cover with the remaining sauce. Bake at 375°F (190°C) for 20 minutes.

WITH POTATO BAKE
Prepare half of the basic recipe. Boil 1 lb. (450 g) potatoes, then mash with 2 tbsp. soy margarine and 4 tbsp. soy milk; season with salt and pepper. Put the chili in a baking dish and top with the mashed potatoes. Cook at 400°F (200°C) for 20 minutes or until golden.

Creamy Vegetable Spanakopita

Dill-flavored vegetables in a creamy sauce contrast with a crispy topping in this recipe.

Serves 6

1 lb. (450 g) fresh baby
    spinach
3½ oz. (100 g) butter, at
    room temperature
2 cloves garlic, crushed
2 tbsp. all-purpose flour
16 fl oz. (475 ml)
    vegetable stock (see
    page 71)
4 fl oz. (120 ml) crème
    fraîche
8 baby potatoes
8 small carrots, peeled
1 onion, chopped

10 green beans, trimmed
2 tomatoes, skinned and
    quartered
2 hard boiled eggs,
    chopped
2 oz. (50 g) grated
    Cheddar cheese
zest of 1 orange
3 oz. (75 g) cooked rice
4 scallions, sliced
2 tbsp. dill, chopped, plus
    extra to serve
10 sheets phyllo pastry
salt and freshly ground
    black pepper

1   Heat a large frying pan over a medium heat.
    Cook the spinach until just wilted. Transfer to a
    colander and press out as much water as
    possible. Steam the potatoes, carrots, onion,
    green beans, and tomatoes until tender.

2   Preheat the oven to 400°F (200°C). Melt 1 oz.
    (25 g) of the butter in the pan and add the
    garlic. Cook for 30 seconds, then mix in the
    flour. Cook for a minute or so, stirring, then
    gradually whisk in most of the stock and bring
    to a boil. Stir in the crème fraîche, scallions
    and dill and remove from the heat.

3   Chop the cooled, steamed vegetables and add to
    the pan with the spinach, eggs, cheese, orange
    zest, and rice. Stir to combine. Add a little
    more stock if the sauce is too thick.

4   Melt the remaining butter. Brush the phyllo
    pastry sheets with melted butter and crumple
    each sheet on top of the filling. Repeat until the
    pan is completely covered. Bake in the oven for
    15–20 minutes, until the phyllo is golden and
    crisp on top. Remove from the oven, sprinkle
    over the additional dill and serve immediately.

WITH MUSHROOMS
Prepare the spinach. Wipe out the pan and place back over a
medium heat. Melt 1 oz. (25 g) of the butter in the pan and add
1½ lb (675 g) sliced mixed mushrooms. Season with salt and
pepper and cook for 2 minutes. Add to the sauce at the same
time as the spinach. Top with pastry as before.

WITH PARMESAN
Prepare the base recipe adding 4 tbsp. grated Parmesan-style
cheese to the sauce with the spinach.

WITH BROCCOLI
Prepare the base recipe adding 5½ oz. (165 g) cooked broccoli
florets to the sauce with the spinach.

WITH MINT
Prepare the base recipe adding 3 tbsp. chopped mint to the sauce
with the spinach.

Whole Roasted Cauliflower with Romesco Sauce

(V)

Romesco sauce hails from Catalonia and is a creamy combination of peppers, almonds, paprika and olive oil. It is commonly served with many tapas and grilled dishes.

Serves 4

1 head or 4 baby cauliflower, trimmed of leaves
2–3 tbsp. olive oil
grated zest and juice of ½ lemon
salt and freshly ground black pepper

for the romesco sauce
5 tbsp. olive oil
2 garlic cloves, halved
2 oz. (50 g) bread, cut into ½-in. (1-cm) cubes
5 oz. (150 g) jarred grilled peppers
3½ oz. (100 g) roasted almonds

1 tsp. dried chili flakes
½ tsp. saffron strands, soaked in 1 tbsp. hot water
2 tbsp. red wine vinegar
1 tbsp. tomato purée
1 tsp. smoked paprika

1 Preheat the oven to 425°F (220°C). Put the cauliflower in a baking tray and rub with oil, lemon zest and juice, then season generously. Cover with foil and bake for 20 minutes, then remove the foil and bake for 10–30 minutes depending on size, or just until tender-crisp.

2 For the romesco sauce, heat the oil in a frying pan over a medium heat and fry the whole garlic cloves for 1–2 minutes until just golden. Remove from the pan and set aside. Add the bread to the oil in the pan and fry for 2–3 minutes until golden, stirring constantly. Remove with a slotted spoon and drain on kitchen towel. Reserve the oil.

3 Put the garlic cloves, toasted bread cubes, almonds, peppers and dried chili flakes in a blender and pulse until the sauce forms a smooth emulsion but retains a little texture from the almonds. Transfer the sauce to a bowl. Add the reserved oil to the saffron and soaking water with the vinegar, tomato purée and paprika. Slowly add this liquid to the almond mixture until you have a loose paste; if it's too thick, add more olive oil or a little warm water. Season with salt to taste. Serve at room temperature with the roasted cauliflower.

WITH TAHINI SAUCE
In place of the romesco sauce, put 4 tbsp. tahini in a bowl and loosen with a balloon whisk. Add 4 crushed garlic cloves and, still whisking, slowly pour in the juice of 2 lemons, which will cause the tahini to lighten in color and thicken. Season with salt and add more lemon juice if you prefer it tangy, or a little warm water if you wish to thin it slightly. Sprinkle with paprika and drizzle with extra-virgin olive oil to serve.

WITH CHERMOULA
Roast the cauliflower as directed, omitting the lemon zest and juice. In place of the romesco sauce, make chermoula by combining a handful each of fresh parsley and cilantro (about 1 oz./25 g), finely chopped; 2 crushed garlic cloves; 1 tsp. each smoked paprika and ground cumin; the zest and juice of 1 lemon; and 3 tbsp. olive oil. Season with salt. Spoon over the cauliflower 5 minutes before the end of the cooking time and return to the oven.

WITH ROMESCO SAUCE
In place of the cauliflower, trim a bunch of large scallions, brush with olive oil and season with salt. Heat a griddle pan or heavy frying pan over a high heat and cook the onions, turning occasionally, until softening and charred at the edges, 1–2 minutes.

Caramelized Onion Polenta Pie (GF) (V)

A great dish to cook ahead of time, and it freezes well, too. Hot or cold, it is great accompanied by a salad, particularly one containing lots of ripe, juicy tomatoes.

Serves 6

1 red bell pepper, halved and seeded
1 yellow bell pepper, halved and seeded
1½ tbsp. olive oil
1½ tbsp. soy margarine
3 large yellow onions, finely sliced
3 tbsp. balsamic vinegar
1 tbsp. brown sugar
2 bay leaves
sea salt and black pepper
2 tbsp. chopped fresh parsley

1 tbsp. chopped fresh thyme or 1 tsp. dried thyme
1 cup (175 g) quick-cooking polenta

for the topping
⅓ cup (75 ml) tomato sauce
2 tbsp. soy cream (optional)
2 tsp. nutritional yeast
1 tsp. paprika
pinch red chili flakes
salt and black pepper

1 Put the bell peppers under a hot broiler and cook until the skin blackens. Turn and repeat until charred. Wrap in plastic wrap, allow to cool, then remove the skin and slice.

2 Meanwhile, heat the oil and margarine in a saucepan, add the onions, and cook for 5–7 minutes until soft. Reduce the heat, and stir in the balsamic vinegar, brown sugar, and bay leaves. Continue to cook until the onions are a rich golden brown, about 20 minutes. Remove the bay leaves and season to taste with salt and pepper.

3 Preheat oven to 400°F (200°C). Cook the polenta according to the package directions. While hot, stir in the peppers, onions, parsley, and thyme. Check the seasoning. Oil a 9-in. (23-cm) round springform pan. Press the polenta mixture into the pan and let cool.

4 Combine the ingredients for the topping, season to taste, and spread over the top of the polenta. To serve, bake at 375°F (190°C) for 20 minutes until the top has browned.

WITH "CHEESE"
Prepare the basic recipe, using 1½ cups (175 g) grated non-dairy "cheese" in place of the onions.

WITH ROASTED VEGETABLES
Prepare the basic recipe, using the roasted vegetables from the Mediterranean Roasted Vegetable Wrap (see page 132) in place of the bell peppers, onions, and herbs.

WITH CARAMELIZED ONIONS & TAPENADE
Prepare the basic recipe, but cook without the topping. Spread tapenade (page 103) over the top of the hot pie and return to the oven for 2 minutes, just to heat through. Serve with a dollop of non-dairy sour cream or soy yogurt.

WITH MUSHROOMS
Prepare the basic recipe, omitting the caramelized onions. Instead, cook 1 chopped onion in 2 tbsp. olive oil, add 1 minced garlic clove and 6 ounces sliced mushrooms. Cook gently until the mushrooms are tender. Add 1 tbsp. balsamic vinegar and cook until the liquid has evaporated. Stir into the polenta with the bell peppers and herbs.

Fennel & Tomato Tart

(V)

Store-bought puff pastry is a gift to vegan cooks as most major brands are dairy-free, but check before purchasing. This pie is particularly attractive and is a taste sensation.

Serves 6

1 x 14-oz. (400-g) can navy beans
2 tbsp. non-dairy milk
2 tbsp. vegan pesto (see page 156)
sea salt and pepper
2 heads fresh fennel
1 red bell pepper, seeded and halved
6 tomatoes, peeled and thickly sliced
½ tsp. cilantro seeds
¼ tsp. fennel seeds
2½ tbsp. olive oil
1 tsp. lemon juice
1 sheet dairy-free puff pastry

1 Preheat oven to 375°F (190°C). In a food processor, combine the beans, non-dairy milk, and pesto, and process until smooth. Season, and set aside. Trim the base of the fennel, and remove and discard the long green stalks. Cut into 8 wedges and place in a saucepan. Cover with boiling water and simmer for 10 minutes, drain thoroughly, and cool.

2 Meanwhile, put the bell pepper under a hot broiler and cook until the skin blackens, turn and repeat until the whole pepper is charred. Wrap in plastic wrap, let cool, then remove the skin and slice. Carefully unwrap the pastry and lay it on parchment paper on a cookie sheet. With a sharp knife, score a border 1 in. (2.5 cm) from the edge—this will rise to form the edge of the tart. Spread the bean purée on top of the pastry, taking care to stay within the scored line. Arrange the tomato slices on top, followed by the fennel and pepper.

3 Lightly crush the cilantro and fennel seeds and sprinkle over the vegetables with a little salt and pepper. Brush the outside border with olive oil, then drizzle over the remaining oil and lemon juice. Bake for about 25 minutes, or until the pastry is risen and golden brown. Slip off the parchment paper and serve warm.

WITH ASPARAGUS
Prepare the basic recipe, using 1 lb. (450 g) asparagus, trimmed (the thinner varieties work best) in place of the fennel and bell pepper. Arrange the asparagus spears in a row, tips in alternate directions, to ensure everyone gets their share of tips and bases.

WITH DILL
Prepare the basic recipe, using 4 leeks, white parts only, in place of the fennel and peppers. Sweat in a covered pan with 1 tbsp. olive oil and 1 teaspoon dried dill tips for 5 minutes, then cool before arranging on top of the tomatoes.

WITH MUSHROOM & THYME
Prepare the basic recipe, using 4 large portabello mushrooms, thickly sliced, in place of the fennel and peppers. Cook in 2 tbsp. olive oil with 1 teaspoon dried thyme then cool before arranging on top of the tomatoes.

WITH ROASTED VEGETABLES
Prepare the basic recipe, using the roasted vegetables from the Mediterranean Roasted Vegetable Wrap (page 132) in place of the tomatoes, bell pepper, and fennel.

Caramelized Onion & Goat Cheese Tart

This tart makes a delicious centerpiece for a summer lunch. Caramelized onions are useful to have to hand, so make double the quantity and cover tightly—they'll keep for up to 3 weeks in the refrigerator.

Serves 3–4

1 tbsp. olive oil
2 red or brown onions, finely chopped
1 tbsp. soft brown sugar
1 tbsp. balsamic vinegar

2 tsp. chopped fresh thyme leaves or ¾ tsp. dried thyme
7 oz. (200 g) ready-rolled shortcrust pastry
2 eggs, lightly beaten

7 fl oz. (200 ml) heavy cream
3 oz. (75 g) goat cheese log, sliced
salt and freshly ground black pepper
salad, to serve

1 Preheat the oven to 400°F (200°C). Grease a 8-in (20-cm) deep, fluted tart tin.

2 Heat the oil in a frying pan and fry the onions for 5–7 minutes until soft. Stir in the brown sugar and balsamic vinegar and season with salt and pepper. Reduce the heat to low, add the thyme and cook for 30–35 minutes, stirring often, until the onions are caramelized. Add a little water if the onions begin to dry out and stick to the pan.

3 Carefully unroll the pastry and use it to line the prepared tin. Prick the base all over with a fork, cover with baking paper, fill with baking beans or dried beans and cook for 10–12 minutes until the pastry rim has dried out and set. Remove the beans and paper, then cook the pastry for a further 10 minutes until the base is dry to touch. Remove from the oven and reduce the oven temperature to 320°F (160°C).

4 Meanwhile, beat the eggs and cream together in a jug and season with salt and pepper. Distribute the onions over the base of the pastry and top with the rounds of goat's cheese. Pour over the egg mixture and use the back of a fork to encourage the egg to pool around the onions. Bake for about 30 minutes, until just set. Serve warm or at room temperature with a salad.

WITH MUSHROOMS & GRUYÈRE
Caramelize 1 onion. Melt 1 tbsp. butter in the pan, then add 3½ oz. (100 g) sliced mushrooms and cook, stirring, until they are soft and the liquid has evaporated. Use to fill the pastry case and proceed as directed. Replace the goat's cheese with 2 oz. (50 g) grated Gruyère.

WITH FENNEL & ONION
For the filling, cook just 1 onion and 1 sliced fennel bulb for 5–7 minutes until soft. Add ½ tsp. each fennel seeds and ground cumin with the sugar and proceed as directed.

INDIVIDUAL PHYLLO TARTS
Make the filling as directed. Melt 2 oz. (50 g) unsalted butter. Take 8 sheets of phyllo pastry and keep covered with cling film while working. Lay a phyllo sheet on a work surface, brush with melted butter, top with a second sheet and brush with butter. Cut into 12 squares. Repeat with the remaining phyllo to create 48 squares. Lay one square into each hole of a greased muffin tin, then add a second square on top at right angles to the other to give a star shape. Spoon 1 tbsp. mixture into each cup and crumble over a little goat's cheese. Repeat with a second muffin tin. Bake in a 375°F (190°C) oven for 10–15 minutes until golden brown.

No-Pasta Spinach & Ricotta Lasagne

(GF)

If you are cooking for people who are gluten-free or watching their weight but still love their food, this lasagne is the answer. It uses sliced zucchini in place of pasta so is much lower in calories but still has that lovely, rich lasagne feel to it.

Serves 4–6

3–4 zucchini, cut into thin strips lengthways
2 oz. (50 g) pine kernels, toasted
7 oz. (200 g) grated mozzarella or Cheddar cheese

for the tomato sauce
2 tbsp. olive oil
1 garlic clove, crushed
4 fl oz. (125 ml) red wine
2 x 14-oz. (400-g) cans chopped tomatoes
2 tbsp. tomato purée
1 tsp. brown sugar
1 tsp. dried Italian herbs or oregano
salt and freshly ground black pepper

for the cheese filling
12 oz. (350 g) ricotta cheese
2 oz. (50 g) grated Parmesan-style cheese
1 egg
6 tbsp. semi-skimmed or whole milk
1 tsp. dried Italian herbs
10 oz. (300 g) baby spinach

1 Preheat the oven to 375°F (190°C). For the tomato sauce, heat the olive oil in a small saucepan and fry the garlic for 1 minute. Add the red wine and bring to a boil. Stir in the remaining ingredients. Simmer for 15 minutes until thickened, then season to taste.

2 In a bowl, combine the ricotta, Parmesan, egg, milk, and herbs, and season to taste. Put the spinach in a colander set in the sink and pour over boiling water to wilt. Cool, squeeze to remove any liquid, and chop finely. Stir into the ricotta mixture.

3 To assemble the lasagne, spread a small amount of tomato sauce in the bottom of a baking dish approximately 13 x 9 in. (33 x 23 cm). Add a layer of the zucchini slices, top with half the ricotta-spinach mixture, half the pine kernels, one-third of the tomato sauce and one-third of the grated cheese. Repeat and finish with a layer of zucchini and tomato sauce and sprinkle with the remaining grated cheese.

4 Bake for about 45 minutes, or until bubbly and golden brown. Remove from the oven and allow to rest for 10 minutes before slicing.

WITH PASTA
Replace the zucchini with 12 fresh gluten-free lasagne sheets. Construct and cook the lasagne as directed.

WITH LEEK & MUSHROOM
Heat 1 tbsp. olive oil in a saucepan. Add 3 chopped leeks and cook gently for 5 minutes, then add 7 oz. (200 g) sliced chestnut mushrooms and continue to cook until the vegetables are soft and the liquid absorbed. Leave to cool until lukewarm. Use this mixture in place of the spinach and construct and cook the lasagne as directed.

WITH ROASTED VEGETABLES
Replace the ricotta and spinach layer with a batch of roasted vegetables (see page 181). Construct and cook the lasagne as directed.

WITH SPRING GREENS
Replace the ricotta and spinach layer with a batch of spring greens (see page 144), using one and a half times the quantities of ingredients suggested. Construct and cook the lasagne as directed.

Dhal Makhani

This is Indian comfort food—a rich, creamy, satisfying dhal that is popular in the northern states. Serve with rice or warmed chapati and a good-quality yogurt.

Serves 4

2 tbsp. sunflower oil
1 onion, chopped
3 garlic cloves, crushed
2 tbsp. grated fresh root ginger
1 green chili, deseeded and finely chopped
2 tsp. ground cilantro
1 tsp. ground cumin
1 tsp. ground turmeric
2 bay leaves
1 x 14-oz. (400-g) can chopped tomatoes

7 oz. (200 g) beluga lentils
1 x 14-oz. (400-g) can kidney beans, drained and rinsed
3 fl oz. (75 ml) heavy cream
1 tbsp. lime juice
½ tsp. garam masala
salt and freshly ground black pepper
chopped fresh cilantro or mint leaves, to garnish

1 Heat the oil in a large frying pan and gently cook the onion for 5–7 minutes until soft and translucent, then add the garlic, ginger, and chili and cook for a further minute. Stir in the cilantro, cumin, turmeric, and bay leaves and cook, stirring, for 1 minute. Add the tomatoes, lentils, kidney beans and sufficient water to just cover.

2 Increase the heat to medium-high and bring the mixture to a boil, then cover, reduce the heat and simmer, stirring occasionally, for 35–40 minutes, until the lentils are tender and most of the liquid has evaporated leaving a thick sauce.

3 Remove the bay leaf. If you like your dhal smoother, transfer half the lentil mixture to a deep bowl and blend briefly with a hand-held blender or purée in a food processor. Return the blended mixture to the saucepan. Add the cream, lime juice, and garam masala, and season to taste with plenty of salt and pepper. Serve garnished with the fresh cilantro or mint.

WITH SPINACH
Add 3 oz. (75 g) bag of spinach to the cooked dhal and allow to wilt before adding the cream and finishing as directed.

WITH RED LENTILS & COCONUT MILK
Replace the black lentils with red lentils. Cook 1 tbsp. mustard seeds in the oil for a couple of minutes until they pop, then add the onions and proceed as directed, omitting the beans and replacing the cream with 3 fl oz. (75 ml) coconut milk. Reduce the cooking time to about 20 minutes. Add 3 oz. (75 g) bag of spinach to the cooked dhal (as above), if desired.

WITH GARBANZO BEANS
Replace the kidney beans with a 14 oz. (400 g) tin of garbanzo beans, drained and rinsed.

WITH CRISPY ONIONS
Thinly slice 1 onion. Heat sufficient sunflower oil to come about ½ in. (1 cm) up the side of a large pan. When hot, fry the onion slices in batches until crisp and golden brown, drain on kitchen towel and sprinkle with salt. Use as a topping for the dhal makhani or any of the above variations.

Gnocchi with Butter Beans, Tomato & Spinach

Rather than spending time making your own, buy ready-prepared gnocchi and enjoy this all-in-one dish on busy week days.

Serves 6

1 tbsp. olive oil
1 onion, finely chopped
2 cloves garlic, crushed
5 mushrooms, sliced
1 x 1 lb 2 oz. (500 g) packet potato gnocchi
1 x 14-oz. (400-g) can chopped tomatoes
1 x 14-oz. (400-g) can butter beans, drained and rinsed
6 oz. (175 g) fresh baby spinach
½ tsp. freshly ground black pepper
3 oz. (75 g) grated mozzarella cheese
4 tbsp. grated Parmesan-style cheese

1 In a large frying pan with a lid, heat the oil over a medium–high heat. Add the onion and fry for 5 minutes, until it begins to soften. Add the garlic and mushrooms and cook for 2 minutes. Add the gnocchi, stir to combine, and cook for a further 5–6 minutes, or until golden brown.

2 Stir in the tomatoes, butter beans, spinach, and pepper, and heat through. Sprinkle the cheeses over the top, cover with the lid, and remove from the heat. Leave to stand for 3–4 minutes, or until the cheeses have melted. Serve immediately.

WITH BROCCOLI
Prepare the basic recipe, omitting the spinach and substituting 6 oz. (175 g) cooked broccoli florets.

WITH PEAS & PINE NUTS
Prepare the basic recipe, omitting the spinach and substituting 2 oz. (50 g) frozen peas added with the gnocchi. Add 4 tbsp. pine nuts with the beans.

WITH SWEET POTATO
Prepare the basic recipe. Roast 1 sweet potato, peeled and diced, in the oven for 20 minutes until cooked. Add to the gnocchi with the butter beans.

WITH BELL PEPPER
Prepare the basic recipe. Add 1 deseeded and chopped green bell pepper to the pan with the onion, and proceed as before.

Rigatoni, Tomato & Cheese Casserole

Serves 8

1 lb. (450 g) rigatoni
2 tbsp. olive oil
1 large eggplant, chopped
8 oz. (225 g) grated mozzarella cheese
8 oz. (225 g) grated Cheddar cheese

1¼ pints (750 ml) passata
5 oz. (150 g) tomato purée
1 x 14-oz. (400-g) can cannellini beans,
    drained and rinsed

4–6 tbsp. water or vegetable stock
    (optional, see page 71)
4 tbsp. chopped fresh basil
salt

1 Preheat the oven to 350°F (180°C). Cook the pasta in salted boiling water in a large, preferably cast iron, casserole dish on the hob, according to the packet directions. Drain well, rinse, and set aside.

2 Wipe out the dish and add the olive oil. Fry the eggplant over a medium heat for about 8 minutes, until starting to brown. Stir in the cooked pasta, cheeses, tomato passata, tomato purée, and beans. If required, add a little water or stock to thin the sauce slightly. Cover and transfer to the oven. Bake for 30 minutes, sprinkle with chopped basil and serve immediately.

WITH PESTO & RICOTTA
Prepare the basic recipe, stirring in 9 oz. (250 g) ricotta cheese with the beans, and add a swirl of pesto (see page 156) with the basil to serve.

WITH GREEN BELL PEPPER
Prepare the basic recipe, adding 1 deseeded, chopped green bell pepper to the pan with the beans.

WITH MUSHROOMS
Prepare the basic recipe, adding 8 oz. (225 g) sliced mushrooms to pan with the passata.

WITH SPINACH
Prepare the basic recipe, adding 2½ oz. (60 g) baby spinach leaves to the pan with the passata.

Pasta E Fagioli

(V)

Serves 6

2 tbsp. olive oil
1 medium onion, finely chopped
1 small carrot, finely chopped
1 stalk celery, finely chopped
4 large cloves garlic, chopped

1 cup (250 ml) canned tomato sauce or
    canned crushed tomatoes
2½ pints (1.5 liters) vegetable stock (see
    page 71)
2 sprigs rosemary, left intact, or 2 tsp. dried
    rosemary

1 large sprig thyme, left intact, or 1 tsp.
    dried thyme
1 large fresh bay leaf or 2 dried bay leaves
11 oz. (300 g) ditalini or other small pasta
2 x 14-oz. (400-g) cans cranberry beans
sea salt and black pepper

1 Heat the oil in a skillet, then add the onion, carrot, and celery. Cook over a medium-high heat for 5–7 minutes or until the onion is soft. Stir in the garlic, tomato sauce or tomatoes, stock, and herbs. Bring to a boil. Reduce the heat, cover, and simmer for 30 minutes, stirring occasionally.

2 Return the stew to a rapid boil and add the pasta and beans. Reduce the heat to medium and cook for 6–8 minutes, until the pasta is just cooked. Remove the herb sprigs, if using, and the bay leaf before serving.

WITH LIMA BEANS
Prepare the basic recipe, using lima beans in place of the cranberry beans.

WITH SMOKED TOFU
Prepare the basic recipe. Stir in 1 x 12-oz. (350-g) package smoked tofu, crumbled, at the end of the cooking time.

PASTA E FAGIOLI SOUP
Prepare the basic recipe. Add about 16 fl oz. (500 ml) stock with the pasta to make the dish more soupy.

SLOW PASTA E FAGIOLI
Soak 7 oz. (200 g) dried cranberry beans overnight, then drain. Prepare the basic recipe, adding the beans to the dish with the tomatoes. Cook for about 1½ hours, until the beans are tender.

Balsamic Mushrooms on Polenta (GF)

This is a good recipe to have up your sleeve and makes a great side with a nut roast or bean burger. Look for tubes of ready-made hard polenta, which can be sliced and grilled for an almost instant replacement for soft polenta.

Serves 2–3

1 tbsp. olive oil
2 small shallots, finely chopped
½ oz. (15 g) butter
1 garlic clove, crushed
7 oz. (200g) mixed wild or portabello mushrooms, sliced
5 oz. (150 g) chestnut mushrooms, sliced
½ tsp. dried thyme or rosemary

1½ tbsp. balsamic vinegar
1½ tbsp. white wine
salt and freshly ground black pepper
1 tbsp. vegetable stock powder
3 oz. (75 g) instant polenta
3 tbsp. grated Parmesan-style cheese
1 tbsp. butter

1 Heat the olive oil in a frying pan and add the shallots. Cook, stirring frequently, until soft and translucent. Add the butter and stir until melted, then add the garlic, mushrooms, thyme or rosemary, and seasoning. Cook, stirring frequently, for 2–3 minutes.

2 Add the balsamic vinegar and wine, reduce the heat to medium–low and continue to cook until the mushrooms are tender, about 2 minutes. Set aside and keep warm.

3 While the mushrooms are cooking, make the polenta according to the packet directions. Stir the stock powder into the specified amount of boiling water. Slowly pour in the polenta, beating with a wooden spoon as you do so. Continue to cook over a moderate heat for 5 minutes, stirring frequently; the polenta is cooked when it leaves the sides of the pan and is a custard-like consistency.

4 Stir in the cheese and butter and season with salt and pepper. Spread the polenta on warmed plates and top with the mushrooms.

WITH HERBS & GARLIC
Omit the balsamic vinegar. Use 2 crushed garlic cloves and increase the quantity of white wine to 3 tbsp. Add 2 tbsp. chopped fresh parsley at the end of the cooking time.

WITHOUT DAIRY
For the mushrooms, increase the olive oil to 1½ tbsp. and omit the butter. Substitute 1 tbsp. olive oil and 2 tbsp. nutritional yeast for the butter and cheese in the polenta.

BAKED MUSHROOMS ON POLENTA
Preheat the oven to 400°F (200°C). Put the olive oil and the butter in a roasting tin and heat in the oven for 1 minute to melt the butter. Cut the mushrooms into chunks and the shallots into quarters. Put all the ingredients into the roasting tin and toss to coat. Bake for 10 minutes, toss again, and cook for another 10 minutes until the mushrooms are tender.

213

(V)

Spicy Spinach & Buckwheat Crêpes

These crêpes are incredibly versatile and can be filled with a wide range of vegetables, dried beans, and nuts. Stuff them with a little leftover stew and you've got a great meal for the family.

Makes 8–10 crêpes

for the crêpes
1 tbsp. egg replacer (see page 223)
4 tbsp. water
1½ cups (350 ml) non-dairy milk
¼ cup (50 ml) canola oil
½ tsp. lemon juice
½ tsp. salt
½ cup (50 g) rice flour
½ cup (50 g) buckwheat flour

for the filling
2 lbs. fresh spinach
2 tbsp. canola oil
1 medium onion, finely chopped
1½-in (4-cm) piece gingerroot, grated
½ tsp. whole fennel seeds
4 cardamon pods, seeds only, crushed
¼ tsp. chili powder
½ tsp. garam masala

for the sauce
1 cup (250 ml) soy yogurt
4 tbsp. chopped fresh mint
2 tsp. lime juice

1 To make the crêpes, whisk together the egg replacer and the water until frothy. Whisk in the other ingredients. Let the batter rest for 30 minutes.

2 Lightly oil a heavy non-stick skillet and place over a medium-high heat. Pour in about 2 tbsp. of batter and swirl to forms a thin layer on the bottom of the pan. Cook until the top is dry and the underside lightly browned, then flip and cook the other side for 15–30 seconds. Stack the crêpes as you make them and keep warm.

3 Cook the spinach in just the water clinging to the leaves until it is just tender; drain, cool, and roughly chop. Heat the oil in a saucepan, then add the onion and cook for 5–7 minutes until soft. Add the gingerroot and spices and cook for 1 minute. Stir in the spinach.

4 Preheat the oven to 425°F (220°C). Put a generous amount of filling down the center of each crêpe, roll, then arrange in an oiled baking dish. Bake for 20 minutes. Combine the sauce ingredients and serve with the crêpes.

WITH GARBANZO BEANS
Prepare the basic recipe, adding 1 x 14-oz. (400-g) can garbanzo beans with the spinach.

WITH ALL-PURPOSE FLOUR
Prepare the basic recipe, using 1 cup (125 g) all-purpose flour in place of rice and buckwheat flours. Or, use ½ cup (50 g) each of all-purpose flour and whole wheat flour.

WITH OVEN-ROASTED VEGETABLES
Prepare the basic recipe, using the roasted vegetables from the Mediterranean Roasted Vegetable Wrap (page 132) in place of the spicy spinach. Serve with the minted yogurt sauce, if desired.

WITH CREAMY MUSHROOM FILLING
Prepare the basic recipe, using the mushroom filling from the Creamy Mushroom Lasagne (page 177) in place of the spinach. Omit the yogurt sauce.

Garlic & Cilantro Naan Bread

Makes 6

2 tsp. sugar, divided
⅔ cup (160 ml) warm milk
2 tsp. active dry yeast
3½ cups (450 g) all-purpose flour

½ tsp. salt
1 tsp. baking powder
2 tbsp. olive oil
⅔ cup (160 ml) plain yogurt

1 egg, room temperature, lightly beaten
3 tbsp. freshly chopped cilantro

1. Dissolve 1 teaspoon sugar in the warm milk, sprinkle the yeast on top, and leave for 10–15 minutes until frothy. In a large bowl, sift the flour, salt, and baking powder. Add the remaining sugar, yeast liquid, and the remaining ingredients, and mix until it forms a soft dough. Knead for 10 minutes until soft, smooth, and elastic. Transfer to a large lightly oiled bowl. Cover and put in a warm place for an hour or so, until doubled in size.

2. Preheat your oven to the highest temperature, and heat a heavy roasting pan. Preheat the broiler. Turn the dough out onto a lightly floured work surface, punch down, and knead again for 2–3 minutes. Divide the dough into 6 equal pieces, and roll each one into a ball. Keep 5 covered. Roll the sixth into a tear-shaped naan, about 10 in. (25.5 cm) long and about 5 in. (12.5 cm) at the widest point.

3. Remove the roasting pan from the oven, and slap the naan down onto it. Quickly put it back and bake for 3 minutes. It should puff up. Remove the roasting pan from the oven and immediately place it under the broiler for about 30 seconds only, or until the top of the naan begins to brown. Wrap the naan in a clean kitchen towel and keep warm. Repeat with the rest of the naan. Serve hot.

WITH ONION
Prepare the basic recipe, adding ¼ of an chopped onion to the flour.

WITH TOMATO
Prepare the basic recipe, adding 2 skinned, deseeded, and chopped tomatoes to the flour.

WITH TOMATO & BASIL
Prepare the basic recipe, adding 2 skinned, deseeded, and chopped tomatoes to the flour. Replace the cilantro with 3 tbsp. freshly chopped basil.

Spaghetti Alla Capricciosa

Serves 6

½ cup (20 ml) extra-virgin olive oil
4 cups (900 g) fresh, ripe tomatoes, peeled and very coarsely chopped
8 basil leaves, torn into shreds

1 tbsp. dried oregano
6 tbsp. freshly grated Parmesan-style cheese
1 lb. (450 g) spaghetti
3¼ cups (700 g) buffalo mozzarella

salt and freshly ground black pepper
18 small, whole, fresh basil leaves, to serve

1. Mix the oil with the tomatoes in a bowl, add the fresh basil, dried oregano, and grated Parmesan cheese. Leave to stand for a couple of hours, or even overnight in the refrigerator.

2. When you are ready to serve, bring a large saucepan of salted water to a boil. Put the spaghetti into the water and stir thoroughly. Replace the lid and return to a boil. Remove or adjust the lid once the water is boiling again. Cook according to the packet instructions until al dente.

3. Meanwhile, cut the mozzarella into small pieces and place in a large bowl. Drain the spaghetti and add it to the mozzarella. Mix together quickly, adding the tomato sauce. Season, garnish with the basil leaves, and serve at once.

WITH ROASTED PEPPERS
To the tomatoes and herbs, add 4 chopped roasted peppers and substitute half of the grated Parmesan cheese for pecorino cheese.

WITH LEMON
To add a lemony note, use 5 tbsp. extra-virgin olive oil, and 5 tbsp. lemon oil, plus ½ teaspoon of grated unwaxed lemon zest to the tomatoes while they are standing.

WITH SMOKED SCAMORZA
For a smoky flavor, substitute the buffalo mozzarella for a smoked scamorza and add a generous sprinkling of smoked paprika to the tomatoes while they are standing. In this case, omit the basil.

Biryani

(GF) (V)

Biryani was originally a dish created for the Moghul emperors and was a very complicated affair. This simple variation, which is very easy to cook, is packed with aromatic spices and makes a great party dish.

Serves 6–8

2 tbsp. sunflower oil
1 large onion, finely sliced
3 garlic cloves, minced
1-in. (2.5-cm) piece gingerroot, shredded
2 tsp. black mustard seeds
1 red chili pepper, finely sliced
3 tbsp. madras curry paste
6 oz. (175 g) each fresh cauliflower, carrot, green beans, and potato, cut into chunks

6 oz. (175 g) whole button mushrooms
4 cups (1 liter) vegetable stock (see page 71)
1 cup (175 g) frozen peas
juice of 2 lemons
large pinch saffron threads
2 cups (250 g) basmati rice, washed
2 tbsp. chopped fresh cilantro
1 cup (150 g) unsalted roasted cashew nuts or almonds

1 Preheat the oven to 350°F (180°C). Heat the oil in a flameproof casserole, then add the onion and cook over a medium-high heat for 5–7 minutes until the onion is soft. Add the minced garlic, gingerroot, mustard seeds, and chili. Continue to cook, stirring, until the mustard seeds begin to pop.

2 Stir in the curry paste, add the mixed vegetables and mushrooms, then stir well to coat. Pour in the stock, and bring to a boil. Reduce the heat and simmer for 10 minutes, until the vegetables are nearly tender.

3 Stir in the peas, lemon juice, saffron, and rice, then season to taste with salt. Cover with parchment paper, then with a tightly fitting lid, and bake for 30 minutes, until the rice is tender and the stock is absorbed. To serve, sprinkle with cilantro and nuts.

WITH RAITA
Prepare the basic recipe, and serve with raita. To 1 cup (250 ml) soy yogurt, add ½ cup (75 g) chopped cucumber, ¼ cup (100 g) finely chopped red onion, 1 tbsp. chopped fresh mint, and salt and lemon juice to taste.

WITH LENTILS
Prepare the basic recipe, adding 1 cup (200 g) rinsed brown lentils with the vegetables.

WITH PUMPKIN
Prepare the basic recipe, using 1 x 12-oz. (350-g) fresh pumpkin, cut into chunks, in place of the cauliflower and carrot.

WITH FRESH MANGO CHUTNEY
Prepare the basic recipe and serve with mango chutney (see page 128).

Vegetable Tikka for a Crowd

GF · V
Serve with
gluten-free
naan bread

This dish is a hybrid and does not follow traditional Indian cooking methods as, for simplicity and flavor, the vegetables are roasted and then added to the sauce. The curry may be made a day ahead, covered, and reheated when required.

Serves 8

1 large potato, diced
1 small butternut squash, peeled, seeded and diced
2 carrots, sliced
1 eggplant, diced
2 red peppers, sliced
6 tbsp. tikka masala curry paste

3 tbsp. sunflower oil
2 onions, sliced
3 garlic cloves, crushed
2 tbsp. grated fresh root ginger
1 tbsp. cumin seeds
1 x 1 lb 8-oz. (680-g) jar tomato passata
1 x 14-oz. (400-g) can coconut milk

5 oz. (150 g) frozen peas
3½ oz. (100 g) frozen French beans
salt
fresh cilantro sprigs, to garnish

to serve
rice or warmed naan breads

1   Preheat the oven to 400°F (200°C). Place the potatoes, squash, carrots, eggplants, and peppers in a large roasting tin and toss with 2 tbsp. of the curry paste and 2 tbsp. of the oil. Season with salt, and roast for about 30 minutes until tender.

2   Meanwhile, make the sauce. Heat the remaining oil in a large saucepan, and gently cook the onion until soft and translucent, about 5–7 minutes. Add the garlic, ginger, and cumin seeds, then cook for 1 minute. Stir in the remaining curry paste, or to taste, and cook, stirring, for 2 minutes.

3   Stir in the passata, coconut milk and half the coconut tin of water. Bring to a boil over a moderate–high heat, then lower the heat and simmer for 5 minutes. Once the vegetables are roasted, add them to the sauce with the peas and French beans and simmer for 10 minutes. Scatter with cilantro sprigs and serve with rice or warmed naan breads.

WITH SQUASH & GARBANZO BEANS
Use 2 butternut squashes and omit the eggplant and carrots. Replace the peas and beans with 2 x 14-oz. (400-g) cans of garbanzo beans, drained and rinsed. Cook the curry as directed.

WITH BAKED TOFU
Preheat the oven to 350°F (180°C). Combine 6 tbsp. sunflower oil, 1 tsp. chili flakes, 2 crushed garlic cloves and 1 tsp. salt. Slice 14 oz. (400 g) firm tofu into ½-in. (1-cm) slices and marinade in the oil mixture for 30 minutes. Drain and roast for 30 minutes until soft and brown.

VEGETABLE BIRYANI FOR A CROWD
Replace the tikka paste with biryani paste, the coconut milk with 10 fl oz. (300 ml) heavy cream and add 3 oz. (75 g) raisins with the squash. Soak ¼ tsp. saffron in 1 tbsp. warm water for 15 minutes. Put 1 lb 2 oz. (500 g) basmati rice, the saffron and its liquid, and 34 fl oz. (1 liter) water in a saucepan and simmer for 10 minutes. Drain, and lay on top of curry. Cover tightly and bake for 20 minutes in a 180°C (350°F) oven until the rice is tender. Serve with toasted almonds and yogurt.

MASSAMAN THAI CURRY FOR A CROWD
Replace the tikka masala paste with 2–3 tbsp. massaman Thai curry paste. Omit the cumin seeds. Mix together 3 tbsp. each soy sauce and lime juice, 3 oz. (75 g) peanut butter, and 1 tbsp. brown sugar. Add to the curry with the peas and simmer for 3 minutes.

Chestnut & Mushroom Bourguignon

(V)

The perfect dish for serving to friends on a winter's day. As with most stews, the flavor matures with keeping, so make it up to 24 hours in advance, cover and chill until required. Serve with creamy potatoes, cauliflower mash, or soft polenta.

Serves 4

2 tbsp. olive oil
4 shallots or 1 onion, chopped
2 garlic cloves, crushed
1 celery stick, finely sliced
2 bay leaves
1 tsp. dried thyme
9 oz. (250 g) chestnut mushrooms, quartered

3½ oz. (100 g) button mushrooms, halved
2 tbsp. all-purpose or gram flour
10 fl oz. (300 ml) bold red wine
7 fl oz. (200 ml) vegetable stock (see page 71)
2 tbsp. tomato purée
9 oz. (250 g) cooked chestnuts from a can or vacuum-packed

7 oz. (200 g) Chantenay carrots, halved, or whole, cut into batons
1 parsnip, cut into batons
handful (about 1 oz./25 g) fresh flat-leaf parsley, chopped
salt and freshly ground black pepper

1 Heat the oil in a saucepan and cook the shallots or onions for 5–7 minutes until soft. Add the garlic, celery, bay leaves, and thyme and cook for 2 minutes. Add the mushrooms and cook, stirring constantly, until they have just softened. Stir in the flour and cook, stirring, for a minute. Slowly add a small glassful of the red wine, stirring to incorporate with the flour.

2 Add the remaining wine, stock, and tomato purée. Break the chestnuts apart into half-walnut-sized chunks and add to the saucepan with the carrots and parsnips. Season with salt and pepper to taste, then bring to a boil over a moderate-high heat. Stir well, reduce the heat, cover, and simmer for 30 minutes.

3 Before serving, stir two-thirds of the chopped parsley through the bourguignon, then sprinkle over the remaining parsley to garnish.

WITH ALE
Replace the red wine with a well-flavored beer.

WITH GNOCCHI
When the stew has finished cooking, add 1 lb 2 oz. (500 g) fresh gnocchi and cook for 2–3 minutes until the gnocchi rise to the surface. If cooking in advance, do not add the gnocchi until just before serving.

WITH WALNUTS
Replace the chestnuts with 4 oz. (125 g) walnut halves.

CHESTNUT & MUSHROOM BOURGUIGNON PIE
Make the bourguignon and leave to cool. Transfer to a 7 oz. (200 g) pie dish or four individual heatproof dishes. Cut a sheet of ready-rolled dairy-free shortcrust pastry to the same size as the pie dish or dishes. Carefully place the pie lid(s) on top of the stew and use a fork to press and seal the edges of the lids around the dish. Cut a vent hole in the center with a sharp knife. Bake in a 400°F (200°C) oven for 20–30 minutes until golden brown.

CHAPTER 8
Sweet Treats

The sweet treats in this chapter show the range of yummy desserts loved by vegetarians and vegans alike—some illustrate how rich and delicious dairy substitutes can be, while other fruit-based desserts require little or no adaptation at all. The advice on substitutions below is invaluable when preparing vegan desserts and cakes, and you'll find that you come back to this time and time again.

CREAM & SOFT CHEESE SUBSTITUTES

Making your own non-dairy cream and soft cheese substitites couldn't be easier and avoids the preservatives and thickening agents sometimes found in commercial versions.

Non-dairy whipped cream

8 oz. (225 g) firm tofu, drained
2 tsp. brown rice syrup
few drops vanilla extract

Blend the ingredients in a blender until creamy and smooth.

Makes 1 cup (250 ml)

Non-dairy sour cream

8 oz. (225 g) firm tofu, drained
¼ cup (90 ml) canola or sunflower oil
2 tbsp. lemon juice
½ tsp. salt

Blend the ingredients in a blender until creamy and smooth.

Makes 1¼ cups (450 ml)

Non-dairy cream cheese

¼ cup (40 g) raw cashews
1 cup (225 g) silken tofu, well drained
1–2 tbsp. soy milk
1 tbsp. brown rice or agave syrup
1 tsp. salt
½ tsp. white pepper

Soak the cashews in boiling water for at least 1 hour, then drain. Blend all the ingredients in a food processor until smooth. Add more salt or syrup to taste. Refrigerate overnight, then use within 5 days.

Makes approximately 1¼ cups (450 ml)

NON-DAIRY PIE CRUST

This is a basic whole wheat pie crust. Shortening is used here because its high fat content makes for a crispy crust, but a solid margarine may also be used. If using for a dessert, add 1 tablespoon sugar.

2 cups (225 g) whole wheat flour
1 tsp. baking powder
1 tbsp. sugar (for sweet crusts only)
pinch salt
½ cup (125 g) shortening
4-5 tbsp. cold water

In a food processor fitted with a metal blade, pulse the flour, baking powder, sugar, and salt until mixed. Add shortening, pulsing until the mixture resembles coarse meal. Add 3 tablespoons of the cold water to the flour mixture, pulsing until clumps form, stopping to test the dough with fingertips to see if it's moist enough to hold together. If the dough is too dry, add a little more water as required. Remove the blade and draw the dough into a ball. Wrap in plastic wrap and refrigerate for 15-20 minutes or until required.

Makes a 8-10-in. (20-25-cm) tart or a 7-in. (18-cm) pie

EGG REPLACER

Commercial egg replacer, consisting of starches and leavening agents, can be bought in health shops. You can also make an egg replacer at home in a large batch.

2½ cups (300 g) arrowroot powder, tapioca starch, or potato flour
½ cup (65 g) baking powder
1 tbsp. guar gum powder or xanthan gum powder

Combine the ingredients in an airtight container and shake vigorously to thoroughly mix. To replace 1 egg, combine 1½ tsp. egg replacer, 1 tbsp. canola oil, and 2 tbsp. water. Whisk together until slightly frothy.

Makes a generous 3 cups (375 g)

Golden Milk

GF V
Use non-dairy
milk and
maple syrup

Also known as a turmeric latte, this recipe is based on an ancient Indian drink that has taken the world by storm in recent years. Turmeric has a long list of associated health benefits, including fighting infection, healthy skin, relieving muscle pain and boosting brain power. Don't leave out the ground pepper—it's essential for the absorption of turmeric into the body.

Makes 2

17 fl oz. (500 ml) milk
    (dairy, soy, almond,
    coconut or oat, or use
    a mixture)
1 tsp. ground turmeric
½ tsp. ground cinnamon
¼ tsp. freshly ground
    black pepper

¼ tsp. grated fresh root
    ginger, or a generous
    pinch of ground ginger
pinch of cayenne pepper
    (optional)
1 tsp. raw honey or maple
    syrup, or to taste

1 Blend all the ingredients in a high-speed blender until smooth; alternatively, whisk all the ingredients together forcefully with a balloon whisk to amalgamate and create a foam.

2 Pour the liquid into a small saucepan and heat for 3–5 minutes over a medium heat, whisking constantly, until hot but not boiling. Drink immediately.

WITH CHAI SPICES
Replace the cinnamon and ginger with ½ tsp. ground chai spice mix.

WITH MATCHA
Replace the spices with 1 tsp. matcha powder and, when hot, sweeten as directed.

WITH OVERNIGHT OATS
Make the bircher muesli on page 16, replacing the apple juice and milk with 7 fl oz. (200 ml) cold golden milk.

OVER ICE
Make the golden milk as directed. Leave to cool, then cover and refrigerate until chilled. Serve over plenty of ice.

MOON MILK
Omit the cayenne pepper and add 1 tsp. ground ashwagandha, ¼ tsp. ground cardamom and 2 pinches ground nutmeg with the spices. Add 2 tsp. coconut oil to the milk while it is heating and, when hot, sweeten to taste as directed. If desired, add 1 tbsp. freeze-dried blueberries or tart cherries to the blender with the spices. You can add a few drops of rosewater too.

Coconut Milk Hot Chocolate

Makes 2

for the coconut chocolate
7 fl oz. (200 ml) coconut milk, refrigerated
1–2 tsp. maple syrup
pinch of salt

1½ oz. (40 g) semisweet vegan chocolate,
  broken into chunks
few drops of vanilla extract or ½ tsp. smooth
  almond butter

for the whipped coconut cream (optional)
2½ oz. (60 g) coconut cream (from the top of
  an unshaken can of full-fat coconut milk)
2 tsp. confectioners' sugar or maple syrup

1 To make the whipped coconut cream, scoop the hardened coconut cream from the refrigerated can of coconut milk into a bowl with the confectioners' sugar or maple syrup and beat using an electric hand mixer. If the mixture is too thick, add a little of the leftover coconut liquid from the tin, a tbsp. at a time, to help the mixture come together.

2 In a small saucepan, combine the chilled coconut milk, 1 tsp. maple syrup and the salt. Simmer, stirring with a whisk, until the salt has dissolved, about 2 minutes. Whisk in the chocolate until smooth. Stir in a couple of drops of vanilla extract or the almond butter, taste, and add a little more if needed; likewise, add a little more maple syrup, if required. Drink while still hot as it is, or top with the whipped coconut cream.

WITH COFFEE
Add a shot of hot espresso coffee once the chocolate has dissolved. Serve with or without the topping.

WITH WHITE CHOCOLATE
Replace the dark chocolate with vegan white chocolate. Serve with or without the topping.

WITH RUM
Add 1 fl oz. (25 ml) coconut- or coffee-flavored rum to the finished hot chocolate. Serve with or without the topping.

WITH ICE CREAM
Replace the chocolate with 1 tbsp. sifted cocoa powder or cacao powder and the maple syrup with 3 Medjool dates. Put the ingredients in a blender with 2 scoops of dairy-free coconut ice cream (or Chocolate Chip Soy Ice Cream on page 237) and blend until smooth. Serve with or without the topping.

Halva Baked Apricots

Serves 2

4 apricots, cut in half lengthways and stoned
8 tsp. halva

to serve
ice cream or crème fraîche

1 Preheat the oven to 375°F (190°C).

2 Place the apricot halves in a baking dish, cut-side up. Drop 1 tsp. of halva into the cavity of each apricot half.

3 Bake until the apricots are tender, around 20–25 minutes, depending on the ripeness and size of the apricots. Serve with ice cream or crème fraîche.

WITH AMARETTI
Instead of the halva, place 8 amaretti biscuits in a plastic bag and crush into fine crumbs. Transfer to a small bowl. Add 1 tbsp. each of softened sweet butter and brandy plus an egg yolk and mix to combine. Spoon into the apricot cavities and bake as directed.

WITH MARZIPAN
Substitute the halva with 8 tsp. shop-bought almond marzipan. Stuff and bake as directed.

WITH ORANGE BLOSSOM SYRUP
While the halva-stuffed apricots are cooking, place 3 oz. (75 g) superfine sugar in a pan with 3 tbsp. lemon juice, ¼–½ tsp. orange blossom water, to taste, and 10 fl oz. (300 ml) water. Heat gently until the sugar has dissolved, then bring to a boil and simmer for about 5 minutes to form a thin, pourable syrup. Drizzle over the baked apricots.

Tropical Fruit Kebabs

Ⓥ

We don't often think about using the barbecue to cook a dessert, but these kebabs make a tasty end to an outdoor meal. If you prepare the kebabs in advance, brush the banana and mango with a little lemon juice to prevent browning, cover with plastic wrap, and keep cool. The syrup can be reheated when required.

Serves 4

for the syrup
⅓ cup (75 g) non-dairy margarine
6 tbsp. maple syrup
6 cardamom pods, seeds only
1 whole clove
1 x 3-in. (7.5-cm) cinnamon stick
½ tsp. vanilla extract

for the kebabs
½ small pineapple
2 ripe mangoes
2 firm bananas
non-dairy ice cream (see page 237), to serve

1   In a small pan, melt the non-dairy butter and stir in the maple syrup. Crush the cardamom seeds with a mortar and pestle, then add to the syrup with the clove, cinnamon, and vanilla. Keep warm to infuse while preparing the fruit.

2   Skin and core the pineapple and cut into 1-in. (2.5-cm) chunks. Cut the mango in half and cut the flesh into large chunks, then remove the skin. Peel and slice the bananas. Thread the fruit onto 8 metal skewers, or wooden skewers that have been soaked in water for 30 minutes.

3   Preheat the barbecue coals or the broiler to medium-hot. Remove the clove and cinnamon stick from the syrup. Put the kebabs on an oiled rack and cook, turning once, and basting frequently with the syrup until the fruit is lightly browned, about 5 minutes. Do not overcook or the fruit will fall apart. Drizzle with any remaining syrup and serve immediately with non-dairy ice cream.

WITH ORCHARD FRUITS
Prepare the basic recipe, replacing the tropical fruit with 1 large apple and 1 large pear, chopped into 1-in. (2.5-cm) chunks and coated with lemon juice, and 6 halved plums.

WITH BAGEL
Prepare the basic recipe. Cut a bagel in half and spread with non-dairy butter, then sprinkle with brown sugar and cinnamon. Cut each bagel half into 6 pieces and thread them on the skewers with the fruit.

WITH ORANGE CINNAMON SYRUP
Prepare the basic recipe, adding 2 tbsp. orange juice concentrate in place of the vanilla in the syrup.

WITH CHOCOLATE SAUCE
Prepare the basic kebabs, and serve with chocolate sauce (see page 237).

Mango Yogurt Parfait

This is a pretty dessert that is ready in an instant.
It tastes delicious with creamy Greek yogurt, but
coconut, vanilla or lemon yogurt also work well.

Makes 2–3

1 medium ripe mango,
   peeled and stoned
3 ginger biscuits,
   crumbled

5 fl oz. (150 ml) Greek or
   non-dairy yogurt
1 passion fruit, halved

1 Put two tall glasses in the freezer while you
prepare the mango. Place the mango in a food
processor and blitz until you have a purée;
alternatively, blitz it in a large bowl using a
hand-held blender.

2 Put half the biscuit crumbs in the base of the
chilled glasses. Spoon half the mango purée
into the glasses, taking care not to let it slide
down the sides. Then divide half the yogurt
between the glasses. Repeat these layers, then
drizzle the pulp of half a passion fruit over the
top of each parfait.

WITH CREAM "CHEESE"
Replace the yogurt with 5 oz. (150 g) vegan cream "cheese"
mixed with 1 tbsp. superfine sugar, 2 tsp. lemon juice, and a few
drops of vanilla extract. Construct the parfait as suggested.

WITH STRAWBERRIES & AMARETTI
Replace the mango with 3½ oz. (100 g) strawberries mixed with
2 tbsp. superfine sugar and a couple of drops of vanilla extract,
and mash roughly with a fork. Use 4 amaretti biscuits in place of
the ginger biscuits.

WITH BERRIES & CHOCOLATE
Replace the mango with 3½ oz. (100 g) frozen mixed berries
that have been allow to partially defrost. Mix with 4 tbsp. non-
dairy semisweet chocolate chips. Layer the parfait as suggested,
using crumbled non-dairy chocolate oat biscuits instead of the
ginger biscuits.

MANGO YOGURT SMOOTHIE
Place the mango, yogurt and a generous ¼ tsp. ground ginger
in a blender and process until smooth. Omit the biscuits and
passion fruit.

Non-Cheesecake with Mixed Berries

(V)

This creamy dessert is stunning—all the joy of cheesecake without the dairy.

Serves 8–10

3 tbsp. soy margarine
8 oz. (225 g) graham crackers, crushed
1 tbsp. cornstarch
3 tbsp. soy milk
12 oz. (350 g) silken tofu, drained

8 oz. (225 g) non-dairy cream cheese (see page 223)
⅔ cup (175 ml) soy yogurt
juice and zest of ½ lemon
egg replacer for 1 egg (see page 223)

1 tbsp. water
¼ cup (25 g) confectioners' sugar, sifted
½ tsp. vanilla extract
1½ cups (225 g) fresh mixed berries
2 tbsp. mixed fruit jelly, melted

1 Preheat oven to 350°F (180°C). Oil an 8-in. (20-cm) cake pan with a removable base. In a saucepan, melt the margarine. Combine 2 tbsp. of the melted margarine with the crushed graham crackers, then press into the cake pan. Bake for 10 minutes, then set aside.

2 Meanwhile, to the remaining melted margarine in the saucepan, stir in the cornstarch, then blend in the soy milk. Cook over a low heat until thickened. In a bowl or blender, beat the tofu, non-dairy cream cheese, yogurt, and lemon juice and zest until smooth. In a cup, whisk the egg replacer with the water (or as directed on the package) until frothy, and stir into the tofu mixture.

3 Mix in the cornstarch mixture, confectioners' sugar, and vanilla. Pour the mixture over the prepared base and cook for 30 minutes, or until the edge of the cheesecake just begins to color. The center will still feel wobbly, but it will firm up when cool. When the cheesecake is cool, arrange the berries on top and lightly brush them with the melted jelly to glaze. Place the cheesecake in the refrigerator to chill. Serve straight from the refrigerator.

WITH PECANS
Prepare the basic recipe, adding 1½ cups (275 g) canned pumpkin purée to the tofu mixture. Replace the vanilla with 1 tsp. ground cinnamon. For the topping, instead of the berries, toss 1 cup (150 g) whole pecans with 3 tbsp. maple syrup, 1 tbsp. sugar, and ¼ tsp. cinnamon. Bake topping mixture at 350°F (180°C) for 10 minutes; cool before using to decorate cheesecake.

WITH GINGER & PINEAPPLE
Prepare the basic recipe, omitting topping. Add 1 tsp. ground ginger to the graham cracker crumbs. Top the cheesecake with slices of fresh or canned pineapple and chopped crystallized ginger.

WITH RASPBERRIES
Prepare the basic recipe, adding 1 cup (125 g) raspberries to the mixture with the vanilla. Use 1½ cups (175 g) raspberries in place of the mixed berries for the topping.

WITH CHOCOLATE
Prepare the basic recipe, replacing the graham crackers with Oreo cookies. To the filling, stir in 6 oz. (175 g) vegan chocolate, melted, in place of the lemon juice and zest, and add 10 broken Oreo cookies.

Toffeed Bananas with Coconut Cream

Serves 4

for the coconut cream
4 oz. (125 g) block creamed coconut
⅓ cup (75 ml) coconut milk
4 tbsp. soy yogurt

4 firm, ripe bananas
1 tbsp. lemon juice
2 tbsp. brown sugar
pinch ground cinnamon

pinch ground nutmeg
toasted coconut, to garnish

1 To make the coconut cream, roughly chop the block of creamed coconut into pieces, and put them in a saucepan with the coconut milk. Heat slowly until the coconut has melted, stirring frequently. Remove and let cool. Add the yogurt to the cooled coconut cream, beating until the mixture resembles whipped cream in texture. Let cool and keep refrigerated until required.

2 Peel the bananas, cut them in half lengthways, brush with lemon juice, and put in a shallow pan. Sprinkle with the brown sugar and a pinch of cinnamon and nutmeg. Put under a medium-hot broiler until the sugar is beginning to caramelize and the bananas are soft. Serve hot with the coconut cream and garnish with toasted coconut.

WITH PINEAPPLE
Prepare the basic recipe, using 8 slices fresh or canned pineapple in place of the bananas. Omit the lemon juice.

WITH NECTARINES
Prepare the basic recipe, using 4 large, ripe nectarines, skinned, pitted, and halved, in place of the bananas.

WITH RED FRUITS
Prepare the coconut cream. To make the salad, combine 12 oz. (350 g) cubed watermelon, 8 oz. (225 g) strawberries, 4 oz. (125 g) raspberries, the seeds from 1 pomegranate, and 2 chopped plums. Sprinkle with 1–2 tbsp. sugar and 4 tbsp. cranberry juice and serve with the coconut cream.

Caramelized Apple Crisp

Serves 6

¼ cup (50 g) soy margarine
¾ cup (175 g) brown sugar
5 tart apples, peeled and sliced

¾ cup (75 g) whole wheat pastry flour
¾ cup (50 g) oat-based muesli
1 tsp. ground cinnamon

½ tsp. ground nutmeg
4 tbsp. canola oil
2 tbsp. almond or soy milk

1 Preheat oven to 400°F (200°C). In a skillet, melt the margarine or non-dairy butter, then add two-thirds of the brown sugar. Cook, stirring constantly, until the sugar has melted. Add the apples and turn to coat in the caramel mixture, then cook for about 10 minutes, stirring frequently, until the apples are cooked but still firm.

2 Meanwhile, in a bowl, combine the remaining brown sugar with the rest of the ingredients, mixing lightly with the fingertips until the mixture becomes crumbly. Add a little more oil if the mixture is too dry or a little more flour if it is too sticky.

3 Transfer the apples to a deep pie dish or casserole and top with the crumb mixture. Bake for 30 minutes, or until crisp and golden. Serve with soy ice cream (page 237, omitting the chocolate chips).

WITH PEACHES
Prepare the basic recipe, using 5 medium, ripe peaches in place of the apples. Add 1 tbsp. rum with the peaches for extra flavor.

WITH GINGER
Prepare the basic recipe, adding 3 tbsp. chopped crystallized ginger to the apple mixture.

WITH SHORTBREAD
Prepare the apples for the basic recipe. Omit the crumb topping and bake as directed. Serve with shortbread (see page 241).

WITH CRÊPES
Prepare the apples for the basic recipe. Omit the crumb topping. Make a batch of crêpes (see page 215). Stuff the crêpes with the apples, arrange in an greased baking dish, and bake at 425°F (220°C) for 20 minutes, or until golden.

Strawberry Tart

Ⓥ

Simple and easy to prepare, a seasonal fruit tart looks and tastes wonderful. Leftover pastry can be made into small jelly tartlets, which are surprisingly popular with young-at-heart adults and children alike.

Serves 6–8

1 recipe whole wheat pie
    crust (see page 223)
1 lb. (450 g) ripe
    strawberries, halved
small fresh mint leaves

for the glaze
½ cup (125 g) sugar
4 tbsp. cornstarch
1 cup (250 ml) water
4 tbsp. strawberry
    preserve
1 tbsp. lemon juice

1   Preheat oven to 400°F (200°C). Lightly butter a 9-in. (23-cm) tart pan. Roll out the pie crust on a floured surface, use it to line the tart pan, and chill for 20 minutes. Line the base of the pie crust with parchment weighted down with pie weights or baking beans, then bake for 12 minutes. Reduce the heat to 250°F (120°C) and bake for 10 minutes more. Remove the parchment and beans and cook for another 10 minutes for the crust to dry out. Cool.

2   To make the glaze, mix together all the glaze ingredients in a saucepan. Bring to a boil and cook, stirring for 1 minute, until thickened. Remove from heat and cool slightly.

3   Spread half of the warm glaze over the cooked crust. Top with the strawberries, then brush the remaining warm glaze over the strawberries. Let cool and serve cold, garnished with small mint leaves.

WITH "CREAM"
Prepare the basic recipe, halving the ingredients for the strawberry preserve glaze. Prepare one portion of non-dairy whipped cream (page 223). Spread a very thin layer of glaze over the base of the tart to seal, then cover with the cream. Top with the strawberry halves, brush with the remaining warm glaze, and garnish with mint leaves.

WITH BLUEBERRIES
Prepare the basic recipe, using 1 lb. (450 g) fresh blueberries in place of the strawberries and blueberry preserve in place of the strawberry preserve.

WITH MIXED FRUIT
Prepare the basic recipe, replacing the strawberries with 1 lb. (450 g) mixed fresh strawberries, blueberries, raspberries, and peach slices.

Use vegan
chocolate

Aquafaba Chocolate & Coconut Mousse

Don't throw away the water from that can of garbanzo beans—it's called aquafaba and forms the basis of an excellent dairy-free chocolate mousse. Chill the bowl and the aquafaba, as it works best when cool.

Serves 4

for the chocolate mousse
10 oz. (275 g) semisweet dark chocolate
liquid from 1 x 14-oz. (400-g) can of
   garbanzo beans (about 3¾ fl oz./
   110 ml), chilled

1 tsp. lemon juice
generous pinch of salt
2 oz. (50 g) superfine sugar

for the coconut topping
1 x 14-oz. (400-g) can full-fat coconut milk,
   refrigerated
1 tbsp. maple syrup
fresh berries, to garnish (optional)

1 Melt the chocolate in a microwave using 20-second pulses, or in a bowl set over a pan of simmering water. Leave to cool slightly, stirring occasionally.

2 In a large bowl, use an electric hand mixer to whisk the aquafaba, lemon juice and salt until it forms soft peaks. While whisking, slowly add the sugar and continue to whisk to stiff-peak stage—the mixture will be glossy and thick and, when pulled to a peak, it will hold its shape. Gently fold in the melted chocolate using a spatula until the mixture is no longer streaky, being careful to knock as little air out as possible. Divide between four small bowls.

3 To make the coconut topping, scoop the hardened coconut cream from the top of the tin of refrigerated coconut milk. Place it in a bowl with the maple syrup and beat using an electric hand mixer; if the mixture is too thick, add a little of the leftover coconut milk, a spoonful at a time, to help it come together. Place a dollop of the topping on the chocolate mousse and decorate with fresh berries, if desired. Eat as soon as possible, or chill until later, but note that this will result in a more dense mousse.

WITH ORANGE CHOCOLATE
Use orange-flavored chocolate (vegan if required) and add 1 tsp. grated orange zest to the mousse with the chocolate.

WITH DARK & WHITE CHOCOLATE
Stir 2 oz. (50 g) white chocolate chunks (vegan if required) into the finished mousse before spooning into bowls. Omit the coconut topping and sprinkle with white chocolate shavings.

CHOCOLATE MOUSSE TART
Using a sheet of puff pastry (vegan if required), bake a pastry shell and cook until golden brown. Leave to cool completely. Fill the pastry shell with the chocolate mousse topped with coconut cream and berries.

AQUAFABA MERINGUES
Whisk the aquafaba to the soft peak stage as directed and add 3½ oz. (100 g) superfine sugar and ¼ tsp. vanilla extract. Whisk until thick and glossy. Drop spoonfuls of the mixture onto a baking tray lined with baking paper. Cook in a 230°F (110°C) oven for about 75 minutes until totally dried out and crisp. Turn off the oven, leaving the tray in place until the oven is cold.

Apple Strudel

(V)

Serves 6–8

½ cup (50 g) finely chopped pecans
½ cup (25 g) soft, fresh breadcrumbs
2 tsp. ground cinnamon
¾ cup (175 g) brown sugar

4–6 sheets phyllo pastry
4 medium Granny Smith apples, peeled and
  sliced
zest of ½ lemon

4 tbsp. canola oil
½ cup (50 g) golden raisins
confectioners' sugar, to finish

1 Preheat the oven to 350°F (180°C). Combine the pecans, breadcrumbs, cinnamon, and half of the brown sugar in a bowl. Put the first sheet of phyllo pastry on a clean kitchen towel on your work surface and brush with oil. Sprinkle with a third of the pecan mixture. Put another sheet of phyllo pastry on top, brush with oil, and sprinkle with another third of the pecan mixture; repeat with the third sheet, then lay the fourth sheet on top.

2 Mix the apples with the remaining sugar, lemon zest, and golden raisins. Lay the apples evenly along the length of the phyllo but no more than halfway across it and leaving a margin around the edges. Brush the edges with a little water. Roll up the dough lengthways, like a jelly roll, using the cloth, and press together gently. Place on a silicone sheet or on parchment paper on a cookie sheet, and bake for about 20 minutes or until golden brown.

3 Serve hot or at room temperature. Serve sprinkled with confectioners' sugar, with a scoop of non-dairy ice cream (page 237). If you wish, the strudel may be made ahead of time and reheated for 10 minutes in a hot oven.

WITH CRANBERRY
Prepare the basic recipe, using dried cranberries in place of the golden raisins.

WITH PEAR
Prepare the basic recipe, using 2 apples and 2 pears.

WITH PLUM
Prepare the basic recipe, using 2 apples and 4 roughly chopped, medium-sized plums.

Baked Rice Pudding

Serves 4

5 tbsp. short-grain rice
3 tbsp. brown sugar or 2 tbsp. agave syrup
1 strip lemon zest or 1 vanilla pod

4½ cups (1.1 liters) soy or other unsweetened
  non-dairy milk
¼ tsp. grated nutmeg

2 tbsp. non-dairy margarine

1 Preheat oven to 300°F (150°C). Generously grease a 1-quart (1.1 liters) ovenproof dish with non-dairy butter or margarine. Put the rice, brown sugar or syrup, and lemon zest or vanilla pod in the dish. Gently pour in the milk and stir. Sprinkle the grated nutmeg over the surface of the milk and dot with butter or margarine.

2 Carefully transfer to the oven and bake for 45 minutes, stir, then let cook for another 75 minutes, by which time a brown crust will have formed and the rice will be fully cooked. Serve hot.

WITH COCONUT
Prepare the basic recipe, using 1½ cups (375 ml) coconut milk and 2½ cups (625 ml) soy milk. Add 2 tbsp. raisins and 2 tbsp. flaked coconut with the rice.

WITH CHOCOLATE
Prepare the basic recipe, using chocolate soy milk in place of the unsweetened soy milk. Use a little of this milk to mix with 2 tbsp. unsweetened cocoa powder to form a paste, then add it to the rice.

EGYPTIAN RICE PUDDING
Prepare the basic recipe, using the lemon zest option. To the rice, add 2 lightly crushed cardamom pods, a pinch of saffron, and 2 tbsp. rosewater.

WITH CARAMEL
Combine 3 tbsp. sugar and 3 tbsp. water in a small pan and cook gently, stirring, until dissolved; increase the heat slightly and continue to cook, without stirring, until a golden caramel is formed. Immediately stir into the milk and continue as with the basic recipe.

Vanilla Fudge

GF V

This fudge makes a terrific gift for vegans and anyone on a dairy-free diet. Give it to non-vegans, and they will express surprise. They never thought vegans could have it so good!

Makes 49 pieces

1½ cups (375 ml) soy
    milk
1 cup (25 g) sugar
½ cup (125 g) non-dairy
    margarine
2 tsp. vanilla extract

1 Grease a 7 x 7-in. (18 x 18-cm) baking pan and line it with parchment. Put the soy milk, sugar, and non-dairy butter or margarine in a very large pan—the mixture expands considerably while boiling. Insert a candy thermometer, and cook over a moderate heat until the sugar has dissolved. Bring to a boil, cover, and cook for 3 minutes.

2 Remove the cover and continue to simmer for 15–20 minutes, stirring constantly, until a candy thermometer reaches 270°F (114°C) (soft ball stage). (If you do not have a candy thermometer, drop a little of the mixture into a cup of cold water. It will form into a soft ball when it is hot enough; until then it will just disperse in the water.) It is extremely important to stir continuously throughout this process, as fudge can easily scorch.

3 Remove the fudge from the heat immediately and put the base of the pan into a bowl of cold water to cool quickly and stop the cooking process. Stir in the vanilla and beat until the mixture thickens and loses its gloss. Pour into the prepared baking pan and put on a wire rack. When almost set, mark into 1-in. (2.5-cm) squares. When it has cooled and set completely, cut into pieces. Arrange in a decorative box or in plastic bags tied with raffia ribbon.

WITH CHOCOLATE
Prepare the basic recipe, using just 1 tsp. vanilla extract. Stir the vanilla and 4 x 1-oz. (25-g) squares vegan semisweet chocolate into the mixture at the same time.

WITH COFFEE
Prepare the chocolate fudge variation above, but use 2 tsp. instant coffee in place of the 2 tsp. vanilla extract.

WITH CHERRY
Prepare the basic recipe, stirring in ⅓ cup (50 g) chopped candied cherries to the mixture at the same time as the vanilla.

WITH RUM & RAISIN
Prepare the basic recipe, using ½ cup (50 g) plump raisins and 2 tbsp. rum in place of the vanilla.

WITH ALMOND
Prepare the basic recipe, using ⅓ cup (50 g) roughly chopped toasted almonds and a few drops of almond extract in place of the vanilla.

Chocolate Chip Soy Ice Cream with Hot Chocolate Sauce

(GF) (V)

A dairy-free indulgence, and it's versatile too. For vanilla flavor, simply omit the chocolate.

Makes 1 quart (1 liter)

2 tbsp. arrowroot
1 cup (250 ml) soy milk
2 cups (500 ml) non-dairy cream
4 tbsp. agave syrup or ⅓ cup (75 g) sugar
2 tsp. vanilla extract
1 cup (175 g) small chips of semisweet
  vegan chocolate

for the chocolate sauce
¼ cup (50 g) non-dairy butter or margarine
¾ cup (175 g) brown sugar
2 oz. (50 g) semisweet vegan chocolate,
  chopped
3–4 tbsp. soy milk

1 Mix the arrowroot to a paste with 2 tbsp. of the soy milk; set aside. In a saucepan, combine the remaining milk, non-dairy cream, and syrup or sugar, and bring to a boil. While stirring, pour the arrowroot paste into the pan, stirring until the mixture thickens slightly. The mixture will continue to thicken as it cools.

2 Cover the surface with greased parchment paper or plastic wrap to prevent a skin from forming. When the mixture is cool, stir in the vanilla extract and the chocolate chips.

3 Pour the mixture into an ice cream maker and process until the ice cream has set. Alternatively, place in a freezer container and freeze for about 6 hours. Remove from the freezer every 1½ hours and mash with a fork to break down the ice crystals to form a smooth ice cream.

4 To make the sauce, melt the non-dairy butter or margarine in a pan, add the sugar, and cook, stirring, over low heat until melted. Add the chocolate and 3 tbsp. soy milk, stir until melted, and add a little more soy milk, if desired. Serve hot over the ice cream.

WITH EXTRA CHOCOLATE
Prepare the basic recipe. Mix 4 tbsp. cocoa powder to a paste with a little of the soy milk and add to the pan with the remaining soy milk. When cool, add 1 cup (175 g) semisweet vegan chocolate chips.

WITH PEPPERMINT
Prepare the basic recipe for double chocolate chip soy ice cream (above), using 1 tbsp. peppermint extract in place of the vanilla.

WITH STRAWBERRY
Prepare the basic recipe, adding 1½ cups (225 g) crushed strawberries with the vanilla. The same principle applies for other berries and for mango or peach ice cream. Serve alone, or if desired, with the chocolate sauce.

BANANA "MILKSHAKE"
Prepare the basic recipe, omitting the sauce. Put in a blender 1 cup (250 ml) ice-cold soy or coconut milk, 4 scoops of vanilla soy ice cream, 1 thickly sliced banana, and ½ tsp. vanilla extract; blend until smooth.

Minted Watermelon Lollies

Once you have a lolly mould, you can turn most drinks into an ice lolly, but remember that alcohol slows down the freezing process and so should be used sparingly. Also note that sugar tastes less sweet once frozen.

Makes about 6

3½ oz. (100 g) superfine sugar
3½ fl oz. (100 ml) water
8 large mint leaves, roughly chopped
grated zest of ¾ lime

1 lb 2 oz. (500 g) watermelon flesh, seeds
   removed, chopped
few blueberries, to decorate (optional)

1 Bring the sugar and water to a boil in a saucepan, then remove from the heat and add the mint and lime zest to infuse. Leave to cool.

2 Place the watermelon in a food processor and blitz to a purée; alternatively, blitz it in a large bowl using a hand-held blender. Place the purée in a sieve over a large bowl and leave to stand until all the juice has run into the bowl; discard the pulp in the sieve.

3 Set the sieve over a second bowl and pour in the cooled sugar-mint syrup to remove the zest and mint. Pour the syrup into the watermelon purée, tasting as you do so until sufficiently sweet and minty. Pour into lolly moulds, leaving a ½-in. (1 cm) gap at the top. Seal with the lid/stick and freeze for at least 4 hours or overnight. After 1 hour, test to see if the lollies are semi-frozen; if so, drop in a few blueberries and push down into the lollies with a knife.

WITH ALCOHOL
Combine the watermelon, sugar, lime zest and a teacupful of ice in the blender and purée. Stir in 3 tbsp. vodka or white rum and serve immediately. If your food processor/blender won't process ice, serve over crushed ice instead.

WITH STRAWBERRY
Use only 9 oz. (250 g) watermelon and purée 7 oz. (200 g) strawberries. Push the strawberry purée through a sieve along with the watermelon and make the lollies as directed.

WITH PEACH & YOGURT
Purée the flesh of 2 skinned and stoned peaches. Half fill the lolly moulds with purée. Sweeten 4 fl oz. (125 ml) plain non-dairy yogurt with agave syrup, to taste, and use it to almost fill the moulds. Using the tip of a knife, gently marble the two ingredients together. Finish the lollies as directed.

WITH HERBAL TEA
Make strong fruit or herbal teas in separate cups, sweeten to taste when hot and allow to cool. Mixed berry tea, cranberry and raspberry, peppermint, lemongrass and ginger, and apple and cinnamon would all work well. Pour into the lolly moulds and finish as directed.

Pistachio Kulfi

(V)

Kulfi is Indian ice cream flavored with pistachio, rosewater, or mango. This version uses coconut and soy milk to replace the traditional slow-cooked sweet milk. It is delicious and lighter than the original. Kulfi molds are conical in shape and can be purchased at some Asian stores; however, silicone muffin pans work really well too.

Makes 6

½ cup (75 g) shelled
  pistachios
1 tbsp. ground almonds
2 cups (500 ml) soy or
  almond milk
1 cup (250 ml) full-fat
  coconut milk
½ cup (50 g)

confectioners' sugar
½ tsp. crushed cardamom
  seeds
1 tsp. vanilla extract
few drops almond extract
fresh mango slices or
  passion fruit pulp,
  to serve

1 Put the pistachios in a blender and process until chopped. Remove about three-quarters of the pistachios and set aside. Process the remaining pistachios until ground, then add the ground almonds and a quarter of the soy or almond milk. Mix in the remaining ingredients by hand, including the chopped pistachios. If the coconut milk remains a bit lumpy, this is good because it adds to the texture of the kulfi.

2 Pour the mixture into an ice cream maker and process until the ice cream has set. Pour it into your molds. Alternatively, place the mixture in a freezer container and freeze for about 4 hours, removing from the freezer every hour and mashing with a fork to break down the ice crystals. Transfer into molds to finish freezing. Remove from the refrigerator 10 minutes before serving. Serve with slices of mango or drizzle with passion fruit pulp.

WITH ROSEWATER
Prepare the basic recipe, adding 2 tbsp. rosewater to the ingredients. Serve sprinkled with a few drops of rosewater and garnished with edible rose petals.

WITH MANGO
Prepare the basic recipe, using only 1 tbsp. pistachios, ground to a powder, and adding the finely chopped flesh from 1 ripe mango to the mixture.

WITH SAFFRON & ALMOND
Prepare the basic recipe, using 1 cup (225 g) blanched almonds in place of the pistachios. Add a pinch of saffron to the mixture and serve garnished with chopped pistachios.

WITHOUT PISTACHIO
Prepare the basic recipe, omitting the pistachios.

Lavender-Dusted Lemon Shortbread

(V)

Lavender sugar is available to purchase, but you can make your own by making a lavender bag from a small handful of lavender petals sewn into a small cotton pouch. Put this into a jar containing 1 cup (225 g) sugar and leave it for 2 weeks, shaking occasionally.

Makes 8 shortbread cookies

1½ cups (175 g) all-purpose flour
½ cup (50 g) cornstarch
pinch salt
½ cup (125 g) superfine sugar

1 cup (225 g) soy margarine
zest of 1 lemon
2–3 tbsp. lavender sugar, to dust

1 Preheat oven to 300°F (150°C). Lightly grease a cookie sheet. Put the flour, cornstarch, and salt into a food processor, and pulse a few times to sift and combine. Cut the margarine or non-dairy butter into chunks and add to the flour with the sugar and lemon zest. Pulse until the fat is fully incorporated. If making the dough without a food processor, rub the margarine or non-dairy butter into the flour, cornstarch, and salt; then add the sugar and lemon zest.

2 Turn the mixture out onto a lightly floured work surface and knead together into a dough. Roll out into a circle about ⅓ in. (8 mm) thick and crimp the edges. Prick the surface of the shortbread all over with a fork and mark into 8 wedges. Alternatively, press the dough into a ⅓-in. (8-mm) thick rectangle, prick all over, and mark into fingers.

3 Transfer the dough onto the cookie sheet and bake for about 25 minutes until very lightly golden. Cool for 5 minutes before cutting into segments and transferring to a wire rack to cool completely. Dust with the lavender sugar.

WITH GINGER
Prepare the basic recipe, using 4 tbsp. finely chopped crystallized ginger in place of the lemon zest. Dust with superfine sugar instead of lavender sugar.

WITH PECAN
Prepare the basic recipe, using ⅓ cup (50 g) finely chopped pecans in place of the lemon zest.

WITH CHOCOLATE CHIPS
Prepare the basic recipe, using ⅓ cup (50 g) vegan semisweet chocolate chips in place of the lemon zest. There is no need to dust these cookies with additional sugar after cooking.

TRADITIONAL SCOTTISH SHORTBREAD
Prepare the basic recipe, using 1 cup (125 g) all-purpose flour plus ½ cup (60 g) rice flour and omitting the lemon zest. Dust with superfine sugar instead of lavender sugar.

Spiced Sweet Potato Cake

This wonderfully moist cake will win you friends.

Serves 8–10

4 oz. (125 g) all-purpose flour
2 tsp. baking powder
2 tsp. cinnamon
½ tsp. ground ginger
½ tsp. ground allspice
1 tsp. salt
3½ oz. (100 g) whole wheat flour
6 oz. (175 g) soft brown sugar

12 fl oz. (350 ml) sunflower oil
4 eggs, lightly beaten
12 oz. (350 g) sweet potato, grated
2 oz. (50 g) pecans
2 oz. (50 g) raisins

for the cream cheese icing
3 oz. (75 g) full-fat cream cheese
2 oz. (50 g) sweet butter, softened
12–14 oz. (350–400 g) confectioners'
    sugar, sifted
½ tsp. vanilla extract
1 tsp. lemon juice
pecans and edible flowers, to decorate

1 Preheat the oven to 350°F (180°C). Grease and line two deep 8-in. (20-cm) sandwich tins.

2 Sift the all-purpose flour into a bowl with the baking powder, cinnamon, ginger, allspice, and salt. Stir in the whole wheat flour and set aside. In a large bowl or food processor, beat together the sugar, oil and eggs. Fold in the flour mixture and beat well. Then stir in the sweet potato, pecans, and raisins. Pour the mixture into the prepared tins. Bake for 35–40 minutes, until a wooden cocktail stick inserted into the center of the cake comes out clean. Leave for 5 minutes, then transfer to a wire rack to cool completely.

3 For the icing, beat the cream cheese until it is soft and creamy. Slowly beat in the butter, then fold in the confectioners' sugar until the mixture is of spreading consistency. Beat in the vanilla extract and lemon juice. Use a little of the icing to sandwich the layers together, and the remainder to cover the top and sides of the cake. Decorate with pecans and edible flowers.

WITH CARROT
Make the cake using 12 oz. (350 g) grated carrots instead of the sweet potato.

WITH PINEAPPLE
Prepare the basic recipe, replacing half the sweet potato with 9 oz. (250 g) well-drained tinned crushed pineapple.

WITH LEMON DRIZZLE
In place of the cream cheese icing, mix together 9 oz. (250 g) confectioners' sugar with just enough lemon juice to make a thick but spreadable icing. Pour over the top of the cake and spread quickly, allowing some of the icing to drizzle down the sides. Decorate with pecans.

WITH PECAN FROSTING
In place of the cream cheese icing, melt 3½ oz. (100 g) butter in a medium saucepan, stir in 2 oz. (50 g) soft brown sugar and 4 tbsp. heavy cream and slowly bring to a boil. Remove from the heat and beat in 4 oz. (125 g) confectioners' sugar and 1 tsp. vanilla extract until smooth. Stir in 2 oz. (50 g) chopped pecans. Cool for 5 minutes, then pour over the cake. Decorate with more pecans.

Carrot Cake with Lemon Frosting ⓥ

Pure dairy-fee indulgence!

Serves 4

1 cup (125 g) all-purpose
 flour, sifted
1 cup (125 g) whole
 wheat flour
4 tbsp. cornstarch
1 cup (250 g) brown
 sugar
½ cup (125 g) granulated
 sugar
1½ tsp. ground cinnamon
egg replacer for 2 eggs
 (see page 223)
4 tbsp. orange juice
1¼ cups (300 ml)
 sunflower oil
1 cup (250 ml) soy milk

1 tbsp. cider vinegar
3 cups (350 g) shredded
 carrots
½ cup (75 g) golden
 raisins
½ cup (50 g) chopped
 pecans or walnuts
4 oz. (125 g) non-dairy
 cream cheese (see page
 223)
¼ cup (50 g) soy
 margarine, melted
1 tsp. vanilla extract
1 tsp. lemon juice
2–2¼ cups (300 g)
 confectioners' sugar

1 Preheat oven to 350°F (180°C). Grease a
 9 x 13-in. (23 x 33-cm) pan and line the base
 with parchment paper. Combine the flours,
 cornstarch, sugars, and cinnamon in a large
 bowl. In a separate bowl, mix the egg replacer
 with 2 tbsp. of the orange juice, and whisk with
 a fork until fluffy.

2 Pour into the dry ingredients with the
 remaining orange juice, sunflower oil, soy
 milk, and cider vinegar. Mix thoroughly, then
 stir in the carrots, golden raisins and nuts.

3 Pour the batter into the prepared pan. Bake for
 40–50 minutes, until firm to the touch and a
 toothpick inserted into the center comes out
 clean. Cool for 10 minutes before turning out
 onto a wire rack to cool completely.

4 To make the frosting, beat the non-dairy cream
 cheese until soft and smooth, then stir in the
 melted margarine, vanilla, and lemon juice. Sift
 in the confectioners' sugar until the frosting has
 a spreadable consistency. Spread over the
 rectangular cake.

WITH PINEAPPLE
Prepare the basic recipe, replacing half the shredded carrots with
1½ cups (225 g) well-drained crushed pineapple.

WITH ZUCCHINI
Prepare the basic recipe, replacing half the shredded carrots with
1½ cups (150 g) shredded zucchini.

WITH PASSION FRUIT GLAZE
Prepare the basic carrot cake, but replace the frosting with a
double quantity of passion fruit glaze (see opposite).

WITH LEMON-COCONUT FROSTING
Prepare the basic recipe. Lightly toast ¾ cup (65 g) shredded
coconut under a medium-hot broiler until the edges become
lightly golden   watch carefully as it quickly burns. Cool and
lightly press into the frosting.

Banana Cake & Passion Fruit Glaze

(V)

Banana cake goes well with the bold taste of passion fruit—vegan cakes needn't be dull!

Serves 8–12

3 large ripe bananas
4 tbsp. sunflower oil
4 tbsp. oat milk
½ cup (125 g) brown sugar
1 tbsp. rum or 1 tsp. vanilla extract
egg replacer for 1 egg (page 223)
1 tbsp. water
1½ cups (175 g) fine-milled whole wheat flour

1 tsp. baking powder
1 tsp. salt
¼ tsp. ground cinnamon
¼ tsp. ground nutmeg
½ cup (75 g) chopped walnuts

for the passion fruit glaze
pulp from 4 passion fruit
6 tbsp. brown rice syrup or light corn syrup
1 tbsp. brown sugar

1   Preheat oven to 350°F (180°C). Oil an 8 x 8 in. (20 x 20 cm) loaf pan. Line the base with parchment. Mash the bananas in a bowl and immediately stir in the oil, oat milk, brown sugar, and rum or vanilla. In a cup, whisk the egg replacer and the water with a fork until frothy. In a separate bowl, combine the flour, baking powder, salt, cinnamon, and nutmeg.

2   Pour the banana mixture and the egg replacer into the flour mixture and stir well. Add the walnuts. Pour the batter into the prepared pan. Bake for 55-60 minutes until firm to the touch and a toothpick inserted into the center comes out clean. Cool for 10 minutes, then turn out and cool completely on a wire rack.

3   For the glaze, combine the passion fruit pulp, syrup, and sugar in a small saucepan. Cook over a gentle heat until the sugar has dissolved. Increase the heat, bring to a boil, and cook, without stirring, for about 2 minutes, until thickened. Remove from heat. When the cake and glaze are fully cooled, spread the glaze over the cake.

WITH CHOCOLATE CHIPS
Prepare the basic recipe, using ¾ cup (125 g) vegan semisweet chocolate chips or chopped vegan chocolate in place of the walnuts. Sprinkle 2 tbsp. brown sugar over the top of the cake before baking. Omit the glaze.

WITH ORANGE
Prepare the basic recipe, using 2 tbsp. orange juice, the zest of 1 orange, and 1 tsp. lemon juice in place of the rum or vanilla extract.

WITH RAISIN
Prepare the basic recipe, adding ¾ cup (125 g) raisins to the batter.

WITH ALMOND
Prepare the basic recipe, replacing ¼ cup (25 g) of the whole wheat flour with ¼ cup (25 g) ground almonds. Also, use ½ cup (75 g) chopped blanched almonds in place of the walnuts.

Apricot Coconut Cookies

V

Use coconut
oil & non-dairy
chocolate

Save a fortune by making your own cookies instead of grabbing one when picking up a coffee. These are exceptionally simple to make and are full of good things.

Makes 10–12

3½ oz. (100 g) coconut
   oil or butter, softened
3½ oz. (100 g) brown
   sugar
1 egg
1 tsp. vanilla extract

2 oz. (50 g) self-rising
   flour
3½ oz. (100 g) porridge
   oats
2 oz. (50 g) desiccated
   coconut
2 oz. (50 g) chopped dried
   apricots

1 Preheat the oven to 350°F (180°C). Grease or line two baking trays with baking paper.

2 Cream the coconut oil or butter and sugar together until light and fluffy, then beat in the egg and vanilla extract. Stir through the flour, oats, coconut and dried apricots.

3 Using a dessert spoon, drop the mixture onto the baking tray, allowing plenty of room to allow the cookies to spread. Flatten with the palm of your hand.

4 Bake for 8–12 minutes until golden brown. Cool for 5 minutes before transferring to a wire rack to cool completely. Store the cooled cookies in an airtight container for up to 2 weeks.

WITH PEANUT BUTTER
Make the base recipe as directed, omitting the coconut and apricots and adding 3 oz. (75 g) crunchy peanut butter following the flour.

WITH CINNAMON & RAISIN
Make the base recipe as directed, substituting 2 oz. (50 g) raisins for the apricots and adding ¾ tsp. ground cinnamon with the oats.

WITH BRAZIL NUTS & MANGO
Make the base recipe as directed, substituting 2 oz. (50 g) chopped Brazil nuts and 2 oz. (50 g) chopped dried mango for the apricots and coconut. Stir 1 tbsp. orange juice into the mixture with the vanilla.

WITH CHOCOLATE DRIZZLE
Make the base recipe as directed, and allow the cookies to cool. Melt 2 oz. (50 g) plain or white chocolate in a bowl set over a pan of simmering water. Use a spoon to drizzle the chocolate over the cookies while still on the wire rack.

Chocolate Cake with Glossy Frosting

(V)

This is such a decadent chocolate cake—even your non-vegan guests will be surprised.

Makes 12 slices

1 cup (225 g) raw sugar
⅓ cup (75 g) shortening, at room temperature
1½ cups (175 g) all-purpose flour, sifted, or whole wheat flour
4 tbsp. unsweetened cocoa powder
1 tsp. baking soda
¼ tsp. baking powder
½ tsp. salt
1 cup (250 ml) cold water
1 tbsp. cider vinegar
1 tsp. vanilla extract

for the frosting
3 tbsp. shortening
3 oz. (75 g) vegan semisweet chocolate
⅓ cup (75 ml) soy milk
1 tsp. vanilla extract
¼ tsp. salt
2 cups (275 g) confectioners' sugar
chopped pistachio or macadamia nuts, to decorate

1 Preheat oven to 350°F (180°C). Grease two 8-in. (20-cm) round pans and line the bases with parchment paper. Combine the sugar and shortening in a bowl or food processor and beat until crumbs form. Add all the remaining cake ingredients and beat well.

2 Divide the batter between the prepared cake pans and bake for 25–35 minutes, or until the cakes feel firm to the touch and a toothpick inserted into the center comes out clean. Cool for 5 minutes, then turn out onto a wire rack to cool completely.

3 To make the frosting, melt the shortening and chocolate in a bowl placed over a saucepan of simmering water. Stir occasionally. Remove the bowl from the heat and stir in the milk, vanilla, and salt. Sift in the confectioners' sugar until the frosting is of spreading consistency. Use to sandwich the cakes together, then spread the remainder on top and side of the cake. Decorate with the chopped nuts.

WITH CAROB
Prepare the basic recipe, using carob powder in place of the cocoa powder in the cake. Use carob in place of chocolate in the frosting.

WITH COFFEE
Prepare the basic recipe, using 2 tsp. instant coffee with the cocoa. Add 1 tsp. instant coffee to the frosting.

CHOCOLATE CUPCAKES
Prepare the basic recipe. Pour the batter into paper liners in a cupcake pan and bake for 20–25 minutes until a toothpick comes out clean. Cool, then decorate with the frosting.

CHOCOLATE SPONGE PUDDING
Prepare a half portion of the basic cake recipe and bake it in a greased and lined 7-in. (18-cm) ovenproof dish. Allow to cool for 5 minutes, turn out onto a plate, and serve hot with vanilla soy ice cream (page 237). Omit the frosting.

Beet Brownies

These rich, smooth brownies are delicious warmed through and served with ice cream or crème fraîche, and equally good cold with a cup of ice-cold milk or a creamy latte.

Makes 12

12 oz. (350 g) unpeeled beets, trimmed and cut into large wedges
3 oz. (75 g) sweet butter, softened
7 oz. (200 g) good-quality dark chocolate, broken into chunks

2 eggs
7 oz. (200 g) superfine sugar
2 tsp. vanilla extract
½ tsp. salt
4 tbsp. all-purpose flour

½ tsp. baking powder
2 tbsp. cocoa powder, plus extra for dusting

1 Preheat the oven to 350°F (180°C). Grease and line a 12 x 8-in. (30 x 20-cm) baking tin with baking paper.

2 Bring a saucepan of water to a boil, add the beets and simmer until very soft and tender, about 1 hour. Drain well and, once cool enough to handle, rub off the skin. Place the beets in a food processor and blitz until you have a purée; alternatively, blitz it in a large bowl using a hand-held blender. Over a very low heat, melt the butter in a medium-sized saucepan. Add the chocolate and, stirring constantly with a wooden spoon, continue to heat until the chocolate has just melted—do not overheat. Remove from the heat and leave to cool slightly.

3 Whisk the eggs, sugar, vanilla and salt in another bowl, then beat into the chocolate mixture in the pan and stir in the beet purée. Sift in the flour, baking powder, and cocoa powder, and fold in until just combined.

4 Pour into the prepared tin and bake for 30–35 minutes, until a crust has formed and the cake is still soft but not wobbly; brownies need to be just cooked, not cake-like. Cool completely in the tin, then dust with sifted cocoa powder to serve, if desired.

WITH WHITE CHOCOLATE
Stir 3½ oz. (100 g) white chocolate, chopped into small chunks, into the mixture with the beets. Melt 2 oz. (50 g) white chocolate in a small bowl over a pan of simmering water and drizzle over the cooled brownies, instead of cocoa powder.

WITH MACADAMIA NUTS
Stir 2 oz. (50 g) chopped macadamia nuts into the brownies with the beets.

WITH CHILI
Add 1 tsp. cayenne pepper, or more according to taste, with the flour.

WITHOUT FLOUR
Replace the flour with 4 tbsp. ground almonds.

Lemon-Poppy Seed Cupcakes

(V)

These cupcakes are delicious with a cup of tea. They have a bright, zingy taste accentuated by the strong crusty syrup on top. The lemon juice activates the baking soda, which makes these cupcakes rise so successfully and gives them a good texture.

Makes 12 cupcakes

2¼ cups (250 g) all-purpose flour
2 tbsp. cornstarch
1½ tsp. baking soda
¾ tsp. salt
½ cup (50 g) semolina or brown rice flour
4 tbsp. poppy seeds

1¼ cups (300 ml) oat milk or other non-dairy milk
½ cup (125 g) soy margarine, melted
¾ cup (175 ml) canola oil
4 tbsp. freshly squeezed lemon juice
zest of 1 small lemon

for the lemon syrup
6 tbsp. freshly squeezed lemon juice
⅓ cup (65 g) sugar

1 Preheat oven to 350°F (180°C). Line a muffin pan with paper muffin cups. In a bowl, sift together the flour, cornstarch, baking soda, and salt. Stir in the semolina and poppy seeds. Make a well in the middle and pour in the milk, melted margarine, oil, and lemon juice. Use a wire whisk to combine. Stir in the lemon zest.

2 Pour the batter into the prepared baking cups to about ½ in. (1.5 cm) from the top. Bake for 20–25 minutes, until a toothpick inserted into the center comes out clean.

3 Meanwhile, stir together the lemon juice and sugar for the topping. When the cupcakes are done, stab them all over with a toothpick. Using a tsp., drizzle the syrup over the hot cupcakes, letting the syrup soak into them. Remove from the pan and cool on a wire rack.

WITH LEMON & LIME
Prepare the basic cupcake recipe, using the zest of ½ lemon and ½ lime in place of the lemon zest. In both the cake and the syrup, use 2 tbsp. lemon juice and 2 tbsp. lime juice in place of the lemon juice.

WITH ORANGE
Prepare the basic cupcake recipe, using 4 tbsp. orange juice and the zest of ½ large orange in place of the lemon juice and zest. In the syrup, use 3 tbsp. orange juice and 1 tbsp. lemon juice.

WITH ALMOND
Prepare the basic recipe, using ¼ cup (40 g) ground almonds in place of the poppy seeds.

WITH ORANGE & ALMOND
Prepare the orange poppy seed cupcakes (above). Additionally, use ¼ cup (40 g) ground almonds in place of the poppy seeds.